THE UNKNOWN GOD.
(Acts 17:23-31)
AND THE END OF
CHURCH AND STATE

Copyright © 2017 by Maurice Louishomme

All rights reserved. No part of this publication may be reproduced, distributed, or transmitted in any form or by any means, including photocopying, recording, or other electronic or mechanical methods, without the prior written permission of Maurice Louishomme, except in the case of brief quotation embodied in critical reviews and certain other noncommercial uses permitted by copyright law.

Verses Quoted are from The KING JAMES Versions of the Bible

First Edition

ISBN-13: 978-0692998380
ISBN-10: 0692998381

This book is dedicated to:

My Family, particularly to my Children,
who are some of the best teachers I have ever known.

And,

My Mother, my Brothers and my Sister, whose conversations
and arguments challenged me, my understanding, and very
often, my ideas of faith.

You all helped to form much of this book's contents.

I thank God for all of you.

Table of Contents

Introduction: The Word of God vs. The Satanic Bible.......7

Chapter 1. The First Murder Was a Suicide: Satan and Man; Looking Back at the Beginning.......33

Chapter 2. The Path of Interpretation: The Creation of the Angels.......63

Chapter 3. The Unknown Truth: The Revelation of God, Genesis 1.......91

Chapter 4. Yeshua is LORD?.......132

Chapter 5. Tradition, The Law, and Faith.......185

Chapter 6. GOD the KING, GOD the PRIEST.......219

Chapter 7. In The Beginning, Revelation: An Interesting Connection Between The Book of Revelation and The Book of Genesis.......220

Chapter 8. God, Satan, and Man: Reflecting On The Beginning and Looking Towards The End.......256

Pages for Notes.......292

INTRODUCTION

The Word of God vs. The Satanic Bible

The Satanic Bible("The Satanic Bible", published by Anton LaVey in 1969) is not a document that came into existence in the year 1969 of the modern era. The Satanic bible is the document that was founded upon the serpent's words to Eve thousands of years ago in the garden of Eden(**Genesis 3:1-5**; The book of **Genesis** chapter **3** verses **1** through **5**). The principles of the Satanic Bible are the pillars that both ancient and modern kingdoms of men stand upon. The teachings of the Satanic Bible thrive upon man's ignorance of the truth, they give life to humanity's fears and prides, and they separate all men and women from God's acceptance(Cross Reference **Genesis 2:17**). The Satanic Bible has survived from the day of its inception in the garden of Eden up to the modern era because it was, it is, and it will always be the misrepresented word of the Unknown God(Cross Reference **Acts 17:23-31**).

When people, usually Christians, ask me if I am myself a Christian, I tell them that I do believe the Bible but that I don't call myself a Christian. "Christian" means so many different things to different people and I try to avoid confusion. Contrary to my intention, my response to their question rarely starts a conversation. Usually, there is an uncomfortable moment of silence between us, they awkwardly smile and then walk away. It's unfortunate, but I generally find that people are not interested in understanding other people. Too often men and women are concerned solely with ourselves or with converting you to our particular way of thinking. We generally want to be right in comparison to others about the stances we take on the issues that affect the world that we each sit at the center of. We need to be right, and not just for the sake of pride but because we are each trying to make the most of or find confirmation in the truths that our individual life experience has always given to us.

I personally look forward to conversations, particularly conversations about religion. Not for the sake of argument, but because I'm curious and I look forward to opportunities to understand and to be understood. I view disagreements as opportunities to understand the unique experience that has led another individual to their particular conclusion and I try to take advantage of the opportunity to better understand my own conclusions. I'm really fascinated with people's minds. Only, that's a hard point to get across to someone who may not have a good grasp on what or on why they believe what they do. More often than not, instead of engaging in mature conversations, we tend to either fight or run when pride, fear, or insecurity leads us to perceive that we are being challenged. The fact is that most men and women who practice one of the many forms of religion rarely knows the facts of whatever truth we happen to be proclaiming. We have all been guilty at some time in our lives of simply believing what someone -a parent or relative, friend, teacher, or a pastor- whom we trust has convinced us to believe. We're fairly simple creatures and we are prone to believe that the people who we put our trust in only have our best interest in mind. That doesn't make them right, but it does make them potentially dangerous. The errors that are committed and believed by the people whom we understand to care for us are often harder to recognize than those of the people whose motives we recognize to be purely self-serving. Adam and Eve fell into this trap in the garden of Eden(**Genesis 3:1-6**).

My Own Path

I was raised by a mother who was determined to see that all her children respected ourselves, honored God, and attended

Church. When I was a young child my mother married a man in the military and as a result we moved regularly from city to city and from church to church. Because of the constant moving and my own personality, I never really developed lasting friendships or felt that any one place was home. As a married adult I wanted my family to be more stationary.

Years ago, when our children were still young, Daniella and I decided that our family would settle into a church. I felt like our family needed a stable foundation and that we would find that stability in a community of people who were devoted to God. I went on a search of the city, attending a number of different church services, trying to find the right fit for my family. Eventually I found a congregation that appeared to be what I believed we had been looking for. It was a diverse fellowship with a strong and stable leadership, and after a few solo visits I felt comfortable enough to bring my family.

On Sunday mornings we would arrive at Church a little early to walk the boys to each of their Sunday school rooms. There were separate daycares available for our girls, who were 1 and 2, but Daniella and I felt more comfortable keeping them with us. Our girls are very close and being separated in a new place felt like too big of an adjustment for them and for Daniella and me. They love to play and talk, so we'd sit apart from the main auditorium in the upstairs cafe, and would watch the television monitors that were tuned in to the downstairs auditorium. This arrangement worked good for the girls and Daniella, but I needed more. After a few weeks of sitting separated from everyone else I began to get an "itch". I needed to sit amongst my brethren and hear the Word of God. So we, mostly I, decided that next week we would try sitting in the main auditorium with the girls.

I hadn't noticed before when I had come alone that there was a section at the back of the auditorium for families with small children. I felt a little silly for not noticing the four or five rows of young children sitting with their parents. That first

Sunday in the main auditorium with the girls went smoothly. The girls only needed to be told to settle down a couple of times.

The second Sunday of my full integration experiment started off smoothly but went sour not long after the service started. Daniella and I were listening to the announcer standing at the podium and the girls were talking their little girl talk. At that young age our girls could just look at each other and get riled up and when I'm focused, I tend to tune the rest of the world out. So, I was a little startled by the man standing next to me who I only noticed after he began to clear his throat loudly and purposefully. Caught by surprise and slightly annoyed, I looked up to see who was standing beside me.

When the older gentleman saw that he had my attention he said in a very matter of fact sort of way, "Your children are too loud. Quiet them down!"

I looked around half expecting to see the girls climbing on other people, but they were just sitting with each other on the floor talking together. The girls may have been loud enough for the couples directly in front of us to hear but no one had given us the "stink eye", and I really hadn't noticed their noise level. I looked around wondering where this guy could have come from. All the people who were sitting around us were looking up at the speaker standing behind the podium, so I wondered how this dude could have been disturbèd.

"Sorry about that, I really didn't notice them.", I said.

Daniella and I decided to hold the girls on our laps for the rest of the service.

The next Sunday while we were still in the car, we decided that we would start off the service by holding the girls and if they were able to keep themselves relatively quiet, we'd let them down to play together.

I scanned the room as we walked in, trying to spy out the old guy from the week before. I didn't see him, but he didn't miss us. As soon as we sat down, he posted up not too far from our seats. It turns out that he was an usher. The Church service started out the same way that it had the week before. The band was playing, the congregation was singing, people were greeting each other, and the other ushers were helping the congregants to their seats. After the singing and music stopped the congregation was greeted by the speaker at the podium and the announcements were made. Our girls were wide eyed with their hands out, still a bit riled up from all the singing and handshaking. Daniella and I smiled and whispered to the girls, trying to get them to follow our quiet voice example. I had spotted the old guy watching us. As the service moved along the girls were actually being very quiet and attentive to what was going on around them. We decided to let them down from the chairs. I didn't want to make eye contact but, out of my peripheral view I could see the old guy trying to burn a hole in the side of my face with his stare. I reminded the girls that as long as they whispered to each other, they could stay on the floor. Every few minutes I peeped down at them, and they both would look up at me with reassuring smiles as if to say, "What could go wrong". I smiled, and they went back to their conversation. Just after my last look down and then back up to the speaker at the podium, one of the girls giggled. It wasn't that loud, but I knew. The old guy was coming over.

  Before he had a chance to get a word out, I said, "Sorry about that, little girls you know.", trying to quickly settle the matter and brush the guy off at the same time.

  At first, he looked at me with a very stern look. Then he smiled in a peculiar way and said, "I have to ask you to leave!".

It took my brain a couple of seconds to register what he had just said.

"Leave.", I said astonished, "Wow.".

At the words "leave" people turned and looked at us. In their faces I read surprise mixed with fear. Some of the parents in the family area whose children were old enough to be mobile unconsciously grabbed their little ones and placed him or her on their laps.

I sat there for a few seconds, letting the usher's words absorb into my brain. I nodded in agreement with myself, and then Daniella and I gathered the girls and our personal effects. We went to the Sunday school rooms to get the boys and, the Louishommes were out.

One of the assistant pastors followed us outside to the parking lot.

"Wait, don't leave.", he said.

I smiled "It's alright we'll just come back when the girls are a little older."

He came back with, "Listen. That usher gives everyone a hard time, it's not you".

"No", I said, "It's alright", and we left. We decided to go to breakfast and beat the after-church crowd. I had an omelet and pancakes.

As small of an incident as that may seem, it was actually a major turning point in my life.

As a young child I was loyal, over-protective, naive, generally disappointed with my life, and I had been conditioned to have very little regard for my own well-being. Throughout my teenage years my disappointment and low self-regard was compounded with an arrogant yet purposefully ignorant demeanor. But now, as an adult, I had a wife and four children. Everything good in my life was bound up in my family.

I had been convinced for some time that my family's eternal security rested in my hands, and now we had just been told to leave a church. I had never seen a family get kicked out of a church. I've seen one or two belligerent congregants get put out, but not a family with small children. I wasn't angry or really even hurt over the incident and I did initially intend to go back to the Church when the girls were older. I wanted the security that I understood to be provided by the church body but, I consented to what I understood to be the fact that our family wasn't yet mature enough to actively be a part of the Christian community.

Throughout my early life I had understood, or at least accepted, the Church organization to be God's proving ground. Men, women, and children who wanted to know God must meet the approval of and pass through God's proving ground in order to be allowed to know Him. I had also been convinced at an early age that the men and women who had received special training to read and understand the bible were the only people who could actually read and understand the bible. But now after getting kicked out of a church, I felt like the door to the entire Church community had been closed to me and my family. Now, new circumstances dictated the manner in which I could relate to the word of God.

As much as I wanted it, I couldn't afford the time, nor did I have the money that would allow me to go to school and learn about God. I figured that studying a few bible-help books that were written by the people who had received special biblical training would suffice in the meantime. With my bible-helps at my side I began to read the bible regularly. I prayed, literally, whenever I had a free moment. And I started asking myself questions about what I was reading. Questions such as "Why wasn't David stoned according to the tenets of the Law for his affair with Bathsheba(**2Samuel 11:1-27**. The book of **2Samuel**, the **11th** chapter, verses **1** through **27**)? Why would David, of all people, be regarded as a man after God's own heart(**1Samuel**

13:14; Acts 13:22)? When did the spiritual powers in the heavens get their positions of authority(Cross Reference **Ephesians 3:10**)? Why is Satan still allowed to harass people? If there is only one Savior, then why are there so many different kinds of Christian churches?" My curiosity seemed to be all over the place and my questions only led to more questions that my bible study-helps couldn't answer.

    I began to take my questions to the few Christians who I knew. But they were only willing to discuss biblical issues that they believed their church had already resolved. And the more probing questions that I asked them the more upset they would get. When I ran out of Christian associates to speak to, I began questioning the Church missionaries who came to my door on the weekends. They'd pull out their pamphlets and start in on their dialog, but I would ask them something that I wanted to know about the bible. I wasn't trying to be offensive, but what I wanted to know about the bible was just more important to me than what their pamphlets had to say.

    I continued to read the Bible fervently and to pray whenever I wasn't sleeping, working, eating, or spending time with Daniella and our children. I bought more bible help-books, bible commentaries, and digital, audio, and DVD bible studies. I listened to local, national, and international online sermons given by different pastors from different denominations. I bought different versions of English translations of the Bible. I read my Bibles, studied my bible-helps, and prayed even more. I waited for the groups of door-to-door Christians. I looked desperately in public for Christians who wanted to save souls. I needed to find someone who understood the Bible that was willing to talk with me. I needed to talk to someone who could respond with something more constructive than anger, or "Because my pastor says so," or with "That's what the Church/Bible teaches." I wanted an explanation. I wanted to talk to someone who was brave enough to have questions about what they didn't understand. But I couldn't find any Christians who had those kinds of questions. In the past I had no trouble finding Christians who wanted to convince me that their brand of Christianity was unquestionably the right one. But now I was questioning Christians about their particular brand and how their particular perspectives corresponded with the Bible. For some reason that seemed to be more intimidating to Christians than an atheist who doesn't believe that God exists.

The more commentaries that I read and listened to, the more sermons that I heard from Catholic, Protestant, Non-Denominational, Messianic, Seventh Day Adventist, whomever, the more that I tried to understand Mormonism and Jehovah's Witnesses, and the more arguments over religion that I got into, the less I understood about God and the Bible. I was stuck and my mind was spinning. My confusion and frustration became aggressive in nature. I felt like no one knew anything about God and that I had been lied to my entire life. I became so aggressive that even my friends and family were hesitant about getting into conversations with me on any topic for fear that the Bible would come up.

Eventually the Christians that I had known were sick of me and the door-to-door evangelists stopped coming by. I was confused. I was upset. And I was hurt. I was searching for God, but I could not find Him. None of the material that I had bought and none of the sermons that I had heard had taught me how to get closer to or how to know God. None of them taught me how to hear from God. All I learned was that I needed more faith and that I needed to put in more service time before God would acknowledge me. I was desperate to hear from God. I was desperate to know the truth. Ultimately, I was desperate to stay out of Hell, and I needed to know that I was accepted by God.

I began to do more and more for God. I believed that if I made a big enough mark in the world and added souls to His kingdom, then God in heaven would have to take notice and speak to me. So, I started telling anyone and everyone that I could about God's grace and love.

Every day I woke up and went to work to provide for my family, pay bills, and keep the economy moving. My motivation to please God, earn heavenly rewards, and spend eternity at God's side was even greater than my desire to keep up with my day-to-day responsibilities. I only wanted to be a good example of godly service, but I was blind to how offensive I had become to most everyone that I knew. I didn't exactly believe that I was righteous, but I knew that I was closer to it than most other people. I saw evil all around me and figured that an ungodly world could only hate the peace, love, and righteousness that could only be found in God. But at the same time, I wouldn't accept that anyone would willingly spend eternity in Hell if they only knew the truth. I had to give them the Truth. But I had no money, no influence, no degree, no diploma, nor any kind of certificate telling people that I was anyone worth listening to. All that I had was a fearful desperation to please God.

More time went by and then reality hit me square in the face. The problem was not with other people. The problem was with me. I was only making a complete fool of myself. Everyone else knew it. And it was time to admit to myself that I was a joke.

The truth was that for all that I was doing to please God, all the trust that I had put in the scholars whose works I had studied, all the biblical debates that I had "won", for all the money that I had spent or given away, and through all the emotional trials that I had experienced, I was still confused about God and the Bible. I hadn't seen any miracles. I hadn't saved one person. And my household wasn't full of spiritual bliss. Day to day life wore on me: Being laid off from my job, arguing with Daniella over her relationship with God, and feeling like I was being laughed at for believing in "fairy tales" was beginning to overwhelm me(after all, I nor anyone that I knew or listened to about God seemed able to really understand the Bible or to prove God's existence). Eventually the weight of it all got to be too much. The struggles I encountered delving into the Bible on my own, continually reflecting on the fact that my family and I had been put out of a church, and normal day to day frustrations coupled with fear and desperation weighed me down continually. Eventually the weight pushed me out onto a ledge(figuratively speaking. Not an actual ledge). I got to a point that I didn't want God to be real. If God was real and I couldn't hear His voice nor understand His word then maybe the reality that I needed to accept was that I, my wife, and our four children were destined to spend eternity in Hell. After all God seemed to be telling me at every turn that He hated me. Feeling hated by God sucked, so I just wanted to be done with it all.

    Well, I wasn't done. God knows why, but I'm finding out as I go along that I'm not allowed to quit. I think that I just needed to take a break. For a time, I stopped worrying about salvation and understanding the bible. I just lived and enjoyed the time with my family. Without the stress of pleasing God, understanding the Bible, or my place in eternity, the weeks went by peacefully. But. More and more as time went by my need to know the truth about God, the bible, life, and death would keep me up at night.
    I didn't realize it at the time, but now looking back I am able to understand that I was being prepared for the path that lay ahead of me. And one positive result of my confrontational approach to witnessing in public is that I gained a good deal of insight into why so many Christians can be so harsh and come across so offensively. Sometimes the best of intentions can result in doing the most harm(Cross Reference **Genesis 3:6**).

Religion to Faith

    I have come to accept that some of us are just wired seek after God. Other people are wired to only reject even the idea of

God. The rest of us fall somewhere in the middle and can be persuaded one way or the other.

From my earliest childhood memory, I can remember believing that God is real. As an adult, I can see the evidence of God all around me. Besides biblical revelation, I understand the observable patterns within nature and in the cosmos, as well as mankind's personal quest to create artificial intelligence as evidence that life and existence can only come about and be sustained with intention. When I was young, I enjoyed thinking of a loving, all knowing, all powerful, fair, and just King of creation. He watched over me when I slept or when I was afraid. He felt pain when I was hurt, and He protected me in situations that could have ended my life. As a young child I believed that every good thing that happened to me came from God and everything bad that happened to me came from the Devil. Even though I often believed then that Satan's hand was more active in my life, I understood that it was God's hand that had always allowed me to learn from my experiences and to survive throughout my youth.

The older I got and the more of life that I experienced the more I began to think that God was not all of those positive things that I had believed Him to be when I was young. Why would a loving and all-powerful God allow little children to go hungry? Or why would He allow a devoted mother and her children to be subject to an abuser? As I matured past adolescence and into my early teenage years, life seemed to be continually explaining to me that God, Who is good, hated me because I was evil. I had been taught at an early age what to expect from God as long as I met His requirements. But for some reason I could never stay in God's good graces long enough to live up to His expectations.

I have always believed in the existence of God, but my belief was immature, misinformed, and purely self-serving. The circumstances of my early life were undesirable, and I needed a way to escape them. I wanted to please God because I needed

Him to be a good luck charm Who gave me an advantage in life. When the blessings that I expected to receive from God didn't come, I questioned His reliability. I know now that most of my misconceptions about God and the relationship that I wanted to have with Him were largely the result of my own unrealistic expectations.

  When I came to a "spiritual" crossroads as an adult I was forced to accept one of two possibilities. I either had to accept that I was just destined to spend eternity in Hell or that what I had learned and understood about God and the Bible from childhood up to that moment in time was completely wrong. On one hand the thought of going to Hell was terrifying but at the same time, the thought was liberating. Being free of God's rules, regulations, and oversight would give me a dangerous kind of freedom that I believe I would at first continually lust after but eventually, I would come to despise. Admitting that I was wrong about God and the Bible was almost harder to accept than the idea of going to Hell because I could only see negatives. Accepting that I had been wrong about God and the Bible meant that I couldn't trust myself to find God. I couldn't trust any of the Bible study helps that I had purchased, I couldn't trust church pastors, Bible teachers, nor any Christian scholar, friend or family member, Catholic, Protestant, or otherwise, who had been schooled in biblical understanding or whom I had relied on in the past to lead me to God. I'd be alone and very uncomfortable entering a world full of unknown possibilities.

  After all of the mental wrestling I simply couldn't accept that I was going to Hell. The thought itself is irresponsible and lazy. It simply defies my nature. I had to fight. But I was very intimidated by the thought of what I might encounter from Christians if I were to understand the text differently than the Church's accepted interpretations. I was also uncomfortable exploring the possibility that the entire Church organization(Catholic, Protestant, non-denominational, etc.) had been teaching the bible erroneously for centuries.

Coming to terms with the Church organizations history of biblical missteps was one obstacle to overcome but accepting that I had personally been wrong about God, life, and eternity was much harder. And besides the fact that I didn't know where or how to start, I was afraid of turning my back on my entire lifetime of experience. I was trapped between what was comfortable to me but I knew wouldn't lead me to God and the uncertainty about what might lay ahead. I was forced to confront myself and to trust that God would lead me in the right direction.

Confronting my fears began to set me free of them and questioning my own points of view pressed me to being honest with myself. Questioning myself forced me to account for my own beliefs. The truth was that for all my passion to glorify God, I had only misrepresented the Truth. The fact is, I was a fraud. I came to recognize that everything that I had been doing to please God really had nothing to do with God. I had only been serving my ego and lashing out when my pride wasn't satisfied. I had never known the word of God because I had no association with the Spirit of God. I was merely repeating the words and perspectives, the meanings of which I didn't fully understand, but that some accomplished pastor, teacher, or Bible scholar had convincingly proclaimed about God. I had to continually accept that everything that I had learned and had been teaching my family about God, every biblical argument that I had beaten people over the head with, and even my own attitude and perspective of life was wrong. The more that I began to see myself as I really was, the more I began to despise myself for being such an arrogant fool.

The disappointment that I felt within myself continued for some time but eventually it manifested into a positive change. I was so disappointed with who I was and how I had bullied so many people that I had no choice but to turn my back and walk away from the man that I had become. Up to that point in my life I had been a modestly proud/arrogant person. I was forced to shed the identity of myself that I had relied on and found comfort in up to that point in my life. But every time that I believed that I was making progress I would stumble over "Me", my own obnoxious self. Daily, I had to continually admit and accept that I was wrong. Every day I had to make a conscious decision not to regress into my old state of being. I still took care of my daily responsibilities but intellectually, emotionally, and spiritually I was stripped bare and exposed. Over the course of time, I was drained completely empty of "Myself". Not long after this difficult purging experience I had a powerful, terrifying, and mind-altering Spiritual experience.

  As a result of that experience, I didn't merely believe that there was a God, I understood that YHWH Elohim had been personally guiding the path of my life. Then the men, women, and stories of the Old and New Testaments began to come alive. At times, the text of the Bible was so vivid that reading it was like watching my grandfather act out the story of his life. Questions that before had only led to more confusing questions began leading to answers. Words and phrases stood out from the pages. Verses of the Bible made sense in light of other verses. The text of the Bible would hum inside my brain and then expand out to my skull, only to then be bounced back onto my brain and fully saturate my mind. At times, an audible voice in my mind/spirit would be reading and explaining the verses to me as I was reading them out loud. I would have dreams of walking between the verses of the Bible whose words appeared and caught fire as they were spoken to me. When I awoke, I not only remembered my dreams, but I also understood what had been taught to me. I was able to ask more informed questions of the text and to receive a response from the Spirit of God. I wasn't being force fed a biblical doctrine; I was being taught how to understand God and the Bible.

  Every day I continued to get more from God than I had ever expected. My thoughts and emotions were constantly being overwhelmed throughout the experience. Only now, the problem was that I was alone. No one was around to confirm what I was understanding. Also, what I was understanding of the Bible had nothing in common with the teachings that are supported upon hundreds of years of Church History and proclaimed by millions of Christians around the world. I would occasionally have a nagging fear of going to Hell for being at variance with Church doctrine but now the fact that I was understanding God's word factored into the equation. I could either trust that my eternity was in God's hands or I could go back to trusting what was familiar to me("Remember Lot's wife" **Luke 17:31-33**{**Genesis 19:26**}). I knew for a fact that I couldn't trust my own rationale to reveal God to me. I was forced once again to confront and come to terms with my fear of opposing centuries of Church history, interpretation, doctrine, and the scholars who had received a formal education in biblical understanding. I overcame my fears and as a result I acquired an entirely different perspective on the entire Church body. Recognizing the multifaceted Church organization for what it actually is has only served to confirm the truth and reliability of the biblical text(Cross Reference **John 16:13**), and the endurance of God's word. The Church's confusion and the divisions that have resulted from its varying doctrines and biblical interpretations testify to the fact that matters of the spirit are not subject to the understanding of man.

    A sobering thought that every Christian should take some time to consider is the fact that each opposing Church congregation can accurately point out the errors in doctrine, interpretation, and practice that are committed by other Christian groups and denominations, yet they have little to no consciousness of their own errors.

Treasure

What you are holding in your hands is a treasure of immense value. I know this because my life has changed ever since I came into possession of it. I cannot measure nor can I estimate the value that this treasure will have in your life. Imagine going to a high-end jeweler with a twenty-pound necklace made up of large foggy white stones, massive red translucent rocks, all held together with large dirty yellow fastenings, and asking the jeweler how much it is worth.

I can only speak for myself, but ask yourself how much would a twenty-pound necklace made up of gigantic uncut diamonds, huge unpolished rubies, with pure gold nugget fastenings be worth to you? From your perspective they may just be rocks, or maybe just knowing that something so precious existed would fill you with satisfaction, or maybe you would love to possess such a treasure because you know that you could make a fortune by selling it off piece by piece.

How would you respond to an even greater treasure that is so immense it can't be measured?

If you could feel the approach of compassion, wisdom, and power, so strong and terrifying that you feared dying on the spot if it were to come any closer, and that is so pure that it feels like fire coursing through your nerves and blood vessels, and so true that its presence is more real to you than your own life. If you could read, study, and understand the Bible with startling clarity or explain Bible verses that only confuse others; if you could know the Truth, what value would you place on the treasure that had been given to you? What would you do if the Spirit of God moved in you?

Though some people have more barriers to overcome than others, it's not essential that you leave your family, your job, or sell all your personal property in order to inherit life.

Luke 14:26-27 and **Luke 18:18-22** are passages about priorities. In order to seek the kingdom of God a man or woman must be willing to forsake all things, even their very own life. God knows what you are in need of, but the question is, are you personally able to come to the end of yourself? Can you forsake the perspectives and the understanding that your own life experience has given to you? Can you reject the lies that define your identity? Are you willing to turn your back on personal possessions, every relationship, and even who you believe yourself to be, in order to come to the Truth?

    For me it wasn't as easy as admitting my mistakes and moving on from them. I had relied on my scarred emotional makeup to shepherd me from my youth into adulthood. My mistakes, my passions, my anger, my pride, my fears, my lusts, my greed and, my understanding of family, friends, enemies, and the world around me defined who I was. To lose those things was to completely lose myself.

    I had to see myself through eyes that were not my own in order to recognize the lies that my own life experience and lifetime of understanding had always and only proven to be true. I had to die to my old life, die to my Satanic identity, and be reborn in the Spirit of God in order to see the lies that my existence was rooted upon. It was not a physical death, but a complete separation from my former state of existence. Another part of my purging experience involved reflecting intellectually and emotionally back to the days of my youth and confronting myself, others, and abusive situations from a mature perspective. I was originally looking for answers in the Bible but discovered that I also needed to understand myself and address how I had become "Me". Mediating between pivotal moments of my own childhood as an adult gave me power in the midst of the experiences that had come to define my identity and allowed me to resolve many of those issues. I don't believe nor do I mean to imply that you have to study the Bible and come to faith in Yeshua in order to deal with issues from your past. I followed that path because the void that had been left within me after I had been drained empty needed to be filled(**Matthew 12:43-45**), and personally, I could only move in that direction. I have also found writing about past experiences to be very therapeutic.

I understand that through reflection I am given a window of insight into my own soul and I accept my personal responses to this life experience as evidence of my place in eternity(**Philippians 2:12**). My actual place in eternity and whether I am destined for Heaven or Hell, is a choice that is larger than my individual existence and is therefore outside of my control. But I do have the power to choose whether to remain intellectually, emotionally, physically, and socially chained to the experiences that the god of this world(**2Corinthians 4:4**), my own insecurities, social biases, and humanity has subjected me to. I can refuse to submit and choose to take advantage of every opportunity to overcome this world(Cross Reference **Revelation chapters 2-3**). Through feast or famine, bumps and bruises, good days and bad, I am thankful for this opportunity of life, and I have hope for what lies ahead.

Conclusion

I do not call myself a Christian. I do accept the Bible as the Truth revealed to man because, I have found it to give the most thorough explanation of life that defines and gives meaning to my own personal experience.

If you already know God, understand the Bible, and know that you have the truth, then praise God you are set. I cannot add anything to you. I only hope to show men and women who are looking for what has been missing in their own spiritual lives what has given me the ability to mature. I am not perfect, and I do not have all the answers. I am a man. A flawed and fairly simple one at that. I don't personally believe that I have any ability to lead another man or woman to the Truth. The Truth simply "**IS**". I only hope to point it out. The Truth itself will either draw or repel you. My life experiences may strike some people as interesting, but those experiences cannot prove God's existence to you. Therefore, I offer this book and its contents as evidence of God and His Holy Spirit's involvement in the human experience.

    I believe that the Old and New Testaments of the Bible are two parts of one message that is meant to be understood. And although we may relate to it differently, there is only one correct interpretation of the scriptures. I believe that the Word of God is the Truth revealed to man and that the Bible is humanity's roadmap back to our common God given manhood that was lost in the garden of Eden(Cross Reference **Genesis 3:1-24**. If you have a Bible then look up the book of **Genesis**, chapter **3**, verses **1** through **24**).

    Two facts become increasingly clear as many of the erroneous interpretations, opposing arguments, and contradictory teachings of the multifaceted Church organization begin to be unraveled in the pages of this book. First, the autonomous Christian Church organizations(Catholic, Protestant, Non-Denominational, Messianic, Independent, Cult, etc. Cross Reference **1Corinthians 1:12-13; 3:1-23**) and individual Church denominations each have interpretations, doctrines, and teachings that not only contradict the interpretations, doctrines, and teachings of other Christian organizations and denominations, each branch of the Church also conflicts with the message of the Bible. Thus, bringing attention to a sobering fact: One and only one branch of the multifaceted Church organization could possibly be right but, each and every one of them can be absolutely wrong.

    The second fact that should become increasingly clear is that the very existence of each opposing branch of the Church organization purposefully albeit unconsciously works to dilute the influence of the Truth by making the scripture's universal application subject to an individual's rational criticism(Cross Reference **Matthew 7:6**).

Post Script

Throughout this book I use the term 'spirit(s)' to identify the initiating principle(s). I understand 'spirit' to be the cause of every effect that shapes the physical world. 'Spirit' is the ultimate reason why. In a similar way to how man's actions first begin as a thought or an impulse in our minds, the origin of all things began in the Spirit.

Throughout this book I use the terms "Faithful Community", "Community of Believers", or terms along those same lines of thought to identify the followers of the biblical Messiah and His teachings, instead of the term Church. "Church" is a broad term that includes Catholic, Protestant, 7th Day Adventists, Messianic congregations, Mormons, Jehovah's Witnesses, proponents of Christian Science, etc. The terms "faithful community", "community of believers", "Messianic community" and similar kinds of terms that are used in this book are intended to convey a message of unity under a common understanding.

My use of the term "Messianic community" bears no association with the modern-day Messianic congregations that aim to teach Christians how to practice the "Law of Moses" alongside their "Jewish brothers" with the aim of "Getting back to their Jewish roots". I simply believe that the term "Messiah" is a more expressive one than is "Christ". Therefore, I tend to refer to the community of God's faithful servants as "Messianic" instead of calling it the Christian community.

Throughout this book I use the name "Yeshua(Strong's Concordance reference number **H3444**. Yehoshua, Strong's

Concordance reference number **H3091**, is preferred by many people.) the Messiah" instead of Jesus Christ. I choose to use the name Yeshua simply because of the names meaning(Strong's Concordance reference number **H3444**) and its association with the Old Testament concept of salvation. "Yeshua" is the transliteration of a Hebrew word that is used many times in the Old Testament. "Yeshua" is found in the Strong's concordance under reference number **H3444**, meaning "He will save". God's Salvation is the cementing concept between the Bible's Old and the New Testaments(**Isaiah 12:2** Cross Reference **Matthew 1:21**). Yeshua of Nazareth is literally the incarnation of God's Salvation. The Greek Iesous and the English term Jesus do not make any such connection between the Old and New Testaments.

I view the term "Christ" much the same as I do the term Jesus. Christ does not convey the idea of the 'Anointed One' nor connect the Old Testament concept of anointing to the New Testament's realization of God's Word in the same manner that the term "Messiah(Strong's Concordance reference number **H4888**: Mishchah)" does.

Throughout this book I use the term Judean in place of the term Jew. The term Jew is confusing and overly inclusive. The term "Jew" fails to distinguish the indigenous Judeans(Yahudim) and their descendants from European Jewish(Ashkenazim and Sephardim) proselytes and their progeny who adopted the religious perspectives, traditions, and practices of the law-abiding ancient Judeans. I use the term Judean because it is clearly defined in the Bible and narrower in my understanding. A Judean is either a descendant of the biblical tribe of Judah or a full-time resident of the ancient land of Judea.

I use the term "YHWH", also known as the tetragrammaton, instead of the terms LORD, Yahweh, Jehovah, or "The Name". **Yod-Hey-Wav-Hey** are the English transliterations of the four Hebrew letters that make up the personal identifier of the God of gods. The term "YHWH" simply takes the first letter of the four transliterated words/letters to make a name. I cling to simplicity, and the use of "YHWH" simply eliminates arguments over the proper way to pronounce God's personal name/identifier.

I use the Strong's Concordance for Hebrew and Greek word definitions only because a friend gave it to me years ago. I am familiar with this particular Bible reference, and it is easy for me to use. I have been told numerous times that other bible reference tools are very good and just as easy to use. I haven't used a different physical copy of a bible reference tool while writing this book only because I haven't needed to. I do also use "E-Sword, the sword of the Lord" online tool to look up word definitions and verses.

I reference the Bible's passages to support my conclusions on what the bible teaches, and I try not to present specific opposing arguments about biblical doctrine in this book. For one thing, there are too many of them. What I present in this book is different enough from what all organized churches that I am familiar with teach. Each reader should be able to compare this book's contents to what his or her congregation teaches. I leave it up to each individual reader to decide whether the contents of this book or your accepted doctrine is more in line with the message and lessons of the bible. You know what you already believe. I'm challenged to effectively communicate new information. With that being said, feel free to use any version or translation of the bible that you are comfortable with. What is presented in this book is not limited by grammatical syntax. I do ask that you look up the verse references that are used in this book, as they witness to the validity of my conclusions. Chapter 1 of this book is more of a psychological examination of Adam, Eve and, Satan and how their characteristics influence humanity in and of every age. If you're more interested in interpretation, discovering answers to questions that you didn't know should be asked, and unraveling confusing biblical passages, feel free to skip ahead to Chapter 2 and beyond. Chapter 4 "Yeshua is Lord" goes point by point to confirm Yeshua's "status". If this is a question for you, then read all about it. If not, skip over the chapter and feel free to come back to it later.

As you go through this book, do keep in mind that blind acceptance is an immature, irresponsible, and ignorant approach to any relationship(Cross Reference **Genesis 3:1-5**). This book is full of new and unfamiliar material, but you don't need to have a college degree or even an open mind to understand what I'm presenting. You should question my conclusions. In fact, if what you read in these pages doesn't agitate, offend, or cause you to research your current beliefs, then all that this book is doing is telling you things that you already know, and you're not learning anything. I've spoken with enough church pastors to gauge the various responses that this information creates. The most disappointing response came from a pastor who was the "Question and answer" guy whom the other pastors at this church went to with their biblical questions. He started off pompous and patronizing but by the end of our conversation he was the eager student full of questions. He asked if he could copy my notes and call me after he had reviewed them, I consented. About a month later he called and excitedly exclaimed, "You're right. The more I tried to prove your conclusions wrong, the firmer your conclusions held". We met again and the first thing I asked was how many of the other pastors he had shared this with. "None." he said, "I'm not getting fired over this". Having my life threated by a different church pastor didn't affect me like that response did. That did really hurt my feelings. I try not to be so vulnerable anymore but still, I'm not asking you to throw your career away. I'm only asking you to take the time that is necessary to understand why you do or do not agree with what I am presenting.

      In life and in Bible study always remain conscious of the fact that whether it be to our own word, that of other men, Satan, or to the word of God, we are all slaves. Freedom, absolute or otherwise, cannot exist until the Truth is known. The day in which we will all know the Truth is prophesied in **Jeremiah 31:34**. But for now the closest that we are able to get to freedom is to trust that God(or the god{religious or scientific} whom you submit to) is right(Cross Reference **John 8:31-32**).

      This book may be a quick read but don't assume that the information came to me over a few days or even a couple of weeks. Also, don't take for granted that every mystery of the bible will be unraveled by the morning. I personally view the bible and the understanding of it similarly to how I look at life itself. I'm still growing and still learning.

Notes:

CHAPTER 1
THE FIRST MURDER WAS A SUICIDE
Satan and Man; Looking Back at The Beginning

At its root, evil is simply a departure from the Truth. Any departure from the truth invariably leads to the "justifiable" acceptance of a "new" or "relative truth". Under normal circumstances men and women generally abhor evil when it is first encountered but, too often when evil is allowed to persist it becomes tolerable. Over time and after it is no longer viewed as being forceful or offensive, evil becomes acceptable. After becoming more or less acceptable, men will defend evil as being viable and will even regard it, in certain situations, as being more constructive than the truth. Inevitably the "new truth" becomes the truth that is endorsed by well-intended men and women, and the actual Truth comes to be regarded as offensive(Cross Reference **Genesis 3:1-6**). This process allowed humanity to accept Satan's great lie(**Isaiah 14:13-14**) and it is because of this process that all too often the best lies don't even know that they are being told.

Satan, father/originator of "The Lie" and founder of the earth's alternate reality, set his word(Cross Reference **Isaiah 14:13-14**) in motion in **Genesis 3:1** when he accosted Eve in the garden of Eden. He changed the course of humanity's future when he convinced Eve that his word was more beneficial than the word of God.

Satan effected so great a change within God's creation but he is mentioned or appears only a few times in the Bible. A simple statement, "The serpent was cunning above every animal of the field that YHWH Elohim had made" introduces Bible readers to humanities greatest adversary. Satan, the Serpent, the Devil, and Great Red Dragon, is mysterious but between the pages of the Old and New Testaments there is enough information about him to give Bible readers insight into the methodology, ambition, and personality of life's mightiest foe.

SATAN:
(Strong's Exhaustive Concordance of the Bible, Reference #**H7854**)
(Cross Reference **Job 1:6-12, 2:1-7**)

The Serpent
Genesis 3:1-5

1. And the serpent was cunning above every animal of the field which YHWH Elohim had made. And he said to the woman, Is it true that God has said, You shall not eat from any tree of the garden?
2. And the woman said to the serpent, We may eat of the fruit of the trees of the garden,
3. But of the fruit of the tree which is in the middle of the garden, God has said, You shall not eat of it, nor shall you touch it, lest you die.
4. And the serpent said to the woman, You shall not surely die,
5. For God knows that in the day you eat of it, your eyes shall be opened, and you shall be as God, knowing good and evil.

Genesis 3:1-5

Genesis 3:14-15

14. And YHWH said to the serpent, Because you have done this, you are cursed above all beasts, and above every animal of the field. You shall go on your belly, and you shall eat dust all the days of your life.
15. And I will put enmity between you and the woman, and between your seed and her seed; He will bruise your head, and you shall bruise His heel.

Genesis 3:14-15

The Willful/Prideful Man
Isaiah 14:4-23

4. You shall take up this proverb against the king of Babylon, and say: How the exacter, the gold gatherer, has ceased!
5. YHWH has broken the rod of the wicked, the staff of the rulers,
6. Who struck the peoples in wrath, a blow without turning away, ruling the nations in anger, persecuting without restraint.
7. All the earth is at rest, quiet; they break forth into singing.
8. Yea, the cypress trees rejoice over you; the cedars of Lebanon say, Since you have lain down, no wood cutter will come up against us.
9. Sheol from below is stirred for you, to meet you at your coming; it stirs up the departed spirits for you, all of the chief ones of the earth. It has raised all of the kings of the nations from their thrones.
10. All of them shall answer and say to you, Are you also made as weak as we? Are you likened to us?
11. Your majesty is lowered into Sheol; the noise of your harps. The maggot is spread under you; yea the worms cover you.
12. O shining star, son of the morning, how you have fallen from the heavens! You weakening the nations, you are cut down to the ground.
13. For you have said in your heart, I will go up to the heavens; I will raise my throne above the stars of God, and I will sit in the mount of meeting, in the sides of the north.
14. I will rise over the heights of the clouds; I will be compared to the Most High.
15. Yet you shall be brought out to Sheol, to the sides of the pit.
16. They who see you shall stare and closely watch you, pondering, Is this the man who made the earth tremble, shaking kingdoms,
17. Making the world like a wilderness, and who tore down its cities; he did not open a house for his prisoners?

18. All kings of nations, all of them lie in glory, each man in his house.
19. But you are thrown from your grave like a despised branch, a covering of those killed, those pierced by the sword, those who go down into the stones of the pit, as a trampled corpse.
20. You shall not be united with them in burial, because you ruined your land; you have slain your people; the seed of evil doers shall never be named.
21. Prepare for the slaughter of his sons, for the iniquity of their fathers; that they may not rise and possess the land and fill the face of the earth with cities.
22. For I will rise against them, says YHWH of Hosts, and cut off the name and the remnant, the son and the grandson, from Babylon, declares YHWH.
23. I will make it a possession of the hedgehog, and pools of water; and I will sweep it with the broom of ruin, says YHWH of hosts.

Isaiah 14:4-23

The Anointed Cherub, Worldly Economist
Ezekiel 28:12-19

12. Son of man, lift up a lament over the king of Tyre, and say to him, So says the Lord YHWH: You seal the measure, full of wisdom and perfect in beauty.
13. You have been in Eden the garden of God; every precious stone was your covering, the ruby, the topaz, and the diamond, the beryl, the onyx, and the jasper, the sapphire, the turquoise, and the emerald, and gold. The workmanship of your timbrels and of your pipes in you; in the day you were created, they were prepared.
14. You were the anointed cherub that covers, and I had put you in the holy height of God, where you were. You walked up and down in the midst of the stones of fire.
15. You were perfect in your ways from the day you were created, until iniquity was found in you.

16. By the multitude of your trade, they filled your midst with violence, and you sinned. So, I cast you profaned from the height of God, and I destroyed you, O covering cherub, from among the stones of fire.
17. Your heart was lifted up because of your beauty; you corrupted your wisdom because of your splendor. I have cast you to the ground, I will put you before kings, that they may see you.
18. You defiled your sanctuaries by the multitude of your iniquities, by the iniquity of your trade; therefore, I brought a fire from your midst; it shall devour you, and I will give you for ashes on the earth, in the sight of all who see you.
19. All who know you among the peoples shall be appalled at you; you shall become a horror, and you will not be forever.
Ezekiel 28:12-19

The Dragon
Revelation 12:3-4

3. And another sign was seen in Heaven. And behold, a great red dragon having seven heads and ten horns! And on its heads were seven diadems,
4. And his tail drew the third of the stars of the heaven. And did cast them to the earth. And the dragon stood before the woman, which was ready to be delivered, for to devour her child as soon as it was born.
Revelation 12:3-4

and,

Revelation 12:7-9

7. And war occurred in Heaven, Michael and his angels making war against the dragon. And the dragon and his angels made war,
8. But they did not have strength, nor was place yet found for them in Heaven.
9. And the dragon was cast out, the old serpent being called Devil, and Satan, he deceiving the whole habitable world

was cast out onto the earth, and his angels were cast out with him.
Revelation 12:7-9
and,
Revelation 12:15-17
15. And the serpent threw water out of his mouth like a river after the woman, that he might cause her to be carried off by the river.
16. And the earth helped the woman, and the earth opened its mouth and swallowed the river which the dragon threw out of its mouth.
17. And the dragon was enraged over the woman and went away to make war with rest of her seed, those keeping the commandments of God, and having the testimony of Yeshua the Messiah.
Revelation 12:15-17
and,
Revelation 20:1-3
1. And I saw an angel coming down out of Heaven, having the key of the abyss, and a great chain in his hand.
2. And he laid hold of the dragon, the old serpent who is the Devil and Satan, and bound him a thousand years,
3. And threw him into the abyss, and shut him up, and sealed over him, that he should not lead astray the nations, until the thousand years are fulfilled. And after these things, he must be set loose a little time.
Revelation 20:1-3
and,
Revelation 20:7-10
7. And whenever the thousand years are ended, Satan will be set loose out of his prison,
8. And he will go out to mislead the nations in the four corners of the earth, Gog and Magog, to assemble them in war, whose number is as the sand of the sea.

9. And they went up over the breath of the land and encircled the camp of the saints, and the beloved city. And fire from God came down out of Heaven and, devoured them.
10. And the Devil leading them astray was thrown into the Lake of Fire and Brimstone, where the Beast and the False Prophet were. And they were tormented day and night forever and ever.

Revelation 20:7-10

      Satan has stood before the Creator of the universe. He is older and more experienced than man's most ancient ancestor. Satan is intelligent and excels in the sciences of man, nature, and economics. He is attractive, persuasive, and able to offer a man or woman what each one believes that he or she most desires. He also operates on a plane of existence that much of humanity is not conscious of. And, Satan is deadly. To say that modern humanity is at Satan's mercy, falls short of even being an understatement. Eve standing alone before the serpent in the garden of Eden was far more capable of defending herself against Satan's attack than humanity is today. Spiritually speaking, modern man more closely resembles an infant covered in deer's blood who is trapped in the mouth of a ravenous wolf, than it does a warrior who is able to stand against his hostile adversary.

      Satan was brought into existence and came into his own standing long before the serpent tempted Eve in the garden of Eden. According to **Ezekiel 28:11-19** the anointed cherub maintained a kingdom with a prosperous economic system. But he profaned his habitation through pride and his kingdom was destroyed. The Bible does not give the date nor the geographic location of Satan's original domain, but the Bible reveals that his kingdom was not of this earth, and it existed before the serpent appeared in the garden of Eden to tempt Eve. The kingdom's name, **Rahab***, is mentioned a few times in the Bible. Each mention of the ancient kingdom of Rahab adds clarity to the puzzle of Satan's past and his plan for humanity's future.

Job 26:11-13
11. The pillars of heaven tremble and are stunned at His(God's) rebuke.
12. He quiets the sea with His power, and by His skillfulness He shatters Rahab.
13. By His Spirit the heavens were beautified; His hand pierced the fleeing serpent.
Job 26:11-13

and,

Psalm 87:4
4. I will mention Rahab and Babylon to those who know me; behold, Philistia and Tyre with Ethiopia; this was born there.
Psalm 87:4

and,

Psalm 89:10
10. You have crushed Rahab as one slain; You have scattered Your enemies with your mighty arm.
Psalm 89:10

and,

Isaiah 51:9
1. Awake! Awake! Arm of YHWH, put on strength. Awake, as in the days of old, of everlasting generations. Was it not You cutting in pieces Rahab, and piercing the serpent?
Isaiah 51:9

This thought is purely speculation: Personally, I have always wondered if the asteroid belt between Mars and Jupiter is the result of a planet, possibly Rahab, being destroyed. A habitable planet that divided the giant gas planets from the terrestrial planets and that could have once been the home of "spiritual" beings who have the ability to communicate with flesh and blood *men and women is at the very least an interesting thought to consider. After all, Satan did rule over a literal kingdom that was destroyed and whose inhabitants were scattered before he arrived in the garden of Eden. The scattered inhabitants of Rahab could very well have been the sinful angels(**Job 4:18; 2Peter 2:4; Jude 1:6**) who were responsible for initiating the perverse cohabitations upon the earth which led to the judgment of the great flood in Noah's day(**Genesis 6:1-7**). Interesting, but purely speculation.*

    The time and place of Satan's reign may have changed over the millennia, but his methodology and aspiration to be compared to the Most High God has not. In order to gain insight into Rahab, a Satanic kingdom that has only a few details given about it, a kingdom(or kingdoms) that is known to have operated under Satanic authority and which has many details provided can be examined to fill in some of the missing information. **Ecclesiastes 1:9**, **Isaiah 28:10**, as well as prophecy itself -which follows observable patterns-, all support this method of interpretation. In **Isaiah 14:4** and **Ezekiel 28:12** Babylon and Tyre/Tyrus respectively, are identified as two such kingdoms, that existed under the leadership of Satan and were prophesied, like Rahab, to be destroyed by God.

    The descriptions given in **Isaiah** chapter **14**(Cross Reference **Matthew 4:8-11**) and **Ezekiel 28** of Satan and his authority over the kingdoms of Babylon and Tyre/Tyrus, taken alongside the temptation of Eve/Adam in **Genesis** chapter **3**(Cross Reference **Matthew 4:1-7**) whilst taking **Genesis** chapter **6** into consideration, provide all of the necessary information to understand the capability, aspiration, and methodology of the cunning old serpent, as well as the modus operandi of all past, present, and future Satanic kingdoms(Cross Reference The Seven-Headed Ten-Horned Beast, the False Prophet of **Revelation 13:1-18**, and the Synagogue of Satan of **Revelation 2:9, 3:9**).

Satan, Satanism, and Man's Suicidal Nature

During a period before written history the being who would come to be known as Satan(Strong's Concordance #**H7854**: Adversary), discovered a righteousness of his own(**Isaiah 14:13-14**) that forever separated him from the way, the truth, and the life that could only be found in his Creator. The anointed cherub's(Cross Reference **Ezekiel 28:11-19**) wisdom, beauty, business acumen, and strength of force only served to foster the pride that he held in his own righteousness. Satan's personal discovery completely consumed his heart, mind, and soul, and made him the creation's original "self-made" man. Satan's imperious self-righteousness spawned the tree of Knowledge of Good and Evil and drove him to blindly pursue his own great lie. When the serpent tempted Eve(**Genesis 3:1-5**) in the garden of Eden with the forbidden fruit, he sincerely believed every word that came out of his mouth. Consequently, when Eve offered the fruit to Adam, she honestly believed that she was helping her husband.

Satan's declaration, "I shall be compared to the Most High(**Isaiah 14:14**)", was repackaged for human consumption and it is that all consuming lie, "You shall be as God(**Genesis 3:5**)", that has been the driving force which has divided humanity in the past and up to the modern day. Being the originator/father of the lie, Satan cleverly positioned himself as the god whom Eve and subsequently all of humanity would come to resemble. And ever since that fateful encounter in the garden of Eden, it has been the spirit of Satan that has dictated over man's perception and understanding of the human experience. Every lie, every theft, every rape, every murder, all the wars of man, and humanity's understanding of God and truth are rooted in Satan's ability to provide each man and woman with their own unattainable standard of righteousness(**Genesis 3:5**).

Satanism allows men and women the justification to lie, or use wealth, beauty, intelligence, emotional manipulation, business acumen, and outright force, in order to usurp the control of human rights and to ruin the earth's habitable environment. In essence, Satanism provides its advocates with the means to "Win" at life. Satanic axioms such as "Survival of the fittest", "Might makes right", and "Money makes the world go round(Cross Reference **Ezekiel 28:15-18**)", only encourage conflict within man and predispose humanity to a perpetual cycle of self-destruction. Satanic kingdoms are rooted in deceit, and they thrive on inequality, competition, desperation, perversion, and injustice. They function as corporate bodies in which success is measured by having more possessions, control, or influence over others and failure is decreed by having less. Skill is determined by comparisons and is measured by ones intellectual, financial, and/or physical mastery over others: winning or being "better". The Satanic corporate body devalues the individual for the sake of the corporation's continuance. Life in a Satanic society is unstable and lived in submission to ignorance, fear, pride, insecurity and the ever evolving will, word, and whims of man. Life itself is valued according to the usage of the ruling class.

In contrast to a Satanic society, a prosperous society operates successfully when it functions like a healthy living body(Cross Reference "The body of the Messiah in the New Heavens and New Earth). Each individual within the society directly and indirectly supplements other individuals of the body for the mutual wellbeing of each individual and for the health of the body. Each individual with their unique individuality, experience, perspective, and knowledge is indispensable to the body. In a healthy society skill is understood to be the physical, emotional, and intellectual mastery of oneself(**Colossians 1:9-11** Cross Reference **Genesis 1:28**: "Be fruitful and multiply"). Challenges and competitions are opportunities for each individual to personally mature and grow. Growth through experience is considered success and stagnancy is failure. Life in a healthy society is lived in continual pursuit of perfection(**Genesis 17:1; Luke 6:40**). A spiritually, emotionally, intellectually, and physically healthy and mature individual, and by extension a society of such individuals, is the picture of godliness. In a godly society life is not lived as a competition. Life is itself the continual opportunity to be fruitful in every good work(Cross Reference the "Tree of life": **Proverbs 3:13-19, 11:30, 13:12, 15:4**) and to increase/multiply in the knowledge of God(**Colossians 1:10**).

Adam and Eve

The story of Adam and Eve's interaction with the serpent is short but it is loaded with insight. Their story exposes Satan's subtle method of achieving world domination and answers the question of why the world at large exists as it does today. Their story also describes man's intrinsic nature, exposes humanity's vulnerabilities, and reveals how we sold/sell out our manhood. The universal qualities of man that are depicted in Adam and Eve provide more than just the back-story for how we progressed from the garden of Eden to the flood in Noah's day, to the time of the Messiah's revelation, and up to the prophesied "End Times". Adam and Eve speak directly to the soul of every individual who has existed on the earth from the time that Adam was placed in the garden of Eden up until this day.

Satan was able to rob Adam of his manhood because he understood the complexity of man. Satan could have witnessed Adam's creation and ordination. He could have observed Adam's life in the garden of Eden and his relationship with YHWH Elohim. Satan also could have witnessed Adam's wonderment when he was presented with Eve. In addition to observing Adam and Eve and acquiring an appreciation for their distinct character traits, Satan, more importantly, understood himself.

Genesis 2:7, 15-25; Genesis 3:1-6; and **Genesis 5:1-2** briefly detail the life, times, and characteristics of Adam and Eve. In addition to identifying distinct qualities of man(Adam and Eve) these passages, in light of **Isaiah 14:13-14**, aide the inquisitive bible reader in understanding why Satan, the anointed Cherub(Cross Reference **Ezekiel 28:14**) who had stood before the throne of God, would even concern himself with a human being.

Genesis 2:7
7. And YHWH Elohim formed the man out of dust from the ground, and blew into his nostrils the breath of life; and the man became a living soul.
Genesis 2:7

Genesis 2:15-25
15. And YHWH Elohim took the man and put him into the garden of Eden, to work and to keep it.
16. And YHWH commanded the man, saying, You may freely eat of every tree of the garden;
17. But of the Tree of the Knowledge of Good and Evil you may not eat, for in the day that you eat of it, you shall surely die.
18. And YHWH Elohim said, It is not good, that the man should be alone. I will make a helper suited to him.
19. And YHWH Elohim formed every animal of the field, and bird of the heavens out of the ground. And He brought them to the man, to see what he would call it. And all which the man might call it, each living soul, that was its name.
20. And the man called names to all the cattle, and to the birds of the heavens, and to every animal of the field. But no helper suited to the man was found for him.

21. And YHWH Elohim caused a deep sleep to fall on the man, and he slept. And He took one of his ribs and closed up the flesh underneath.
22. And YHWH Elohim formed the rib which He had taken from the man into a woman and brought her to the man.
23. And the man said, This now, at last, bone of my bone, and flesh from my flesh. For this shall be called Woman, because this has been taken out of man.
24. Therefore, a man shall leave his father and his mother, and shall cleave to his wife; and they shall become one flesh.
25. And they were both naked, the man and his wife, and they were not ashamed.
Genesis 2:15-25

and,

Genesis 3:1-6

1. And the serpent was cunning above every animal of the field which YHWH Elohim had made. And he said to the woman, Is it true that God has said, You shall not eat from any tree of the garden?
2. And the woman said to the serpent, We may eat of the fruit of the trees of the garden,
3. But of the fruit of the tree which is in the middle of the garden, God has said, You shall not eat of it, nor shall you touch it, lest you die.
4. And the serpent said to the woman, You shall not surely die,
5. For God knows that in the day you eat of it, your eyes shall be opened, and you shall be as God, knowing good and evil.
6. And the woman saw that the tree was good for food, and that it was pleasant to the eyes, and the tree was desirable to make one wise. And she took of its fruit and ate; and she also gave to her husband with her, and he ate.

Genesis 3:1-6

and,

Genesis 5:1-2

1. This is the book of the generations of Adam: In the day that God created Adam, He made him in the likeness of God.
2. He created them male and female, and blessed them, and called their name Man in the day when they were created.

Genesis 5:1-2

Satan knew that Adam's role within the garden of Eden served a purpose within God's creation. When God created man(**Genesis 1:27**) male and female, Satan seized on the opportunity to set his plan in motion. His desire to kill humanity's first man and take possession of his identity(Cross Reference **Revelation 2:9, 3:9[Luke 20:13-14]** the "synagogue of Satan, who say they are Judeans and are not, but lie") as the mediator between man and the word of God, was just one step in his campaign to position himself in the place of the Most High(Cross Reference **Isaiah 14:13-14**).

The Male and Female, and The Tree of Knowledge of Good and Evil

The terms **'male'** and **'female'** first appear in the biblical text in **Genesis 1:27** when man was created on the sixth day of the creation. The two terms as they are used in **Genesis 1:27** have been, much like the phrase "Be fruitful and multiply", misinterpreted. This point may not resonate with you until you know what the first chapter of Genesis actually is(described in Chapter 3 of this book) but, the terms 'male' and 'female' are not used in **Genesis 1:27** to reference a man or a woman's physical anatomy. In the 2nd chapter of the book of Genesis, Adam and Eve should most certainly be understood as having been two flesh and blood individuals but, in **Genesis 1:27** the terms 'male' and 'female' are used to identify the **masculine** and **feminine** qualities of a man's soul. The masculine and feminine qualities of man's soul are similar in scope yet of a diminished magnitude to the spiritual qualities that are found in the **Image** and **Likeness** of God(**Genesis 1:26, 27; 5:1**; described in Chapter 2 of this book). Just as the **image** and **likeness** of God impart distinct spiritual qualities on man, the masculine and feminine characteristics of man impart their own distinct qualities on the human soul.

The masculine characteristic of a man's soul is literal, logical, protective, and accords a degree of accountability. The feminine character trait of man is volitional, imaginative, expressive, and imparts a degree of distinctiveness. Both the male and female characteristics of man's soul have their own distinct qualities but, a man cannot be complete, whole, nor balanced in the absence or neglect of one of these two essential characteristics(Cross Reference **Romans 1:24-27**). In the absence or neglect of one of these two qualities an individual will become insecure, aggressive, overbearing, abusive, compulsive, and/or violent. This form of corruption took root in the human soul when Eve was tempted by the serpent in the Garden of Eden(**Genesis 3:1-8** Cross Reference **Genesis 4:1-8, 23-24**).

Before Eve was tempted and Adam sinned(**Genesis 3:1-6**) YHWH Elohim had told Adam in **Genesis 2:16** that he could freely eat of every tree of the garden of Eden. In **Genesis 2:17** YHWH Elohim appeared to contradict His own word when He commanded Adam not to eat the fruit of the tree of knowledge of good and evil. The confusion is cleared up by recognizing that the tree of knowledge of good and evil was not a tree that was native to the garden of Eden, it was not a creation of God, and it was not placed in the garden paradise by God to test Adam.

Adam was forbidden to eat the fruit of the tree of knowledge of good and evil(**Genesis 2:17**) because its qualities are contrary to the nourishment that God Himself provided for His living souls(**Genesis 1:29-30** Cross Reference the tree of life: **Proverbs 3:13-18, 11:30, 13:12, 15:4).** The very existence of the tree of knowledge of good and evil defies the quality of life that is offered to man by the Most High God. It was spawned in the lie of Satan(**Isaiah 14:13-14** "I will be like the Most High"), it matured in the serpent's rebellion(**Genesis 3:5** "You shall be as God"), it bore additional fruit in Adam's sin(**Genesis 3:6-8** Cross Reference **Genesis 2:17**), and it will continue to exist until the Devil is cast into the lake of fire and brimstone(**Revelation 20:10-15**).

The serpent recognized the significance of Adam's relationship with YHWH Elohim and he understood the reason for YHWH Elohim's prohibition against the fruit of the tree of knowledge of good and evil(**Genesis 2:17**). Adam had been placed in the garden of Eden to stand before God as humanity's representative and, he stood before humanity as the picture of godliness. Adam and Eve also existed in the garden of Eden as literal personifications of the human soul. Satan intelligently attacked the foremost man of the earth to separate Adam from his position of favor, to corrupt the likeness of God in man, to subjugate the soul of man to the spirit of adversity, and to anoint himself as god over the corrupt existence.

When the serpent decided to attack Adam, he acted from a position of understanding. The dragon had watched Adam and Eve, studied their behaviors, and had analyzed their relationship. After all they were completely naked -that is to say, fully exposed and having nothing to hide- and they were both content(**Genesis 2:25; Philippians 4:11-12**) with the life that had been provided for them. The serpent convinced Eve that she had a deficiency, which created a desire in her imaginative mind. He was then able to proposition Eve with the fruit of the tree of knowledge of good and evil in full confidence of Adam's subsequent response.

Satan's understanding of Adam and Eve's individual strengths and weaknesses did not only serve Satan's purpose in the garden of Eden. The exploitation of humanity's universal character traits continues up to the modern age.

Eve

Eve had been taken out of Adam's body, formed, and presented to him as the indispensable feminine counterpart(**Genesis 2:21-24**) to his masculine nature. Eve is on record as the first human being to encounter the serpent and the first to eat the fruit of the tree of knowledge of good and evil. Interestingly, Eve did not recognize that she had committed a mistake, nor did she become aware of her nakedness until after both she and Adam had eaten the forbidden fruit. If nothing else, this fact supports the argument that we may never be able to see ourselves as we truly are until after we have completely died to our old way of life(Cross Reference "Born Again" **John 3:5-8**).

Genesis 3:1-5 is the record of the serpent approaching man in a vulnerable state of mind, and offering her(Eve) the means to alleviate her condition. Eve was powerless to defend herself against the foe whom she believed offered her salvation in her moment of confusion.

Genesis 3:1-5
1. And the serpent was cunning above every animal of the field which YHWH Elohim had made, and he said to the woman, is it true that God has said, You shall not eat from any tree of the garden?
2. And the woman said to the serpent, We may eat the fruit of the trees of the garden,

3. but of the fruit of the tree which is in the middle of the garden, God has said, You shall not eat of it, nor shall you touch it. Lest you die.
4. And the serpent said to the woman, You shall not surely die.
5. For God knows that in the day you eat of it, your eyes shall be opened, and you shall be as God, knowing good and evil.
Genesis 3:1-5

Eve's response in **Genesis 3:3** to the serpent's question shows her to have been honest, sincere, and trusting. Eve's openness is admirable but, what she failed to recognize is that the serpent proposed a loaded question. It was Eve's disclosure about how she understood the two trees that were in the midst of the garden of Eden that gave Satan all of the ammunition that he needed to recreate man according to his own image and likeness(**Isaiah 14:13-14** Cross Reference **Genesis 1:26**). By considering how she approached the opportunity to partake of the fruit of the tree of knowledge of good and evil in **Genesis 3:6**, curiosity, desire, imagination, assertiveness, and decisiveness(in addition to her previously stated feminine qualities) can also be read into Eve's personality.

Genesis 3:6
6. And the woman saw that the tree was good for food, and that it was pleasant to the eyes, and the tree was desirable to make one wise. And she took of its fruit and ate; and she also gave to her husband with her, and he ate.
Genesis 3:6

It was Satan's recognition of Eve's personal characteristics coupled with her naivety to his sinister ambition that allowed the serpent to manipulate her expectation to his advantage. Eve was simply caught at a disadvantage. She apparently had little to no appreciation of evil and could therefore have no conception of the lengths that it would go to accomplish its objectives.

After Eve submitted to the serpent's temptation and ate the fruit of the tree of knowledge of good and evil, she in turn submitted Adam to her new understanding. Thereby making the head of her community subject to her will and disrupting God's established order(Cross Reference **Psalm 82:5**). As a result of her actions Eve was disciplined by YHWH Elohim in **Genesis 3:16** and became subject to Adam's authority. Eve's discipline is severe, but she is held less accountable than Adam for her part in the rebellion, because she had not been personally commanded by YHWH Elohim to watch over the garden of Eden nor had she been personally cautioned against eating the fruit of the tree of knowledge of good and evil(**Luke 12:47-48**).

There is nothing in the Bible that would suggest that YHWH Elohim has anything personal against women. After all, from the beginning of the creation God made Man both male and female(**Genesis 1:27; Mark 10:6**). The fact of the matter is that YHWH Elohim is a masculine(Cross Reference "Father" in relation to God, throughout the Bible.) and objective God. The universe is the fruitful and life-giving feminine expression God's own individuality. It only follows that the maintenance of God's creation would require an authoritative and accountable administration to oversee its orderly operation, a literal understanding to maintain its functional dynamics, and the meticulous execution of duty to precede personal expression or individual ambitions -if for no other reason than to prevent chaos(Cross Reference Satan/the Adversary). It is for this reason that the image of God(**Genesis 1:27** Cross Reference **Genesis 1:26**) needed to precede the likeness of God(**Genesis 5:1** Cross Reference **Genesis 1:26**) when man was originally created. And why the masculine trait of man needed to precede the feminine characteristic when Adam was formed(**Genesis 2:7, 21-22** Cross Reference **Genesis 1:27, 5:2**). God's creation was established in order(Cross Reference The seven-day creation **Genesis 1:1-2:4a**) and within it humanity was given liberty. Satan is responsible for disrupting God's order, and for the creation and human relations degenerating into a system of inequality and control.

    Satan introduced control into the creation and redefined the human experience through manipulation. The serpent accused God of withholding the truth from Eve and stood convincingly before her as "living" proof of his assertion. He pressed his argument further by offering Eve the fruit of the tree that he knew contradicted the understanding of the word that she was looking for. Yet it wasn't until Eve handed Adam the forbidden fruit and he willingly chose to stray out of the 'way of life', that Satan's prideful ambition to be comparable to the Most High(**Isaiah 14:13-14**) began to fully materialize.

Adam

    Adam was not born in the garden of Eden, he was placed there in **Genesis 2:15** as a mature, intelligent, and capable adult male after he had been formed in **Genesis 2:7**. Adam did not work for compensation or a reward. He performed his duties in the garden of Eden because he was a literal, rational, protective, devoted, and task oriented man who had been commissioned by his Creator(**Genesis 2:15-24**) to execute the duties associated with the office of a priest(before sin). Adam was content with his life in the garden of Eden, his wife, and the relationship that he had with his Creator. He knew the word of God, he was committed, and single minded in performing the duties(Cross Reference **1Timothy 2:14**) associated with his office. Adam did not only stand before YHWH Elohim as the righteous representative of humanity and before all of mankind as the example of godliness. Adam also stood before Satan as an unapproachable obstacle.

Unfortunately for Adam, he was the coveted prize of a clever being who was in possession of exceptional capabilities(Cross Reference **Ezekiel 28:12**). Adam may personally have been an unapproachable obstacle to the serpent but Eve, the glory of Adam's life(**1Corinthians 11:7** Cross Reference **Ephesians 5:25,28-29**), could serve Satan as the perfect means to his desired end. Satan was able to succeed in the garden of Eden by dividing Adam's loyalty and presenting him with a choice where no choice had ever existed before.

"Choice" itself is not the root cause of man's problems, it is only an effect or consequence of an individual's ignorance(Cross Reference the temptation of Yeshua of Nazareth: **Matthew 4:1-11; Luke 4:1-13**. There was no choice for Yeshua to make.). Our susceptibility to be misled in any situation is due to our ignorance of all the pertinent facts. When the serpent tempted Eve, he attacked her confusion regarding the two trees that were in the midst of the garden of Eden. He was able to create an emotional response in Eve by promising her what she believed to be a solution to her problem. Eve became a liability when she took the lead and spoke with the serpent instead of deferring to Adam who had received the command from God. Adam was not deceived. He fully understood the word of God, but he still chose to follow Eve's example.

Although prideful chauvinists have used **Genesis** chapter **3** to demean the mental fortitude of women, the message of **Genesis** chapter **3** was never intended to lead people to conclude that women are incapable of handling confrontation. Eve was deceived(Adam sinned in full knowledge of the word of God). The message of **Genesis** chapter **3** is a universal address to man(**Genesis 5:2** "He created them male and female, and He blessed them, and called their name Man.") that speaks to the human soul. What should be understood from **Genesis** chapter **3** is that in the midst of a(or any) confrontation, an individual's(whether they be male or female) emotional response that is procured by the adversary must become subject to the individual's informed rationale(**Genesis 3:16** Cross Reference **Genesis 4:6-7**) or, that individual will suffer the greater risk of succumbing to the adversary's will(Cross Reference **Genesis 3:1-8**).

      Adam was forced to choose between the helpmate who defined a portion of his own identity or an existence apart from her. Adam loved Eve. He valued her word and the relationship that he shared with her(Cross Reference **Ephesians 5:25,28-29**). His life was literally over when Eve ate the forbidden fruit. Now, after Eve had eaten the forbidden fruit, Adam only needed to come to terms with severing the relationship that he had with YHWH Elohim, Whom he eventually blamed for his sin(**Genesis 3:12**). Adam's attempt to justify himself by blaming God reveals the level of desperation that has been imbued within humanities fallen nature. The immediate gratification of having his wife initially outweighed Adam's fear of losing his life. But when Adam came to his senses in **Genesis 3:7** and heard YHWH Elohim in the garden of Eden(**Genesis 3:8**) he hid out of fear. I imagine that the prospect of facing his Creator and the idea of death, an unknown existence apart from God, must have been just as terrifying for Adam in that moment as it is for many people today.

      Adam's sin and the effects of it were not confined to the garden of Eden. **Romans 5:12** and **Romans 6:16** explain just how far the repercussions of Adam's sin have reached.

Romans 5:12

12. Because of this, even as sin entered the world through one man, and death through sin, so also death passed to all men, inasmuch as all sinned;
Romans 5:12

and,

Romans 6:16

16. Do you not know that to whom you yield yourselves slaves for obedience, you are slaves to whom you obey, whether of sin to death, or obedience to righteousness?
Romans 6:16

     Adam was justified by his Creator from the day that he was formed. He was deemed righteous by his innate nature as the likeness of God. He stood before God as the representative of humanity, and all of humanity was thereby justified by God through Adam. When the seed of rebellion that took root in the pride of Satan infiltrated humanity through Adam, we all, in turn, were alienated from the Light and Life of God, and we all became subject to sin and death. Adam may not have plunged a knife into anyone's heart, stolen another man's property, cast spells, or summoned demons to do his bidding but, according to **Romans 6:16**, when Adam submitted himself to the serpent(**Genesis 3:4-7**), the Spirit of Life was taken from him(**Genesis 2:17** Cross Reference **Genesis 3:6-24**), and he(subsequently, we) became a Satanist(s). Humanity's alienation from the Spirit of Life allowed the many and varied expressions of fear, pride, and insecurity to infiltrate the human psyche.

     In the very day that Adam ate the fruit of the tree of knowledge of good and evil he died(Cross Reference **Genesis 2:17**). The Spirit of Life was taken from Adam, man's God given identity was compromised, and the Satanic spiritual identity was unopposed in filling the void that had been left within the human nature(Cross Reference **Romans 6:16**). Thus, by elevating his own word to the place of God's(**Genesis 3:4** "You shall not surely die" vs. **Genesis 2:17** "You shall surely die".) and having Adam removed from his anointed position in the garden of Eden, Satan was able position himself as the mediator between humanity and the word of Truth(**Genesis 3:1-7** Cross Reference **Romans 5:12**). Furthermore, by convincing man to eat the fruit of the tree that was spawned in his own lie, Satan was able to seat himself as the god whom mankind would resemble(**Isaiah 14:13-14** Cross Reference **Romans 6:16**).

As sinister a move as it was, I feel no shame in saying that Satan's appeal to man's feminine psyche was a stroke of genius. Corporations, advertisers, entertainers, clerics, and politicians so often capture our support by bypassing our rational thinking, taking advantage of our emotions, and provoking our imaginations, that we fail to appreciate the brilliance of Satan's maneuver.

In the past I had often wondered if Adam had stood idly by watching the serpent tempt Eve or, if he had been off somewhere else tending to the needs of the garden. I've asked myself, "If Adam was present, then how could he have allowed Eve to be tempted? But if he was not there, then why hadn't he done more to secure the garden before leaving her alone?" Now that I am older, have been married and have children, and some experience on my side, my perception of Adam and his failure has changed. I now wonder what Adam could have done to have stopped the woman he loved and whom he respected, from eating the forbidden fruit once she was determined to have what she had been convinced would give her the "thing" -knowledge, position, distinction, authority, relationship, self-worth, etc.- that God had kept from her(Cross Reference **Genesis 3:1-5**). I don't believe that Eve was a selfish, impulsive, nor an irresponsible woman and I don't think that Adam was a weak man for following her example. I do believe that Eve was deceived because she had no conception of the genius that she was being confronted with, and that Adam, who may have been flooded with remorse and guilt, and the fear of losing the most precious part of his life, faltered because he chose to compromise.

Religion Proper:

If the greatest lies don't know that they are being told, then it only follows that the greatest liars don't know that they are(**Matthew 24:24**).

All pursuits of righteousness (**Genesis 3:5** Cross Reference **Genesis 4:1-16**) and for justification(Cross Reference Genesis **4:19, 23-24**), every form of control, act of aggression, theft of man's rights, and even modern man's yearning to create his own sentient being(Artificial Intelligence) are founded upon Satan's lie, "I shall be compared to the Most High(**Isaiah 14:14**)". When Eve was deceived by the serpent into pursuing a caricature of her inherent nature(Cross Reference **Genesis 5:1** "The Likeness of God") the foundations of God's established order were shaken(**Psalm 82:5**), the truth became ambiguous, and righteousness having become subject to each man or woman's individual justification(**Genesis 4:23-24** Cross Reference **Genesis 3:5** "You shall be as God, knowing good and evil."), allowed religious chauvinism to take hold of all humanity.

I understand every institutionalized system of belief that men and women adhere or refer to in order to understand ourselves and the world around us, or which justifies the manner in which we relate to other people and our surroundings, to be religion. God instituted life. He offered man a relationship and the freedom to explore a world full of opportunities(**Genesis 2:7,15-16**). Satan orchestrated religion(Pursuits of righteousness for the sake of justification; Cross Reference **Genesis 3:5** "You shall be as God") in order to subject mankind to his identity. It is through religion that Satan institutionalized control(Satan came in his own name, anointed himself to the position of mediator between man and truth, and humanity submitted to his authority. Cross Reference **John 5:43**; **Romans 6:16**).

Conclusion

Satan is evil, and he is the most diabolical being ever created, but not necessarily for all the reasons that mankind attributes to him. We often assume that Satan is a hideous monster who scares the life out of us, but we fail to appreciate the fact that Satan has never aspired to be an evil version of the Most High God. Satan is the initiating principle who established 'the Lie' that he, and by extension we, could be compared to the Most High(**Genesis 3:5; Isaiah 14:13-14**). That 'Lie' is the unattainable notion of self-righteousness that convinced Eve to eat the forbidden fruit and, that which man has chased after ever since Adam's fall from grace in the garden of Eden.

Satan is powerful and deadly, but neither he nor his power is absolute. And though he is allowed to persist in authority over the earth, his spirit has been overcome(Cross Reference the "Death and Resurrection of the Messiah" and **Revelation 3:21**). Satan's power over humanity is founded upon our ignorance of the Truth and our continued submission to his lie(Cross Reference **Genesis 3:1-5**). In the day that the Truth, which is absolute(Cross Reference "I Am": **Exodus 3:14; John 8:57-59**), is known by all of humanity and when man has been imbued with the Spirit of Life, humanity's subjection to sin and death will end, and the power of Satan will cease to exist(**John 8:31-32** "The truth shall make you free" Cross Reference **Matthew 4:1-11, Luke 4:1-13**).

Adam and Eve's encounter with the serpent in the garden of Eden(**Genesis 3**) and the Devil's temptation of Yeshua of Nazareth in the wilderness(**Matthew 4:1-11; Luke 4:1-13**) are two of the Bible's definitive examples of spiritual warfare. Adam and Eve, who were presented with an opportunity and a choice, sinned. In Yeshua's case there never was a possibility of Him rebelling against His own identity. Yeshua of Nazareth stood before the Devil as the literal manifestation of the Truth, the living Word of God. Satan's ambition to seat himself as the creation's exalted god, "life" giving spirit, and chosen man was thwarted by the birth, ministry, death, and resurrection of Yeshua of Nazareth. The appearance of the Messiah, Who is the prophesied seed of the woman and the eternal Israel of God(Cross Reference **Genesis 3:15** and **Galatians 6:16** with **Galatians 3:16** and **Isaiah 49:1-10**) convicted Satan of his own lie. Satan is brilliant and cunning, he is intelligent and beautiful but, when he was confronted with God's living Word(Cross Reference **Matthew 4:1-11; Mark 1:12-13; Luke 4:1-13**) he was forced to accept that he could never be equal(**Isaiah 14:13-14**) to the God that he idolized.

In retrospect; as physically, emotionally, mentally, and spiritually exhausting as Yeshua's forty-day trial in the wilderness(**Matthew 4:1-11; Mark 1:12-13; Luke 4:1-13**) must have been, I believe that the experience would ultimately have been a great deal more debilitating for Satan, who was put on notice that the time of his judgment was drawing near.

Postscript

For a secular man or woman to misunderstand Adam and Eve's confrontation with the serpent in the garden of Eden is one thing. But, for a servant of the Messiah to presume that Satan, life's most hostile adversary, had been unleashed upon two naive adolescents may, in fact, be blasphemy. A wise and all-powerful God could not be so careless with His likeness, neglectful of His human creations, nor irresponsible with the earth's one sacred location.

The simple truth is that Adam and Eve prefigure the Messiah and His messianic body of believers(**Romans 5:14, Revelation 2-3**). Eve's confusion concerning the word of God, her subsequent trial, and submission to the serpent's misrepresentation of God's word are prophetic of the Christian Church's own experience with God's word, subsequent trial throughout the earth's great tribulation, and submission to false messiah's. Adam and Eve's experience in the garden of Eden even goes so far as to directly address the question of why there are so many types of Christian fellowships in the world today(**Genesis 3:1-24** Cross Reference **Revelation 2-3**).

Notes

CHAPTER 2
THE PATH OF INTERPRETATION
The Creation of the Angels
(Cross Reference **John 9:39-41**; "Blind Religious Leaders")
This chapter is a recap of the main topic of my first book "The Naked Truth of Angels and Man".

For years I had heard two reoccurring arguments from the pastors who I listened to at church, on the radio, and on the internet. The first and most frequent argument concerned the "Rapture" of the Messianic Body of believers. Pastors who I personally spoke with would continually say, "No one, except for the Father in Heaven knows the days or the times of the end. Therefore, the timing of the rapture cannot be known". To which I would always respond, "Those who are watching during those days will know." While I had then and have no interest now in the day, month, or year of the event, or even what it will look like, I could show those pastors exactly where the "Rapture" of the Messianic body takes place in the book of Revelation(Cross Reference **Matthew 24:30-31; Mark 13:26-27; 1Corinthians 15:51-55; 1Thessalonians 4:16-17**). In the book of Revelation after the seven believing communities are addressed in **Revelation 2-3**, after the scroll that is sealed with seven seals is completely unsealed in **Revelation 8:1**, after the seventh angel sounds his trumpet in **Revelation 11:15**, and after the shout is made in **Revelation 14:15**, to the One like the Son of man sitting upon the cloud(Cross Reference **Revelation 14:14**), for Him to reap His harvest, the "Rapture" of the Messianic body does take place in **Revelation 14:16**.

Man vs. Man

The second argument(really just a statement) that has come from church podiums is that the creation of the angels is not mentioned in the Bible. I enthusiastically disagree. If you have ever wondered when the "kings of the earth*" and the "powers in heavenly places*" received their positions of authority, the answer is found in the first chapter of the book of Genesis.

***Psalm 2:2; Daniel 10:11-21; Ephesians 3:10, 6:12** Cross reference **Deuteronomy 32:8**{English translations of v.8 in the Septuagint version of the Bible use "sons of God" instead of "sons of Israel", that is found in the Masoretic texts}.*

     For many centuries within church communities around the world, Adam has been understood to be the man who was created in **Genesis 1:27**. This interpretation appears to be supported by **1Corinthians 15:45-47** in which Adam is referred to as the "first man". But contrary to accepted church doctrine, the bible emphatically declares that Adam was not the man who was created in the image of God on the sixth day of the creation. According to **Genesis 2:7-8**(Cross Reference **Genesis 2:15-16**, and **Genesis 5:1**) Adam was formed as the likeness of God after God's initial six days of work and the creation's seventh day of repose. After being formed by YHWH Elohim, Adam was transported from his native land into Eden. Adam was then placed in Eden's garden paradise, given responsibilities, a word of caution, and a helpmate with whom to live out his existence. In addition to being given life and his unique existence within the garden of Eden, Adam was also privileged to commune with the Creator of the Universe.

     The belief that Adam was the man who was created in **Genesis 1:27** is simply one of the Church organization's(Catholic, Protestant, non-denominational, Messianic, Cult, etc.) long standing errors. This misguided interpretation of the man who was created in **Genesis 1:27** is aided by the Church's bewilderment over the first two chapters of the bible and prevents Christians from ever coming to the truth. The fact is that any undertaking in biblical comprehension that begins with misinformation simply cannot result in understanding(Cross Reference **Genesis 3:1-5**). The confusion surrounding Adam, who was formed from the dust of the ground in **Genesis 2:7**, and the man who was created in the image of God in **Genesis 1:27**, must therefore be eliminated before a faithful heart can be set on the path to understanding the Bible.

Adam Was First But, He Was Not the Original "Man"

In the Bible, the term "first" can be used to refer either to a progressional sequence or to an individual's positional distinction. The two sons of God, the Angels and Adam, are the Bible's most underappreciated examples of this occurrence. Chronologically the angels of God, who are always referred to and represented in the bible as men(**Genesis 6:2-4; Job 38:4-7; Psalm 82:6; Daniel 9:21**), were created by God before Adam was formed(**Genesis 2:7,15**) and given his positional distinction in the garden of Eden, or deemed the creation's first man.

Adam's creation and advancement to the position of distinction established a biblical precedent, but the bible is full of subsequent examples that show the younger siblings being given the position of distinction that is presumably reserved for the firstborn child. Two fairly well-known examples of the younger siblings receiving the blessing of the firstborn can be found in **Genesis 27:1-29** and **Genesis 48:13-20**(Cross Reference **Genesis 21:1-13** "Isaac and Ishmael"). In **Genesis 27:1-29**(Cross Reference **Romans 9:13**) after Esau had previously sold his birthright to his younger brother(**Genesis 25:33**) Jacob, Jacob then disguised himself as Esau to receive the blessing of the firstborn directly from the hand of their father, Isaac. In **Genesis 48:13-20** Jacob, adopting and blessing the two sons of Joseph, intentionally crossed his hands and placing his right hand upon the head of Ephraim, blessed his younger grandson ahead of Manasseh the elder grandchild. A few other biblical examples of the younger brother being placed ahead of the elder sibling can be found in **Genesis 4:1-7**(Abel and Cain), **Genesis 49:1-12**,(Judah), and in the book of Exodus. In **Genesis 4:1-7** Abel was preferred ahead of his older brother Cain, in **Genesis 49:1-12** Judah(See also **Genesis 49:22-26**; Joseph), the fourth born son, was blessed to receive the preeminent position among his brethren, and in the book of Exodus Moses was given the distinguished position as head of the nation of Israel, instead of his older brother Aaron.

The belief that Adam was the man who was created in **Genesis 1:27** has not only sent Christians and Jews off looking in the wrong direction for biblical understanding, this erroneous belief has also resulted in faulty conclusions concerning world and human history. For instance, the long-held belief that the universe is between 6,000-8,000 years old is founded upon the assumption that Adam was the man who was created on day six of the creation. Besides the fact that the bible refutes this claim, archaeology has proven that Central, Eastern, and North Eastern African civilizations were relatively well advanced in the sciences of anatomy, mummification, agriculture, language, math, writing, art, architecture, metallurgy, oceanography, and astronomy by the time that religious Jews and Christian congregations assume the creation to only have just begun. Archaeologists have even discovered anatomically modern human fossils in Herto Bouri, Ethiopia*, that predate the Jewish and Christian presumed creation start dates by over a hundred thousand years.

The fossils which were discovered in 1997, should also force educationalists to reevaluate modern conceptions of man's evolution as the Ethiopian Homo-Sapien fossils also predate the fossils of European Neanderthals by thousands of years. Note: There are many scientists who believe that the Neanderthal skeletons are simply the remains of Homo Sapien-Sapiens who suffered from rickets and osteoporosis.

http://www.berkeley.edu/news/media/releases/2003/06/11_idalt u.shtml

In light of the Herto Bouri fossils, the fact that Neanderthal fossils have only been found in Europe and Asia, and the fact that the indigenous African does not have any Neanderthal DNA, I believe that it is safe to assume that the Neanderthal species did not originate in nor did they migrate out of Africa. These facts, taken in consideration of a 2010 study that was published in Science Magazine reveals a bit of irony in American history. According to the study, Neanderthal DNA is only 99.7 percent identical to Homo-Sapien Sapien DNA. For comparison sake, chimpanzees are believed to share around 98.8% DNA with modern humans. The irony is that in the days of Euro-American slavery, the slave traders and purchasers who participated in the inhumane practice of subjecting supposed "sub-human" African men and women to forced servitude, were technically descendants of beings who were 0.3 percent less human than their 100% Homo-Sapien Sapien African captives. Given the racist implications of European imperial ideologies that have been used throughout modern history to justify the subjugation of tan, black, brown, etc.; i.e. melanated peoples around the planet, evolutionary theorists need to offer some sort of response to the discoveries that reveal Africans to be the earth's only purely Homo-Sapien Sapien species of man.

See: Press release (Max Planck Society) "The Neandertal in us" (07 May 2010).

Another error that has resulted from the belief that Adam was the original man of the creation, is the assumption that Adam was the only human being to exist on the earth at the time of his supposed creation in around 4004 B.C(by Christian dating). The presumption is simply wrong and this erroneous claim, also contradicts the biblical text. The Bible's books of Genesis and Job both give supporting evidence to prove that flesh and blood men and women inhabited the earth in the days when Adam and Eve were expelled from the garden of Eden.

In **Genesis 4:9-17**, after Cain had murdered his younger brother Abel, he was driven out of the land of his nativity and told by YHWH that he was to live out his existence as a vagabond and a fugitive on the earth. In response, Cain stated his fear of being killed by anyone who may find him. The obvious question is "Who did Cain fear would kill him?" Had Adam and his descendants been the only men living upon the earth at that time, Cain would have had a greater chance of being killed in his native land by one of his own siblings, than if he had wandered abroad(Note that Seth, Adam and Eve's third son, was not born until after Cain had been banished). Contrary to popular belief, Cain's fear did not result from any guilt that he may have felt for murdering Abel. Cain shared a fear with his father. He feared wandering abroad because he was recognizable as the son of Adam(Cross Reference **Job 31:33-34**), humanities high priest and representative who had been discharged from the garden of Eden for rebelling against the word of God. Men and women living on the earth understood that a dramatic change in their lives had taken place and that Adam was the man responsible for subjecting the world to a new state of existence.

Genesis 4:17 also records that Cain had a wife who bore him a son after he had been banished from his native land. Assuming that God gave Cain time to go back home, pack, and collect his wife it is reasonable to believe that Cain had previously married an unmentioned sister of his(Cross Reference **Leviticus 18:9**), but it is more probable that Cain took a wife from an existing population after he left his native land.

The book of Job also has a comment on the life and times of Adam after he was banished from the garden of Eden. The book of Job focuses on a man of God named Job, who was personally tormented by Satan. After Job and his family are subjected to a series of calamities three associates of Job's come to visit with him and to discuss the cause of his recent misfortune. Ultimately, Job's three associates believe that his distress is the result of his own unrighteousness. Near the end of Job's discourse in defense of his way of life he affirms the claim of his righteous existence by referencing Adam, "Who hid the guilt of his iniquity from the multitudes and from families by refusing to go outside of his door(**Job 31:33-34**)."

The bible does not record any conversation between Adam and another man or woman but his fear of the multitudes and of other families, Cain's fear of being killed by anyone who might find him outside of his native land, the mark of protection that was placed on Cain by YHWH, and the fact that Cain married a woman who bore him a child after he was banished from his native land, speaks volumes. The bible is clear on the fact that the angels of God were the first sons of God to come into existence and that Adam was deemed the creation's first man by his positional distinction in the garden of Eden. The bible also provides enough evidence to support the fact that Adam and Eve were not the only human beings living upon the earth in the day that they were sent out of the garden of Eden. It is easier to gain an appreciation for these facts as well as the differences between the two sons of God after **Genesis** chapters **1** and **2** are understood in their proper contexts.

A Few Subtle Differences Between Genesis 1 and 2

I will go into a little more detail on the nature of the realities that were created in Genesis chapters 1 and 2 in a later chapter, but for this particular chapter I would like to primarily focus on the men who were created in Genesis chapters 1 and 2. I am only mentioning a few of the differences between the two so-called creation accounts in order to highlight the differences between the men who were created in each.

It has been universally understood that Genesis chapter 1 describes the creation of the universe and its living organisms. And Genesis chapter 2 has been accepted by the Church community as a retelling of the Genesis chapter 1 creation account that happens to focus on the earth and Adam's role within the garden of Eden. I had been raised on this understanding and had accepted it as a reasonable explanation for the opening two chapters of the bible.

The bible does not agree with this understanding. According to the bible, **Genesis 1:1-2:4a** and **2:4b-25** do share a mutual dependence but, they are also two different and independent histories*.

*In **Genesis 2:4b-25**, *YHWH Elohim builds upon God's foundation that was established in* **Genesis 1:1-2:4a***{Cross Reference* **John 5:17-19***}. And God's word from* **Genesis 1:1-2:4a** *is authenticated by the ministry of YHWH Elohim that began in* **Genesis 2:4b-25**. *The Old and New Testaments of the bible share the same kind of relationship.*

The most obvious difference between the two "Creation" accounts is how each took shape. The **Genesis 1:1-2:4a** creation was spoken into existence by God. But the **Genesis 2:4b-25** "creation" was personally molded by the hand of YHWH Elohim after He had come down to the surface of the earth. One specific example of the differences between the two Genesis "creation accounts" is found in the vegetation that God spoke into existence in **Genesis 1:11-12** and the vegetation which YHWH Elohim planted in **Genesis 2:8-9**. The **Genesis 1:11-12** vegetation not only entered existence differently than the **Genesis 2:8-9** vegetation, but the former vegetation also continued its existence differently than the earth's latter greenery. The **Genesis 1:11-12** vegetation preceded the sun, moon, and stars, which did not appear until day four(**Genesis 1:14-19**) of God's seven-day creation, it was not dependent upon a man to till the soil, nor was it dependent upon rain to water the ground. According to **Genesis 2:5** the earth's latter plant-life was yet to spring up because, although the sun, moon, and stars had previously been created, YHWH Elohim had not yet sent rain upon the earth and there was no man to till the ground.

    How the vegetation came to exist and the many other differences between the **Genesis 1:1-2:4a** and **2:4b-25** accounts are and have been fairly obvious, but the lack of understanding the reason for those differences coupled with our blind acceptance of improper interpretations has nullified the effectiveness of God's message(Cross Reference **Genesis 3:4-5**). It is only after the differences between Genesis chapters 1 and 2 are recognized and understood in their proper contexts that they are able to reveal the distinct natures of each "creation" account. By extension, recognition of the differences between **Genesis 1:1-2:4a** and **2:4b-25** also reveals the distinct natures of the men who were created in each chapter.

The Man

    After God had created the vegetation, the sun, moon, and stars, the aquatic animals, the birds, and the land animals, God declared in **Genesis 1:26** that He would create man. God said that He would create man in His image and according to His own likeness. The man would be given authority to rule over the fish of the sea, over the birds of the air, and over the animals upon the earth.

Genesis 1:26
26. And God said, Let Us make man in our image, according to Our likeness; and let them rule over the fish of the sea,

and over the birds of the heavens, and over the cattle, and over all the earth, and over all the creepers creeping on the earth.
Genesis 1:26

In **Genesis 1:27** God created a man. Most people assume that God had completed the work which He said He would accomplish in **Genesis 1:26**. But according to the details of **Genesis 1:27-28** God's work was not yet complete.

Genesis 1:27-28
27. And God created the man in His image; in the image of God, He created him. Male and female He created them.
28. And God blessed them; and God said to them, Be fruitful and multiply, and fill the earth, and subdue it, and rule over the fish of the sea, and over the birds of the heavens, and over all living things creeping on the earth.

Genesis 1:27-28

I had read **Genesis 1:26, 27-28** dozens of times in the past and had never appreciated the significance of what had been said. I hadn't noticed that the image of God was stated twice in **Genesis 1:27** and that the likeness of God was not mentioned at all. When I did notice the repetition of the image of God and the omission of God's likeness, I simply regarded the matter as curious and moved on. It wasn't until I had been purged of my former understanding and after the bible had "come alive" that God's not doing exactly what He said He would do in **Genesis 1:26** began to matter to me. Not long after **Genesis 1:26, 27-28** became a matter of personal interest I came across **Genesis 5:1-3**. Then **Genesis 1:26, 27-28**, and the image of God being stated twice, changed from being an interesting puzzler into a great source of frustration.

Genesis 5:1-3

1. This is the book of the generations of Adam: In the day that God created him, He made him in the likeness of God.
2. He created them male and female, and blessed them, and called their name Adam/Man in the day when they were created.
3. And Adam lived one hundred and thirty years and fathered a son in his own likeness, according to his image, and called his name Seth.

Genesis 5:1-3

As a child I had been told many times that the bible occasionally contradicted itself and **Genesis 5:1-3** in respect to **Genesis 1:26,27-28** clearly appeared to be one of those times. Only now I was reluctant to just accept that explanation and move on. If Adam was the man who had been created in the image of God in **Genesis 1:27** I needed an explanation for why the bible would say in **Genesis 5:1** that he was made in the likeness of God. I read and reread **Genesis 1:27** and **Genesis 5:1**, and the verses that immediately followed each account of man's creation. There were many clear differences between the two accounts, only, I couldn't understand why there should be any.

In time I came to appreciate the fact that I couldn't see nor understand the message of the bible because I had been following an erroneous traditional teaching that was being taught as the word of God(**Matthew 15:7-9, Mark 7:6-9** Cross Reference **Genesis 3:2-3**). Forcing an interpretation upon the text that simply wasn't right was like trying to force the wrong key into a lock and expecting it to open(Cross Reference **Matthew 11:12**). I was rescued from my confusion on the issue and from my frustration with Church doctrine by the Spirit of God and led back to **Genesis 1:26**.

Genesis 1:26

26. And God said, Let Us make man in Our image, according to Our likeness...
Genesis 1:26

When I let the bible speak for itself, I was able to recognize that **Genesis 5:1-2** did not contradict **Genesis 1:27-28**, but in fact, it substantiated **Genesis 1:26**. In **Genesis 1:27** God had created a "man in His image, in the image of God He created him". In **Genesis 2:7**, as it is recounted in **Genesis 5:1**, God had created Adam "In the likeness of God". **Genesis 5:1-2** simply testified that God was completing His word(Cross Reference **Genesis 1:26**). **Genesis 1:27-28** and **Genesis 5:1-2** are the details of God creating two different men. It wasn't until much later that I understood that the life, death, and resurrection of the Messiah, the last Adam, was the actual and eternal fulfillment of God's word(Cross Reference **Genesis 1:26**; and Chapter 6 of this book on the ministry of the "King and Priest").

My excitement was off the charts. I had found something in the Bible that hadn't been known for only God knows how long. The discovery was sweet; it was like new life had been breathed into me. I wanted to tell the whole world, but I didn't know where to start. Then as the next couple of days went by, the sweetness of the discovery changed to bitterness in my stomach. I became infatuated with wondering, "Why? After hundreds and hundreds of years of church history and teaching, why is it that churches don't know this?"

I began to perceive an unsettling answer to my "Why" questions about the Church organization's shortcomings. As I delved deeper in thought and in research on the past 2000 or so years of the spread of Christianity I was again rescued by the Spirit of God and my focus was diverted from Church history back to the Bible. It dawned on me that recognizing the creation of two men in the opening chapters of the book of Genesis without having any supporting evidence amounted to just another interesting interpretation of the text. Fortunately, the supporting evidence for the creation of two distinct men in the opening chapters of the book of Genesis is given in the blessings that directly follow the verses that state the condition in which each man entered existence.

The man who was created in the image of God in **Genesis 1:27** was blessed in **Genesis 1:28**.

Genesis 1:28
28. And God blessed them; and God said to them, Be fruitful and multiply, and fill the earth, and subdue it, and rule over the fish of the sea, and over the birds of the heavens, and over all living things creeping on the earth.
Genesis 1:28

The man who was created in the image of God was blessed with authority over the earth and over all the living creatures upon it. The same point, regarding the authority that is associated with the image of God, is reiterated in **Genesis 9:1-7** when, after the great flood, Noah and his sons come to be in the image of God.

The creation of Adam, the preeminent man of existence who was formed as the likeness of God, is recalled in **Genesis 5:1**. In **Genesis 5:2** Adam received his blessing from God.

Genesis 5:2
2. He created them male and female, and blessed them, and called their name Man in the day when they were created.
Genesis 5:2

Much like the times that I had read **Genesis 1:27** and missed the repetition of the image of God, I had read over

Genesis 5:2 many times and never recognize that Adam had received a blessing from God. When I did eventually take notice of the reference to Adam's blessing in **Genesis 5:2** I remember thinking that Adam was lucky to have received such a good blessing back in **Genesis 1:28** because he got hosed in **Genesis 5:2**. But now, after becoming conscious of the fact that **Genesis 1:27-28** and **Genesis 5:1-2** were addressing the creation of two different men, I needed to understand what blessing Adam had received.

There didn't appear to be much information to go on in **Genesis 5:2**. God made a man as His likeness(**Genesis 5:1**), He created them male and female, and He blessed them and called their name Man. I didn't understand what I was looking at. The blessing that had been given in **Genesis 1:28** to the original man was fairly obvious. The image of God carried authority. But Adam and Eve's blessing didn't include any details that I could see. Without being able to see anything obvious, I decided to compare the differences between the blessings(**Genesis 1:28; 5:2**) associated with the image and likeness of God.

Genesis 1:28
28. And God blessed them; and God said to them, Be fruitful and multiply, and fill the earth, and subdue it, and rule over the fish of the sea, and over the birds of the heavens, and over all living things creeping on the earth.
Genesis 1:28

and,

Genesis 5:2
2. He created them male and female, and blessed them, and called their name Man in the day when they were created.
Genesis 5:2

The man created in the image of God was blessed, told to be fruitful and multiply, and he was given authority over the earth and all living things upon it. Adam and Eve were blessed and together they were called Man.

I was stuck. I then referred to **Genesis 9:1-7**, which is the second time in the bible that the image of God was given to man. **Genesis 9:1-7** also includes the second and third times that man is given the command to be fruitful and multiply.

Genesis 9:1-7
1. And God blessed Noah and his sons. And He said to them, Be fruitful and multiply, and fill the earth.
2. And your fear and your dread shall be on all the animals of the earth, and on every bird of the heavens, on all that moves on the earth, and on all the fish of the sea. They are given into your hands.
3. Every creeping thing which is alive shall be food for you. I have given you all things, even as the green plant.
4. But you shall not eat flesh in its life, its blood.
5. And surely the blood of your lives I will demand. At the hand of every animal I will demand it, and at the hand of man. I will demand the life of man at the hand of every man's brother.
6. Whoever sheds man's blood, his blood shall be shed by man. For He made man in the image of God.
7. And you, be fruitful and multiply. Swarm over the earth and multiply in it.
Genesis 9:1-7

In light of the fact that two distinct men were created in the opening chapters of the book of Genesis(**Genesis 1:27; 2:7**), the command to be fruitful and multiply served as an indispensable clue that not only helped to unlock the meaning of the image and likeness of God, the phrase also unraveled several of the Bible's other mysteries.

A first thing that I noticed about the command to be fruitful and multiply is that it was only associated with the image of God and the authority that follows with that image.

The man who was created in the image of God in **Genesis 1:27** was told in **Genesis 1:28** to be fruitful and multiply, and then he was told to subdue the earth and its living creatures. In **Genesis 9:1**(and **Genesis 9:7**) God commanded Noah and his sons to be fruitful and multiply, He then gave them authority over the creatures of the earth and the right to administer capital punishment. In **Genesis 9:6** Noah and his sons are told that this authority and responsibility had been given to them because they had been made to be in the image of God.

The second discovery associated with the command to be fruitful and multiply is that, and although the point may already be clear, Adam was never commanded to be fruitful and multiply. The details of Adam's creation(**Genesis 2:7**), his appointment(**Genesis 2:15-17**), disgrace(**Genesis 3**), blessing(**Genesis 2:15-25, 5:2**), and family history(**Genesis 4:1-17, 5:3-32**) are given in the Bible but, there is no time in the life or history of Adam that he was ever commanded to "be fruitful and multiply."

In light of the verses that follow the Bible's first instance of the command to "be fruitful and multiply" in **Genesis 1:28**, Adam never being given the command, the family history that follows Adam and Eve's blessing in **Genesis 5:2**, and the fact that Noah and his wife already had three sons before God's command to "be fruitful and multiply" was given for the second and third times in **Genesis 9:1** and **7**, one fact came to be increasingly clear. The fact being that, contrary to universally accepted Church doctrine, the command to "Be fruitful and multiply" is not God's endorsement for man to reproduce children. In consideration of the fact that the man who had been created in the image of God and commanded to be fruitful and multiply was wiped off of the earth because he did procreate(Cross Reference **Genesis 6:1-4**), had the Church organization understood the Bible's opening chapters, just the opposite conclusion regarding God's command would have been reached.

Cutting to the chase, the biblical explanation for the command to "Be fruitful and multiply" is expanded upon in **Colossians 1:9-11**("Be Fruitful in good works and multiply in the knowledge of God.") and **2Peter 1:2-8**. God's command to "Be fruitful and multiply" that is given in **Genesis 1:28** and **Genesis 9:1,7** to the men who were created and those who came to be in His image are calls to godliness and accountability to uphold God's Holy standard(Cross Reference **Romans 1:18-19**).

The recognition that Adam was never told to be fruitful and multiply highlighted one of the many differences between Adam, God's likeness(**Genesis 5:1**), and the man who had been created in the image of God in **Genesis 1:27**. And while that recognition did not give me exactly what I wanted, it did lead me closer to understanding the defining attribute of God's likeness and the blessing that Adam and Eve had received from God in **Genesis 5:2**. The 5th chapter of the book of Genesis is crucial to unraveling the rest of the mystery.

In **Genesis 5:3** it is stated that Adam fathered a son in his own likeness and according to his image, and he called his name Seth. If **Genesis 5:3** does nothing else, it should cause a reader to pause and to consider that the "image and likeness" of God may not necessarily be synonymous designations. The terms "likeness" and "image" were used in **Genesis 1:26** when God said that He would create man, only the terms were used in the reverse order. The use and reversal of the two terms reinforces the fact that the image and the likeness of God(**Genesis 1:26**), or of Adam(**Genesis 5:3),** each bestow their own distinct qualities. The two terms are not used poetically as affirmations to overemphasize one characteristic of God or man.

Genesis 5:3

3. And Adam lived one hundred and thirty years and fathered a son in his own likeness, according to his image, and called his name Seth.
Genesis 5:3

In fathering Seth in his own likeness and according to his image, Adam had apparently accomplished a feat similar to what God had said He would do in **Genesis 1:26**.

I understood that Adam's likeness and his image(**Genesis 5:3**) were meant to convey a similar if not the same meaning as the image and likeness of God. I Therefore felt safe in assuming that Adam's image, like God's, carried a degree of authority. The two instances in the book of Genesis that the image of God was bestowed on man provided enough information to understand that quality of God, but the references to the likeness of God and of Adam were not so forthcoming. I needed some additional help to understand what quality was in the likeness of God, and now the likeness of Adam, and to understand the significance of God calling Adam and Eve "Man" in **Genesis 5:2**.

I thank God for my family, particularly in this instance, because it was my own children who helped me to get the clarity that I needed in my time of frustration.

Daniella and I have four children. Even though each one of them is their own unique person with their own individual characteristics and personalities, each one of our four children share, to varying degrees, some of the physical characteristics and personality traits of Daniella and myself. Our children are all fairly young, and we as parents are doing the best we know how to nurture their individuality and to raise them each to be responsible men and women. When they do grow up and leave the house, they will no longer be subject to Daniella's and my authority. They will be independently responsible and accountable for their own words and deeds.

Similar to my own family situation, Seth, Adam's son, was born with a physical, mental, and emotional resemblance to his father and mother. And as Seth grew older, he matured into a responsible man who was accountable for his own words and deeds.

That recognition, of my own family and of Adam's relation to Seth -who was Adam's own likeness and image- solved the mystery of the likeness of God and answered my question of why Adam was never told to be fruitful and multiply. Adam, the son of God(**Luke 3:38**), had been formed by the hand of YHWH Elohim, he had the Spirit of Life/God breathed into him, and he existed on the earth as the literal likeness of God. Righteousness was attributed to Adam because he was the flesh and blood replica of his creator. Adam was the personification of godliness and the only way that he could cease to **be fruitful and multiply** was if he were to lose the Spirit of Life that had been breathed into him in **Genesis 2:7**. I had the answer that I had been searching for and my excitement was again, through the roof.

The blessing that God had given to Adam and Eve in **Genesis 5:2** far exceeded the blessing that had been given to the man created in the image of God in **Genesis 1:27**. Adam had been formed to resemble His Creator. He was created as an independent identity. When God blessed Adam and Eve and called their name Man He bestowed personal sovereignty upon them.

Whereas Adam, the likeness of God who was appointed to be humanity's representative, was given personal sovereignty and a command(**Genesis 2:17**) that was intended to protect his life and the relationship that he had with his Creator, the man who had been created in the image of God was given universal authority and commanded to be fruitful and multiply because he was bound to and made accountable to an ordinance, a law, that made him responsible to uphold God's holy standard(Cross Reference **Genesis 1:28** and **Genesis 9:6-7** "Be fruitful and multiply" in light of **Psalm 2:2-3; Psalm 82:1-8**).

The men who were created in the image of God on the sixth day of the creation are associated with the principalities and the powers in heavenly places spoken of in **Ephesians 3:10**, they are the kings of the earth referred to in **Psalm 2:2-3**, and **10**(Cross Reference **Daniel 10:13,20**), and they are the gods and the sons of God who are being reprimanded in **Psalm 82**(Cross Reference **Genesis 6; Romans 1:18-32**).

Both men, the man created in God's image and in the likeness of God, were created to represent God and to stand as examples/gods before all of mankind(Cross Reference **Exodus 4:15-16, 7:1; Psalm 82:6**). Man failed on both accounts.

Adam, God's likeness, was expelled from the garden of Eden and the flood of Noah's day was sent as judgment upon the man who had been created in the image of God. Man, save eight people, was wiped off the face of the earth but the damage had already been done. The angelic likeness(Cross Reference **Romans 1:23**) -their physical, emotional, and mental perversion- was embedded within humanity's psyche and genetic makeup. In coordination with the spiritual calamity caused by Adam' sin in the garden of Eden, it is this genetic seed of corruption that continues to influence all manner of human interaction up to this very day(**Genesis 6:1-7,11-12; Romans 1:18-32**; and the book of Revelation Cross reference "the Abomination of Desolation").

The recognition that two distinct men were created in the opening chapters of the book of Genesis is an invaluable bit of information. Besides clarifying the identity of the kings of the earth(**Daniel 10:13,20** Cross Reference **Deuteronomy 32:8** of the Septuagint version of the Bible) and illuminating the difference between the image and likeness of God, the revelation also resolves the apparent contradiction between **Genesis 1:27** and **Genesis 9:1-7**. In **Genesis 1:27** and in **Genesis 9:1-7** the image of God is given to man, with no obvious explanation provided to explain why this attribute of God was given to man on two different occasions. A quick comparison between **Genesis 1:27** and **Genesis 9:1-7** reveals the subtle difference between how the image of God was received by man in each chapter. The man who came into existence in **Genesis 1:27** was created, meaning that he originated, in the image of God. In **Genesis 9:1-7** Noah and his sons were made, meaning that they came to be after the fact, in the image of God. The fact being that the man who was created in the image of God in **Genesis 1:27** had been physically removed from the earth by the flood(Cross Reference **Genesis 6:7**).

Before moving on, a subtlety of Adam's existence that it is necessary to be conscious of is the timing of his creation. Adam was formed in **Genesis 2:7**. He is the son of God who came into existence after God had finished His seven-day work of the Heavens and the Earth(**Genesis 2:4a**). Adam was formed by YHWH Elohim and existed on the earth after the work of the earth and heavens had commenced in **Genesis 2:4b**. Adam was formed outside the parameters of the Heavens and the Earth(Cross Reference **Genesis 2:4a**). Therefore, humanity not only had God's acceptance through Adam's ministry in the garden of Eden, we also initially* existed outside the realm of the authority that had been given to and exercised by the man who had been created in the image of God in **Genesis 1:27**.

Note: *The <u>underlines</u> are used to mark the reversals of "<u>Heavens</u> and <u>Earth</u>, and <u>earth</u> and <u>heaven</u>" that the Bible uses in **Genesis 2:4a** and **2:4b** to designate between two different epochs of the creation's history.*

Modern man willfully subjects itself to the man who was created in **Genesis 1:27, by accepting that we are nothing more than evolved animals.*

Adam: What's In A Likeness?

The first likeness that humanity inhabited was of YHWH Elohim(**Genesis 2:7,15-17,21-25** Cross Reference **Genesis 5:1**). After Satan overcame Adam in the garden of Eden humanity's God given likeness became subject to sin and death(**Genesis 3:1-7** Cross Reference **Genesis 2:17; Romans 5:12**). As time went by the human identity fell under the influence of the sinful sons of God who took it upon themselves to spread their seed and corrupt nature throughout the earth(**Genesis 6:1-7** Cross Reference **Psalm 82:1-8; Romans 1:18-32).** After the flood of Noah's day, Nimrod the Ethiopian* rose to become the first human being to subject men and women to his own will. And taking up this identity, humanity collectively sought, as it is stated in **Genesis 11:4**, to establish its own sovereign identity that stood independent of and as an affront to the God of gods(Cross Reference **Revelation 13:1-10**).

Cush is synonymous with Ethiopia -Genesis 10:8-12**. Cross Reference "The Wonderful Ethiopians of The Ancient Cushite Empire" by Drusilla Dunjee Houston, published in 1926. The book is a very interesting composition written by an American woman born in 1876, who was a teacher, a journalist, a musician, and a historian. To put her work and*

accomplishments in perspective consider that Ms. Houston was born only 11 years after slavery officially ended in the United States -December 6, 1865-, and at a time when the rights of dark brown, brown, tan, and copper complexioned indigenous and imported Americans as well as the rights of pale skinned(European) women were subject to the ideals and perspectives of men who were of European descent.

Genesis 11:4

4. And they said, Come let us build a city and a tower with its top in the heavens, and make a name for ourselves, that we not be scattered on the face of all the earth.
Genesis 11:4

In **Genesis 11:1-9** the time is recalled when the whole earth was of one lip and one tongue, and all were gathered together in the valley of Shinar. The men collectively decided to build a city, and within the city a tower, and to make a name for themselves. YHWH came down to see the city and the tower that the men were building. Upon seeing what the men had done YHWH decided to confound the language of the peoples and to disperse them abroad. The languages were confused, the people were dispersed, and the city, which came to be known as Babel, was left unfinished.

Many bible teachers tend to only focus on the building of the tower of Babel and the desire of the men to reach to heaven. Although these are important issues to consider, there are equally important ones to understand from **Genesis 11:4**. The men who were gathered at the tower of Babel had relinquished the identity of Adam's sons and the image of God that had been given to Noah and his son's when they had come out of the ark after the flood(**Genesis 8:18, 9:1-19**). The men gathered at Babel were taking authority over law and order into their own hands and establishing themselves as the identity for humanity to follow in(Cross Reference **Revelation 13** and **17**, and "the Abomination of Desolation" that is referred many times in the Bible). The confusion of the languages and the dispersal of the peoples who were gathered around the tower of Babel was a temporary measure meant to forestall humanity's descent into a unified rebellious and Satanic state(Cross Reference the Beast and False Prophet of **Revelation chapter 13**).

After humanity had been allotted to the nations in the 11th chapter of the book of Genesis(Cross Reference **Deuteronomy 32:8; Psalm 2:1-12; Daniel 10:13,20-21**), Abram was called out unto YHWH in the 12th chapter of the book of Genesis. Abram was told by YHWH that if he would obey the Word of YHWH and go out of his native land into a land that YHWH would show him then he would be made into a great nation, he would be blessed, his name would be made great, he would be a blessing to those who blessed him, those who cursed him would be cursed, and in him the families of the earth would be blessed(**Genesis 12:1-3**).

Abram then went out of the land of his nativity into the land of Canaan(**Genesis 12:4-5**). In the 15th chapter of the book of Genesis the word of YHWH came to Abram in a vision and told him not to fear for YHWH is his shield and great reward(**Genesis 15:1**). Abram, who was advanced in age and childless, was then promised in **Genesis 15:5** a great multitude of descendants. Abram believed the word of YHWH and his belief was counted to him as righteousness(**Genesis 15:6**). In **Genesis 15:7-21** Abram entered into a covenant with YHWH and in **Genesis 17:1-4** Abram was told to walk before YHWH and be perfect, and that YHWH would confirm His covenant with Abram, and that he, Abram, would be the father of many nations. In **Genesis 17:5** YHWH gave Abram, a name meaning "high father", a new identity by changing his name to Abraham which means "father of a multitude". Then in **Genesis 17:7**, Abraham was promised the Seed who would inherit all of the promises of YHWH and in whose identity men and women from all nations of the world would be able take refuge(Cross Reference **Isaiah 49:1-26; Luke 1:54-55; Galatians 3:16, 6:15-16; Revelation 3:12**).

Genesis 17:1-7

1. And when Abram was ninety-nine years old, YHWH appeared to Abram and said to him, I am the Almighty God! Walk before me and be perfect;
2. And I will make My covenant between Me and you, and will multiply you exceedingly.
3. And Abram fell on his face. And God spoke with him, saying,
4. As for Me, behold! My covenant is with you and you shall be a father of many nations.
5. Neither shall your name be called Abram any longer, but your name shall be Abraham; for I have made you a father of many nations.
6. And I will make you exceedingly fruitful, and I will make nations of you, and kings shall come out of you.
7. And I will establish My covenant between Me and you and your seed after you in their generations for an everlasting covenant, to be a God to you, and to your seed after you.

Genesis 17:1-7

In the seed promised to Abraham(Cross Reference "the Israel of God" **Isaiah 49:1-6; Romans 4:16; Galatians 3:29, 6:15-16**) men, women, and children of all nations, backgrounds, and languages are given the opportunity to enter into the one unadulterated identity that supersedes the identity that was forfeited by Adam(**1Corintians 15:45-47** Cross Reference **Genesis 2:17; 3:1-24**) in the garden of Eden and that which was mired by the children of Jacob(Cross Reference **Matthew 23:37-38; Luke 13:34**).

In the new heavens and new earth, the men, women, and children who have taken shelter in the Salvation(Yeshua: Strong's Concordance Reference #**h3444**) of God will have their identity in the name of God, the name of the city of God which comes down out of heaven, and in the name of the Messiah of God(**Revelation 3:12** Cross Reference **Zechariah 14:9**), who is the eternal fulfillment of God's word. In the prophesied days to come all the servants of YHWH will have their identities in the One Who is the literal embodiment of the Image and Likeness of God(Cross Reference **Genesis 1:26**).

Notes

CHAPTER 3
THE UNKNOWN TRUTH
The Revelation of God: Genesis 1

Reading the Bible without understanding its opening chapters is like starting a road trip heading in the wrong direction. Where you end up will not be where you planned on going. Misunderstanding the Bible's foundational lessons has done just that to the Church organization. Resulting in misplaced devotion within Christian fellowships and reducing God, Satan, and the heavenly host to little more than vague notions that generally serve to excuse individuals from personal responsibility.

Fairy Tales

Growing up your family may have practiced traditions, believed superstitions, or had certain ways of saying and doing things that only made sense in your home. As a child my family had many such practices. We submitted to, created our own, and fought against seemingly unassailable obstacles. We protected the people and ideas that did us the most harm and we trusted the Church to lead us, after we had been set free of this current existence, to a life that would be worth living. My family tolerantly lived a comfortably ignorant existence. Circumstance taught me to blame myself for the confusion and contradictions that surrounded me throughout my early life. Unfortunately, life rarely ever made sense and circumstances being as they were, I missed much of my childhood waiting to be an adult. I figured that life would make more sense when I was older and when I had control over the direction that it took.

When I was young my family situation was unstable but, Church provided a haven for me. Our family would frequently move and change churches, but I was always able to find stability in familiar Church doctrines. I had been told many times that "Jesus Christ was the same yesterday, today, and forever(**Hebrews 13:8**)", and it was that kind of consistency that gave me a sense of security. Because of the consistency and the security that I felt, and the fact that what I learned came from adults, I accepted Church doctrine as truth even though there were teachings and messages of the Bible that I didn't understand, or which seemed to contradict each other. At times, my confusion and curiosity would get the better of me. The few times that I had gathered enough courage to question something that seemed to contradict or conflict with another teaching, or which defied all rational explanation, I was quickly put in my place by an adult who knew what was best for me. I had been raised to show respect to anyone who was older than me and I was too afraid of letting my curiosity take me too far outside of their graces. As I got older and the more I understood of life, death, and Hell, the more anxiety I felt questioning Church doctrine.

      I had learned early on in life that the Christian Church and the Jewish people were God's chosen people. I believed that Christian pastors and Jewish Rabbis were God's personally ordained representatives who alone had the right to teach His word. To doubt the church's conclusion on any matter was essentially the same as doubting God. To doubt God would only land me in Hell. And Hell was a dark pit that was made of fire and filled with screams and monsters, and that was ruled by a giant disfigured beast called Satan who loved nothing more than to scare, torture, rape, eat, and laugh at men, women, and children who could never die but lived eternally so that they could be continually reconfigured in order to suffer the same torment daily. As a child these dark fears kept my inquiring mind in check, and for a while I stopped openly questioning what I had been told to just accept.

One question that I had a hard time accepting and that continually tormented me concerned the two opening chapters of the book of Genesis. From my earliest memory of going to church it had been drilled into my head that Genesis chapter 1 was the creation of the universe, and that Genesis chapter 2 was a retelling of the Genesis 1 creation story that happened to focus on the earth and Adam's life in the garden of Eden. I had read each of the first two chapters of the Bible many times and had trouble agreeing with that conclusion. I could see that there were some similarities between the two chapters, but I could also see that there were even more differences.

As an adult, when I began focusing on the opening chapters of the Bible to understand man's creation in the image and as the likeness of God, my questions about the differences between Genesis chapters 1 and 2 resurfaced. I could see that two different things were going on in Genesis 1 and 2. Only I still couldn't understand why or what the two different things were.

I couldn't understand why Moses would say in **Genesis 2:1-3** that God had finished with His work and decided to take a day off, and then, only a few verses later tell a story similar to the one that he had just told. Only in the second telling of the story, Moses, who must have been very tired while he was writing(I tend to do this myself), reversed the order of some of the events, left out a few of the earlier details, and added a couple of different ones. In Moses' second creation account the sun is not recreated. Apparently, it already existed because we find out in **Genesis 2:5** that the plant life had not sprung up because it was dependent on rain and a man to till the ground. The sun is not mentioned at all, but I assumed that it existed because as any gardener knows, sunlight is just as necessary as water to grow a garden. My mind swirled with questions like: Why isn't the seventh day mentioned in the Genesis 2 account? Why are there differences in how the animals came to exist. For example: In **Genesis 1:21** the birds are associated with the sea creatures that come out of the waters. In **Genesis 2:19** the birds are associated with the animals that are formed out of the ground. Why have man created after the animals in the Genesis 1 creation and before the animals in the Genesis chapter 2 account? Why not just finish the creation all in one snap instead of taking six days?

At first, I thought that I was reading too much into the text and just creating problems for myself where none really existed. But then again, I could clearly see that there were differences between the two accounts. In the past I had accepted the Church's explanation, that there were some things in the bible that could not be understood until God returned to the earth in the prophesied last days. But that answer couldn't hold off my inquiries any longer. I needed a solution to the problems that were keeping me up at night.

The Reality

Genesis chapters 1 and 2 are similar but they do differ. The differences between the two chapters are essentially the same as the differences between the men whom God had created in each chapter. In the Genesis 1 creation God is speaking space, matter, and life into existence. In the Genesis 2 account YHWH Elohim is physically manipulating preexisting matter. Genesis 1 is a grand display of God's power, intelligence, and organizational skills. Genesis 2 is an intimate display of YHWH Elohim's benevolence, conviction, and compassion. Genesis 1 is almost like seeing an interesting man or woman at a distance. In that scenario, Genesis chapter 2 would be that same compelling individual walking directly to you, offering their hand, and introducing themselves.

In short, **Genesis 1:1-2:4a** is the foundation of the animated universe and material existence. **Genesis 2:4b-25** is a physical existence with spiritual overtones. A subtitle for the first chapter of Genesis/Bereshith(**Genesis 1:1-2:4a**) could possibly be, "The Book of Essence". I haven't thought of a cool subtitle for the second chapter of Genesis.

Genesis 2:2 informs readers that after six days of creating, God completed His work on the seventh day. **Genesis 2:3** marks the day of God's repose, the Sabbath, as the creation's significant day(Saturday is the Sabbath, the seventh day of the week. But to avoid getting hung up on the proper day to worship Cross Reference **Mark 2:27, Romans 14:5-6**, and **Galatians 4:9-10**. *Existence was created to be malleable*).

Genesis 2:4a summarizes what had occurred in the previous verses.

Genesis 2:2-4a

2. And on the seventh day God completed His work(**h4399** m'la'kah: deputyship, ministry) which he had made. And He rested on the seventh day from all His work which He had made.
3. And God blessed the seventh day and sanctified it, because He rested from all His work on it which God had created to make*.
4. These are the births/generations of the heavens and the earth when they were created.

Genesis 2:2-4a

In the midst of **Genesis 2:4** there is a change of focus and a dimensional shift from the all-encompassing Heavens and Earth to the surface of the physical Earth looking up at the visible Heavens. The initial work of God having been completed and summarized in **Genesis 2:4a**, God's work to complete His word commenced in **Genesis 2:4b**(**Genesis 1:26** Cross Reference **John 5:17**).

Genesis 2:4b-7

4. In the day that YHWH Elohim made <u>earth</u> and <u>heaven,</u>
5. and every shrub of the field was not yet on the earth, and every herb of the field had not yet sprung up; for YHWH Elohim had not sent rain on the earth, and there was no man to till the ground.
6. And midst went up from the earth and watered the whole face of the ground.
7. And YHWH Elohim formed the man from the dust of the ground, and blew into his nostrils the Breath of Life; and the man became a living soul.

Genesis 2:4b-7

After the commencement of the age of the <u>earth</u> and <u>heaven</u>(**Genesis 2:4b**), yet before any shrub or herb, animal of the field, or bird of the air had appeared on the earth(**Genesis 2:5-6,19**), the man Adam was formed by YHWH Elohim in **Genesis 2:7**. In **Genesis 2:8** Adam was taken from the land of his nativity to the land of Eden. Then in **Genesis 2:15** Adam was placed within Eden's garden paradise to commune with his creator. Adam was given a blessed existence that offered him everything except a life of inactivity. In addition to providing Adam with physical tasks, mental stimulation, physical and emotional companionship in Eve(**Genesis 2:21-25**), and a sanctuary in which to commune with His Creator, Adam's life in the garden of Eden provided him with a profound opportunity. Adam could observe, study, and make use of his immediate environment, but more importantly Adam's life in the garden of Eden provided him with the opportunity to understand God's initial work. The creation -aka the kingdom of Heaven(**Genesis 1:1-2:4a** "The heavens and the earth.").

    Genesis 1:1-2:4a is the creation of space and matter, but it -i.e. the universe- was intended to serve the man of God as more than just a habitable environment. It's not obvious but the word "work" in **Genesis 2:2** is key to unlocking the message of

Genesis 1:1-2:4a.

Genesis 2:2
2. And on the seventh day God completed His **work** which He had made.
Genesis 2:2

    The Hebrew word that has been translated as "work" in English versions of **Genesis 2:2** is pronounced M'lak-toe. M'lak-toe is a variation of another Hebrew word that is pronounced in English as M-la'kah. M-la'kah can be found in the "Strong's Hebrew Dictionary" under the reference number **H4399**(M-la'kah). It is derived from another Hebrew word which is transliterated as Mal'awk(Strong's reference number **H4397**), which has the simplified meaning: to dispatch as a deputy; a messenger.

    The Hebrew word that is pronounced as Mal'awk is translated into English versions of the bible as "angel" or "messenger". The three words Mal'awk, M-la'kah, and M'lak-toe are all derivatives of the same unused Hebrew "root word". Although the three words differ in spelling and pronunciation, they are all essentially related to a **message**, a **messenger**, or to the **ministering** work of either.

*Definition for Strong's **H4397**(Mal'awk): from an unused root meaning to dispatch as a deputy; a messenger; specifically of God, i.e. an angel(also a prophet, priest or teacher):- ambassador, angel, king, messenger.*

*Definition for Strong's **H4399**(M'la-kaw): from the same root as **H4397**; properly deputy-ship, that is ministry; gen. employment (never servile) or work (abstract or concrete); also property (as the result of labor):-business, +cattle, +industrious, occupation, (+ -pied, + officer, thing (made), use, (manner of) work ([-*

man], -manship).

By replacing the word "work" in **Genesis 2:2** with the more descriptive term we are better equipped to see how the seven-day creation was intended to be understood by Adam.

Genesis 2:2
2. And on the seventh day God completed His ministry(M'lak-toe) which He had made.
Genesis 2:2

The seven-day creation would function as a habitable environment and it would serve empirically as God's ministry. The seven-day creation of the universe is literally a message to the one man within the creation who, having been filled with the Spirit of God(**Genesis 2:7** Cross Reference **Exodus 31:3, 35:31**) had the eyes to see and the ears to hear that message(Cross Reference **John 15:26, 16:13; 1Peter 1:12**). **Genesis 1:1-2:4a** is God's personal revelation of Himself to Adam, the man who was created in **Genesis 2:7** to be God's likeness.

By understanding the vitality, diversity, and enormity of the creation Adam could use the universe as an analytical study tool to appreciate the benevolence, wisdom, and power of his creator. Adam could also utilize his understanding of nature and the cosmos to make technological use of his own environment. But even more importantly, by reflecting on his own existence as the likeness of God, the creation would serve Adam as a metaphysical analysis of himself(Cross Reference **Luke 17:21** "The kingdom of God is within you.").

Although the term "metaphysics*" has come to be associated with a wide range of practices and philosophies, I am strictly interested in the dictionary's usage of the term.

Met-a-phys-ics (met'e-fiz'iks) n. pl. (construed as singular) 1. The systematic study or science of the first principles of being and of knowledge; the doctrine of the essential nature and fundamental relations of all that is real. Webster Comprehensive Dictionary

The Message

The **Genesis 1:1-2:4a** creation of the universe is the "body", the feminine expression, of the masculine Godhead(Cross Reference Adam and Eve). It is the all-encompassing macrocosmic reality that is, relatively speaking, mirrored within the microcosm of Adam, the likeness of God*.

Occult groups may not openly credit the Bible for recognizing that the macrocosmic reality is mirrored within the microcosmic existence, but the corresponding understanding of this relationship is reflected in the phrase "As above, so below".

When we look at the six-day creation as the model for Adam's soul and inner spiritual reality, the picture of what Adam was to understand about himself begins to materialize.

In the beginning God impregnated the void with space/plasma and matter: The Heavens and the Earth(**Genesis 1:1**). God then brought the plasma and matter to life by calling for light/life to animate the new creations(**Genesis 1:2-5** Cross Reference **John 1:4-5**). Next an expanse, corresponding to the divide between the higher and lower nature, was created to divide the upper habitable waters from the lower habitable waters(**Genesis 1:6-8**). The lower waters were collected to one place and dry land appeared. The dry land, itself a seeded and living organism, was called upon to produce a self-renewing life-giving tree and other plant-life(**Genesis 1:9-13**). God then introduced two major lights in the heavens to divide between day and night, to be for signs and seasons, and to mark days and years. The greater light was set in the heavens to illuminate and rule over the day, the lesser light was placed to shine and rule over the night(**Genesis 1:14-19**). The lower waters of the creation were then populated by a multitude of marine animals - the mightiest being the Leviathan(**Job 41:1-34;** corresponding to the Ego)-, amphibious animals, insects, and birds(**Genesis 1:20-23**). And on the sixth day of the creation, land animals -the strongest of which is the Behemoth(**Job 40:15-24;** corresponding to emotional fortitude)-, reptiles, insects, mammalian creatures, and finally the man in God's image, were all created(**Genesis 1:24-27**).

      There are four groups of living organisms within the Genesis 1 creation. The plant life accounts for the first group. The marine animals, birds, and amphibious creatures make up the second group. Reptilian, insect, and mammalian animals make up the third group. And the angels of God make up the fourth group. The four separate groups of living organisms of the Genesis 1 macrocosm correspond to the functional and involuntary, chemical, emotional, and rational composition of Adam's genetic makeup. The flora or plant-life of the larger creation corresponds to Adam's involuntary bodily functions such as the production and reproduction of cells, his heart beat, digestion, breathing etc. Coming into existence after the flora of Adam's inner universe, the sun, moon, and stars appear in the heavens as governing bodies over Adam's conscious and unconscious mind. The cycles of the heavens and the seasons of the earth correspond to Adam's own daily, weekly, monthly, and yearly hormonal cycles. The celestial bodies are followed on day five by the sea creatures which correspond to Adam's survival instincts and the base levels of his psyche(Cross Reference **Job 40:15-24, 41:1-34; Ecclesiastes 10:20; Mark 4:4,15**). The land animals correspond to the emotional and intuitional areas of Adam's mind. All of Adam's inner heavenly kingdom was put under the authority of his own personal angels/messengers. Adam's inner man was made responsible to oversee his various chemical urges and responses, hormonal balance, bodily functions, and to support Adam's emotional and mental health. Adam's personal messengers were essentially made responsible to maintain Adam's wellbeing(and his sanity) by overseeing the various components of Adam's inner kingdom and by relaying internal and external information or stimuli to Adam's "godhead/mind"(Cross Reference **Job 1:6-7, 2:1-2**). Adam's governing principles and complex thinking processes such as self-awareness, speech, language, and comprehension were processes of Adam's own mind(Cross Reference "Likeness of God").

Some modern scientists, namely proponents of evolutionary theory, and even some Christian ministries suggest an explanation for the innate nature of humanity that at first glance appears to share an affinity with biblical teaching. Genesis chapter 1's creation of sea creatures, amphibious lifeforms, reptilian creatures, and land animals that precede the creation of man does in fact appear to be similar to evolutionary theory's progression-of-life from the ocean to homo-sapien man. But the presumed similarities between the two belief systems end there. The distinguishing difference between what the bible and evolution theory teach is the manner by which man and the human nature came to exist.

According to the Bible, man was created independent of the animal kingdom and then charged by God to rule over the other species within the creation(Cross Reference **Genesis 1:27-28**). Adam, the likeness of God, was created with a lower nature that was governed over by his own inner man who relayed internal information to Adam's mind(or godhead). Adam was personally held responsible to govern himself and to respect the rights of other men and women(**Genesis 2:7-8, 15-20; 3:1-7** Cross Reference **Genesis 4:7, 5:1, 6:13, 9:6**). Satan, a spiritual entity, initiating principality, and hostile adversary to humanity, is held responsible for corrupting the innate spiritual nature of man(**Genesis 3:1-24** Cross Reference **Genesis 2:7,17; 5:1-2**). The angels who sinned and had sexual relationships with human women, during the era leading up to the flood of Noah's day, are held responsible for convoluting the nature of the human soul(Cross Reference **Genesis 6:1-7; Psalms 2:1-12 and 82:1-8; Romans 1:18-32; 2Peter 2:4; Jude 1:6-7**). Man, and human nature were originally created to resemble God and His nature(Cross Reference **Genesis 1:26**: "the image and likeness of God"), but the nature of modern man is the result of subsequent meddling by nefarious spiritual beings.

Evolutionary theory posits that all life on earth began in the ocean, it evolved into amphibious creatures, which evolved further into the reptilian animals. Life then continued to evolve into various types of land animals and eventually resulted in the evolution of homo-sapien man. Because humanity presumably evolved out of the animal kingdom, human nature can only be rooted in the animal nature of our earliest ancestors(I am overly simplifying). By equating humanity to an evolved animal evolutionary theory undermines biblical teaching and personal responsibility by inadvertently justifying* the corrupt state of mankind.

Animals murder, devour, rape, and steal, therefore it only follows that humans, a rational and self-conscious animal, would connive ways and justify the means of accomplishing the same(See: European Colonialism).

The bible may seem to imply a similar kind of justification, e.g. Satan and the fallen angels, but, besides the fact that man is a rational being who was created independent of the animal kingdom and who has retained aspects of his original God given nature, the law of God implicitly holds each man and woman *responsible for their own actions -Cross Reference **Genesis 4:7, 9:5-6***.

The theory of evolution also denies the existence of an infinite, intelligent, just, and all-powerful Creator. By this denial evolutionary theory ordains man, despite our ignorant nature, destructive pursuits, and religious insecurities(i.e. seeking justification for the sake of pride, fear, or insecurity through man-made religious systems: skin color, gender, socioeconomic standing, cultural heritage, national pride etc.; all dividing factors which man is willing to die and to kill for.) to be the earth's ultimate authority(Cross Reference **Daniel 9:24-27, 11:36-45**). Among its other deficiencies the theory of evolution's denial of a spiritual reality defies inspiration, ingenuity, and the attainment, retention, the usage of knowledge and the 'mind' itself. Another problem with evolutionary theory is that, besides intraspecies adaptations to specific environments(for instance the Bengal vs the Siberian Tigers) or to acquire food sources(Such as the observable variations in the Galapagos Island's tortoises), I am personally unaware of any "missing links" or multiple generations of transitional animal species. But I am also not a scientist out looking for missing links or generations of transitional animals and though they may exist, they have yet to be found.

I personally believe that it is completely unscientific for anyone who knows less than everything to presume to put a limit on what is or is not possible. I also believe that it is cruel and inhumane to invalidate another individual's existence by dismissing the experiences that have only served to confirm the perspectives that have brought them to the present moment, simply because your experiences are not compatible, and your perspectives are not in agreement with theirs. We're all ignorant. The closer humanity moves to the truth of our existence the better off we'll all be.

Demons and other Spiritual Beings

The angelic beings who were created in the image of God were given the right to exercise authority over the created order(Cross Reference **Genesis 1:28**; and **Daniel 10:13,20-21; 12:1** Cross Reference **Deuteronomy 32:8*** of the Septuagint version* of the Bible). At this very moment they are spiritual beings who act as initiating principles to unite, inspire, compel, and buffer the hearts and minds of nations(**Daniel 10:20-21**) and even of individual men, women, and children(Cross Reference **Genesis 10:8-12** "Nimrod"). Ever since their physical removal from the earth they have acted through human emissaries who, because they are human, die and must be replaced by other human rulers(Cross Reference **Genesis 10:8-12**). It is through the succession of human rulers that the kings of the earth(Cross Reference **Psalm 2:2-3,10**) are able to hold sway over a given human population for centuries of years(Cross Reference **Daniel chapter 7**).

Just as spiritual rulers are attached to nations and human empires, other spiritual beings such as demons and familiar spirits can attach themselves to or manifest within families as well as individual men, women, and children(Cross Reference familiar spirits: **1Samuel 28:7-11; 2Chronicles 33:6; Isaiah 19:3**). Demons are the result of spiritual perversions within the animal kingdoms of the macro and microcosms of reality(Cross Reference **Genesis 6:1-7; Romans 1:18-32**; As Above, So Below). Demons can manifest and/or express themselves through intellectual, psychological, emotional, physical, and sexual means. Demons are essentially corruptions of our biological, chemical, and/or electrical makeup that result in disease/diseases to varying degrees. Our internal messengers(See **Genesis 1:27-28**) can also succumb to corruption(**Genesis 6:1-6**).

The Behemoth and The Leviathan

The micro and macrocosmic spiritual relationship existing between man and the kingdom of heaven(Cross Reference **Genesis 1:1-2:4a**) is briefly touched upon in the book of Job.

In the book of Job, a conversation about God's interaction in the lives of men takes place between Job and four of his associates. Job's righteousness is the main topic of the conversation. In chapters **38-42** after **Job** has shut the mouths of his associates in defense of his way of life, YHWH intervenes. And beginning with examples of the many ways in which God interacts within His own creation -each example being too grand for Job and his associates to understand-, YHWH enlightens Job's mind to the ordering of the macrocosmic reality. In **Job 40:6-14** YHWH introduces the climax of His discourse by first asking Job whether or not he can master himself, and declare himself truly righteous, or adorn himself with majesty and excellence, and be truly glorious and beautiful("Himself" being the key word). Or if he can judge righteously in face off all mankind, and even before God Himself.

Beginning in **Job 40:15** and continuing through **Job 41:34** YHWH draws Job's attention to two incredible beasts, the Behemoth and the Leviathan, which God has made and which only God Himself has the ability to approach or to master. The beasts are so incredible that some men and women have assumed that the beasts could only be mythical creatures. Considering that the bible only addresses spiritual and physical reality and, given the fact that Job is told to consider these two incredible beasts alongside other common animals that he is familiar with, some men and women understand the references to the incredible beasts to be descriptive of actual marine and terrestrial dinosaurs. Whether or not these animals were real or fictional has been and will continue to be debated, but what is more important for the purpose of this chapter is how their references speak to man's fundamental instincts and the egotistical and emotional areas of the human psyche.

In **Job 40:15-24** the Behemoth is said to be first in the ways of God. It is this mighty beast that rules over the emotional and intuitive areas of the human psyche.

Job 40:15-24

15. Now behold Behemoth, which I made along with you; he eats grass like an ox.
16. See, now, his strength in his loins, and his force in the muscles of his belly.
17. He hangs his tail like a cedar; the sinews of his thighs are knit together.
18. His bones are like beams of bronze, his ribs like bars of iron.
19. He is the first in the ways of God; only He who made him can bring near his sword.
20. For the mountains yield food for him, and all the beasts of the field play there.
21. He lies under the lotus trees, in a covert of reeds and marsh.
22. The lotus trees cover him in their shade; the willows by the brook surround him.
23. Indeed the river may rage, yet he is not disturbed; he is confident, though the Jordan gushes into his mouth.
24. Shall any take him before his eyes, or pierce through his nose with snares?
Job 40:15-24

Just as God is the only one who can bring His sword(**v. 19**) against this mighty beast, only a mature and responsible man or woman has the fortitude to gain mastery over their own tongue and to gain control of their emotional outbursts. Our tongue gives "life" to the thoughts of our hearts and the Behemoth within each of us can destroy in seconds a relationship that may have taken years to build. The power of the tongue is often underestimated but **Proverbs 18:19-21**(Cross Reference **Matthew 15:18-20**) plainly states just how much strength there is in our words.

Proverbs 18:19-21
19. An offended brother is worse than a fortified city; yea contentions are like the bars of a castle.
20. A man's belly shall be satisfied with the fruit of his mouth; he shall be satisfied with the produce of his lips.
21. Death and life are in the power of the tongue; and those who love it shall eat its fruit.
Proverbs 18:19-21

Respect goes a long way. A mature man or woman can engage in a conversation with another mature individual, if only to gain an appreciation for the other individuals personal experience. This can be accomplished without feeling the need to attack nor having any fear of being personally compromised. Understanding should never deteriorate into competition. The worst thing that should ever occur between two mature individuals who are conversing is the failure to effectively communicate. But the fear of poor communication is superseded by the possibility of growth through a better understanding of their individual selves and of one another.

In **Job 41:34** the Leviathan is called "king over all the sons/children of pride". It is this mighty beast that is associated with the human ego.

Job 41:1-34

1. Can you draw out Leviathan with a hook, or hold down his tongue with a cord?
2. Can you put a reed rope into his nose, or pierce his jaw with a thorn?
3. Will he multiply pleas for help to you? Will he speak softly to you?
4. Will he make a covenant with you? Will you take him as a servant forever?
5. Will you play with him as with a bird, or will you tie him up for your maidens?
6. Will your companions bargain over him? Shall they divide him among the merchants?
7. Can you fill his skin with harpoons, or his head with fishing spears?
8. Lay your hand on him; remember the battle, you will never do it again!
9. Indeed, any hope of overcoming him is false; shall one not be overwhelmed at the sight of him?
10. No one is so fierce that he would dare stir him up. Who then is able to stand against Me?
11. Who has preceded Me, that I should pay him? Everything under heaven is Mine.
12. I will not keep silent about his limbs, his mighty power, or his graceful proportions.
13. Who can remove his outer coat? Who can approach him with a double bridle?
14. Who can open the doors of his face, With his terrible teeth all around?
15. The rows of his scales are his pride, shut up tightly as with a seal;
16. One is so near another that no air can come between them;
17. They are joined one to another, they stick together and cannot be parted.

18. His sneezings flash forth light, and his eyes are like the eyelids of the morning.
19. Out of his mouth go burning lights; sparks of fire shoot out.
20. Smoke goes out of his nostrils, as from a burning pot and burning rushes.
21. His breath kindles coals, and a flame goes out of his mouth.
22. Strength dwells in his neck, and sorrow dances before him.
23. The folds of his flesh are joined together; they are firm on him and cannot be moved.
24. His heart is as hard as stone, even as hard as the lower millstone.
25. When he raises himself up, the mighty are afraid; because of his crashings they are beside themselves.
26. The sword, the spear, the dart, and the javelin overtake him, but they will not hold.
27. He counts iron as straw, bronze as rotten wood
28. The arrow cannot make him flee; sling-stones become like stubble to him.
29. Darts are regarded as straw; he laughs at the threat of javelins.
30. His undersides are sharp like potsherds; he spreads pointed marks in the mire.
31. He makes the deep boil like a pot; he makes the sea like a pot of ointment.
32. He leaves a shining wake behind him; one would think the deep had white hair.
33. There is nothing like him on earth, one made without fear.
34. He beholds all high things; he is king over all the children of pride.
Job 41:1-34

Only God(or god, meaning Adam) can bring His sword against the Behemoth and only God, in the macrocosm of reality, and Adam, within his own microcosm, have the ability to approach the Leviathan. The ego is at the foundation of each man and woman's individuality. The corrupted human ego has provided men, women, and children with the justification to encroach upon the rights of other individuals, and to even disregard the authority of God. It is the self-righteous self-image, the ego, of Satan and of man that is responsible for every conflict, form of control, and abuse of power that have come to define the human experience(**Job 41:34** Cross Reference **Genesis 4:1-26**).

It is important for all men and women to appreciate the fact that we are all composed of at least a spirit, a soul, and a physical body. Understanding of these aspects of our human nature is important for personal growth and preceding interactions with other men and women(**Ephesians 3:9-10**). We are each driven by forces that do not appear to the naked eye(**Ephesians 6:12**). We each have the ability to affect other people, and the moods and emotions, outbursts, and the actions of others have the power to positively or negatively affect our personal disposition. This subtle "energy" can inspire tears, drive us to extreme happiness, or even move us to compromise our own wellbeing and incite us to mob violence(For an example of this subtle energy in action consider the ebb and flow of emotion and momentum at a sporting event. Both, the crowd and the athletes "feed or are fueled" off this energy).

Eve's confrontation in the garden of Eden with the serpent and Yeshua of Nazareth's trial in the wilderness with the Devil are the bible's two definitive examples of the battle that is waged for control over the macro and microcosmic realities: aka, Spiritual Warfare. Both Adam and Eve's, and Yeshua's confrontations show how the spirit and soul of man is attacked by our common adversary. Eve succumbed but, contrary to perspectives that have been inspired by masculine pride(Cross Reference the "Leviathan" **Job 41:1-34**), she was no fool. The serpent did not approach Eve because he believed her to be gullible. The truth of the matter is that the serpent approached Eve in the garden of Eden, not because he saw her as weak or foolish but because he recognized aspects of her personality that were compatible with his own.

    The Devil's temptation could not work in his confrontation with Yeshua of Nazareth(**Matthew 4:1-11; Mark 1:12-13; Luke 4:1-13**), and not just because Yeshua is the God Who is responsible for existence(Cross Reference **John 1:1-5**). Yeshua of Nazareth is God and the author of the Heavens and Earth, but he was also a man Who knew Himself and, Who understood the truth of His own internal kingdom(**Luke 17:20-21**).

GOD'S FORMAL INTRODUCTION
(Genesis 2:4b-25)
And The Identity of Man

In **Genesis 1:1-2:4a** God commanded His creation into existence. Starting in **Genesis 2:4b** God began to be personally identified because His relationship with the creation had changed. God is formally introduced first, by His personal identifier/name -YHWH Elohim-, secondly by the creation of Adam and the garden of Eden, and lastly by the relationship that He established between Himself and the man whom He had formed to be His likeness. What Adam had received from God: his life and independence, the garden paradise, his companion, and the word of God; provided Adam with enough information to recognize the power, benevolence, and majesty of his Creator. But Adam had been given more than just information concerning God. In being given the name of God, Adam was given the right to draw near and speak face to face with YHWH Elohim(Cross Reference **Exodus 33:11**). Adam was granted access to YHWH Elohim so that he could know, understand, and appreciate the God who had given of Himself to provide Adam with existence and, as God's likeness, an identity*.

*After Adam had been formed and YHWH Elohim breathed His Spirit of Life into the man but before Adam was placed in the land of Eden, Adam was given time to appreciate and reflect on his Creator as well as his independence when YHWH Elohim left Adam on his own for a time to go and plant the garden of Eden(Cross Reference **John 14:2-3**).*

The name of God did not give Adam a license(**Romans 6:15-16**) but, it did provide him with an opportunity.

A name, in any capacity, can serve as an invitation or it can simply be a matter of recognition. But the circumstance of having a name can change considerably when we must look to others to name, identify, describe, or define other men, women, objects, or ideas for us(Cross Reference the "Ego" in light of Eve's confrontation with the serpent and her subsequent subjugation of Adam in **Genesis 3:1-19**). Anyone who wishes to relate to what you have created, named, or understand, must submit themselves to your definition and method of relating to it. For example, to understand the qualities and characteristics of YHWH Elohim one must look to God, His word, and to what He has revealed of Himself for understanding. To understand the qualities and characteristics of the man who was created as the likeness of God we must look to YHWH Elohim who created, named, and defined the qualities and characteristics of that man. To understand the qualities and characteristics of a patriot or rather of a so-called nigger, one must look to the European imperialists, colonists, slave marketers, slave drivers, and slave owners who were responsible for kidnapping, selling, transporting, raping, murdering, enslaving and poisoning, and who denied the history, who denied the heritage, who denied the humanity, who malevolently disrupted the family continuity*, who created distrust and hate by purposefully setting dark brown, brown, and copper skinned men and women at variance with each other, who prohibited the right to pursue knowledge, and who through terrorism, brutalization, centuries of misinformation and disinformation, and generation after generation of indoctrination redefined and reclassified God's creation's -indigenous American and African men, women, and children- as niggers, coons, coloreds, negroes, blacks, and/or African-Americans(Cross Reference the legal definition of Civiliter Mortuus: Civil Death is the legal status of all of the afore mentioned "Identities". Eve was also deceived into pursuing a caricature of her God given identity by Satanic intervention: Cross Reference **Genesis 3:1-7; Revelation 2:18-29**). Men and women who conform to the "Nigger" identity are exactly what the prideful, arrogant, thieving, money hungry, possession and sex crazed, hostile, deceitful, greedy and antithetical Colonial "Land of the free and home of the brave" has convinced them to be. Niggers have sold out their God given identity and submitted to an identity that was created by a colonial corporate establishment that can only hate them.

Male slave owners would routinely set aside their prejudices and, at times, their marriage vows to take young black and brown skinned girls from their families as well as women from their spouse's beds, to rape them. When the rape resulted in pregnancy the "illegitimate" child would often be sold away in order to hide the insult inflicted upon the rapist's spouse, who otherwise would be continually subjected to the humiliation of seeing the evidence of her husband's infidelity. Indigenous men and boys were also subjected to being raped by European men as part of a dehumanizing process that is known as "Buck Breaking".

Although the "Nigger" is looked on as a bastard by the United States corporate establishment It has been useful for selling pride and guns, arousing fear and selling more guns, and for fostering insecurity, sustaining intellectual slavery, and promoting a perception of inferiority among indigenous peoples. The "Nigger" has been accused of inspiring domestic terrorists, such as the KKK, to violence. The "Nigger" has been the United Incorporated States' greatest advocate for passing laws to restrict "Niggers" and, for limiting the potential of men and women who have been wrongly perceived as "Niggers". The "Nigger" is a useful distraction that has served as a watchdog within communities of indigenous Americans and peoples of African descent. The "Nigger" has kept watch over dark brown, brown, and copper skinned American citizens to assure its corporate patron that none within the indigenous communities would dare aspire to be anything more than a Nigger. The Nigger(Spic, Red-Man, Chink, Gook, Towel Head, Wetback,

Dike, Fag, etc.) is an essential dehumanizing component of the colonial culture, economy, and the colonial identity(Satanism thrives on ignorance, comparisons{**Isaiah 14:14**}, competition{**Genesis 3:5**}, inequalities{**Genesis 3:6**}, and injustice{**Genesis 3:7**}).

    The state sponsored and church supported defecation upon Aboriginal identities, and the indoctrination of European superiority is deeply rooted within the American psyche. From the days of American slavery, the re-engineering and misconceptions of the indigenous American and African identity has served as a foundation for the establishment's provisional government. Two key issues, caste status(which is perceived and marketed as racism) and nationality, are necessary to understand before any serious undertaking can begin to rectify American culture. Even the governments patronizing promoting of "Black History Month" is a mockery of aboriginal people's contribution to human society, as it only recognizes the achievements of slaves, former slaves, and their descendants within the context of the colonies that have oppressed them and misappropriated their human identity. Archaeological and eyewitness historical accounts attest to the *brilliance, wealth, and expansion of ancient African empires such as Kush, Axum/Ethiopia, Phoenicia/Canaan, Carthage, Numidia, ancient Ghana, Mali, Songhai, Great Zimbabwe, Munhumutapa, and most notably of the ancient native Egyptian dynasties. The Olmec civilization in central America is also worth noting.

*Cross Reference "When We Ruled" -a must read- written by Robin Walker; "They Came Before Columbus, The African Presence In Ancient America" by Ivan Van Sertima; "Christopher Columbus and The African Holocaust" by John Henrik Clarke; and "The African Origin Of Civilization, Myth Or Reality" by Cheikh Anta Diop.

Even though their African heritage has been denied in the modern age by European and Arab scholars, whose ancestors readily attested to the monetary wealth and advanced cultural heritage exhibited by the many varying African societies throughout the African continent, the ancient Egyptians more than any other witness testified, through their artwork and sculptures, to the fact that they did not resemble Egypt's current Arab rulers whose progenitors invaded and conquered the land in the 7th century of the modern era, nor did the indigenous Egyptians resemble the Europeans actors who are so often cast to impersonate Egyptians in secular artwork and modern cinema. The "whitewashing", misrepresentation, and destruction of historical artifacts, such as the chiseled off lips and noses of Egyptian sculptures, the blasted off features of the Sphinx, as well as European and colonial scholarly attempts to convert black and brown skinned African men and women into "dark-skinned Caucasians" testify to the literal and physical Satanic community's hatred of the truth(**Genesis 3:15** "And I will put enmity between thee and the woman, and between thy seed and her seed…").

No other peoples on earth have had such a debate over their ancestral identity to the extent that the ancient Egyptians have. The debates continue only because of the bias of European imperialists, historians, scholars, archaeologists, and scientists who continue to promulgate emotional arguments, argue against collected data, and who refuse to accept hard evidence as fact*.

Internet search: Dr. Cheikh Anta Diop and Dr. Theophile Obenga's presentation at the 1974 Cairo Symposium sponsored by the United Nations Educational, Scientific, and Cultural Organization: UNESCO. News of the symposiums findings were chronicled by UNESCO in a 1978 publication entitled, Ancient Civilizations of Africa, Vol II. There are numerous videos available on different social media platforms of Drs. Diop and

Obenga speaking about their findings that confirm the African identity of the ancient Egyptians. Dr. Cheikh Anta Diop and Dr. Theophile Obenga's conclusions that were presented at the 1974 Cairo Symposium stood unopposed at that time and stand unopposed to this very day.

The great mystery of how the Egyptian's Pharaonic society could miraculously appear with its educational and civil institutions, religious, and masonic orders intact and fully operational reaches a preposterous height as some historians, upon finding no evidence for the origins of Egyptian civilization in Europe nor in Asia, will go even as far as attributing Egypt's technological achievements to visitors from space, before considering to look deeper into the African continent(Cross Reference "Black Genesis: The Prehistoric Origins Of Ancient Egypt" by Robert Bauval & Thomas Brophy, Ph.D.). But of course, "Old habits die hard". The justification for the brutality of the European slave trade is rooted upon the doctrine that the indigenous Americans and Africans were little more than brute beasts and that offering them the European civilization and culture, which had been appropriated from North and North-West African Moors, was for their own betterment(not to mention the free labor, sexual exploitation, and Africa's mineral wealth that the European colonialist were and still are able to take advantage of in modern times). How would modern reflections on history look upon the many hundreds of years of unimaginable atrocities committed against the mothers and fathers of civilization if we all knew their true contribution to humanity(Pythagoras and Plato are only two of the many notable examples of educated Greeks whose knowledge was bestowed on them by the ancient Egyptians/Kemetians{Kemet, an ancient name of "Egypt", is where the word "Chemistry" comes from}. Also, ancient Greek and Latin alphabets were both adopted from the ancient Phoenicians, who were themselves the descendants of Africans who migrated into the land of Canaan).

The great mystery behind the origin of Egypt's advanced society is answered simply by looking to the south and southwest of Egypt(Cross Reference "Black Genesis: The Prehistoric Origins of ancient Egypt" written by Robert Bauval and Thomas Brophy, PhD.). It is irresponsible for archaeologists, anthropologists, and historians to even suggest, first, that any society of men and women could simply "appear" on the earth in such an advanced state of existence as has been exhibited by the ancient Egyptians. Second, it is preposterous to suggest that such an advanced society would leave no evidence pertaining to the development of its religious or civil institutions. Third, it is obnoxious to even suggest that it is probable that Egyptian society migrated to Africa from Asia or Europe without leaving prior evidence or before establishing settlements on either continent. These types of claims are simply offensive.

The social injustice of misappropriating the ancient Egyptian's ancestry takes another sinister turn in consideration of Europe's Ashkenazim(Ashkenaz son of Gomer, son of Japheth, **Genesis10:2-3**) and Sephardic Jews. While men and women in Western Society have no problem prostrating themselves before a European representation of Yeshua of Nazareth, these same individuals take no consideration of the fact that they are worshiping a manmade image, nor do they consider the fact that the ancient Israelites and Judeans did not resemble either of these two groups of European Jews(Cross Reference "The Thirteenth Tribe" by Arthur Koestler).

The truth as attested to by the Old and New testaments of the bible is that the children of Israel(the **Israelites** and **Judeans**) resembled, except for their grooming preferences, the indigenous heavily melanated Egyptians in physical appearance. The bible records many instances in which the children of Israel were themselves believed to be native Egyptians. In **Exodus**

2:15-19 Moses, a descendant of the tribe of Levi, helped the daughters of the priest of Midian who upon returning home told their father that an Egyptian had aided them. In **Acts 21:38-39** the apostle Paul, a descendant of the tribe of Benjamin, was believed by the Roman soldiers to be an Egyptian. In **Matthew 2:13-15** Joseph and Mary, both descendants of the tribe of Judah, took the young child Yeshua to Egypt to hide away where they would not stand out and easily be recognized when king Herod sought to kill the young Messiah. Besides those direct comparisons, **Genesis 41:50-52** relates the fact that the descendants of the tribes of Manasseh and Ephraim were Egyptian in appearance as the birth of both children were the result of Joseph's marriage to Asenath who was the daughter of Potipherah, an Egyptian priest of On(**Genesis 41:45,50; 46:20**). The only physical depictions of the ancient Judeans that specifically identify them as Judeans, that I am personally aware of, are housed in the British Museum in London. The "Lachish reliefs(Search the internet: "Images Lachish Reliefs")" which date to 701 B.C. and which once decorated the Assyrian king Sennacherib's palace in Nineveh, show all of the Judean men adorned with knotted beards and knotted "Afro" hairstyles, being led captive into Assyria. Men, women, and children resemble their ancestors, we all wear our "passports" on our faces. European's living in America are easily identified as European colonists because they resemble their European ancestors who colonized the America's. European Jews living in the land that is called Israel today are easily identified by their passports, their faces, as European colonists whose ancestors were given authority to colonize the land by other Europeans(See the "Balfor Declaration of 1917").

It is simply a fact that the ancient Israelites and Judeans resembled the black and brown skinned indigenous Egyptians. Emotional arguments are what stand between that fact and men and women's acceptance of the Truth. The repetitive display of a European Messiah is just the capstone upon the dishonest misrepresentations of a people who have been robbed, disrespected, abused, vilified, sold and slaughtered like animals, kidnapped and led captive throughout the earth(Cross Reference **Deuteronomy 28:15-68**) by both the European Church* and State. The boiled down and condensed reason why Europeans need the ancient Egyptians to be seen and understood by the public as anyone except for men and women who are of heavily Melanated African descent is because the bible, the stick of authority that the European Church and State uses to support their claim of a "Superior Race(See 'Curse of Ham/Canaan')", says time and time again that all of the children of Jacob, the Children of Israel, resembled the indigenous Egyptians who were and have conclusively been proven to be heavily Melanated/Dark Skinned African men and women. The ancestors of European Ashkenazim and Sephardic "Jews" simply appropriated pre-existing knowledge. Understanding of the Truth can open the gates and set one free of the ideology of European superiority that has been imposed on our minds from the first time that we saw a naked, bloody, and disfigured European hanging on a cross at a church. And being told that this grotesque image represents the God who became flesh to die in your place to appease the requirements of a law that you didn't know that you were bound to uphold.

Have you ever questioned, "Why does every church have the image of a European savior hanging in it?" Not even considering the fact that **Exodus 20:3-5** says not to create any image and not to bow down or wordship it. Not considering the fact that Satan's stated aspiration is to put himself before the eyes of the world and be recognized and accepted as God. Not even considering the fact that ultimately, the biblical text acknowledges only two seeds, two distinct groups of men and women inhabiting the earth; the seed of the Woman and the seed of the Serpent(**Genesis 3:15**). Consider within yourself, what does seeing the image of a European as God do to your personal Heavenly Kingdom?

If you have the inkling, research the Christian ideology that is referred to as the "Curse of Ham". The curse upon Canaan - who was the grandson of Noah-, has been used by Catholic, Protestant, and so-called Christian cults to justify the brutality and injustices that have been inflicted upon dark skinned, i.e. melanated, peoples and their descendants around the globe. The lie of the "Curse of Ham" is easily exposed.

*In **Genesis 9:25** Canaan, Noah's grandson, was cursed by Noah and declared to be a servant of servants first to his own brothers, Ham's three other sons, Kush, Mizraim, and Phut. Next, in **Genesis 9:26** Canaan was declared to be subject to Shem, and lastly in **Genesis 9:27** Noah declared Canaan to be subject to Japheth. Only Canaan was cursed. He alone was cursed by Noah to be servant of servants first to his own brothers and then to his two uncles. Neither Kush, Mizraim, Phut, nor Ham fell under Noah's, not God's, curse upon Canaan.*

*Contradicting the deceitful "Curse of Ham" doctrine that has been foundational to the Christian colonial establishment, **Genesis 10:8-12** states that Nimrod, son of Kush, son of Ham, began to be mighty in the earth. Nimrod was a mighty hunter before YHWH who was responsible for the establishment of many mighty and enduring empires. Furthermore, **Isaiah 19:25** reveals YHWH's affection for Mizraim -another son of Ham- and the existing affinity between Mizraim(Egypt) and Israel. In **Isaiah 19:25** YHWH refers to Mizraim/Egypt as "My people" and in the same verse He refers to Israel as "My inheritance".*

God's Formal Introduction Continued:

Back in **Genesis 2:4b** after God is formally identified as YHWH Elohim, His first work in **Genesis 2:7** was to form Adam from the dust/clay of the ground. God's second act was to breathe His Spirit of life into the man. Next YHWH Elohim planted a garden and placed Adam within the land of Eden(**Genesis 2:8**). YHWH Elohim then moved Adam into the garden paradise(**Genesis 2:15**) that had been personally planted by the hand of God. For a time, Adam existed alone in the garden of Eden but he had been given responsibilities that would stimulate his mind, invigorate his body, and occupy his time. Through observing the earth, the heavens, the animals, and his own manner of carrying on and relating to the world around him Adam should have grown in appreciation for the wisdom, capabilities, and genuine compassion displayed by his Creator. It is apparent that one thing that Adam did come to appreciate through his observations was the fact that he was the only man who existed in the garden of Eden(**Genesis 2:20**). Adam apparently only found contentment in the life that had been given to him after Eve was taken out of his body and presented to him in **Genesis 2:22**. Still, in all of these things, from the time of his creation until Eve was presented to him, Adam was allowed to personally see how God's hand was active in his life.

Each day spent in the garden of Eden provided Adam with the opportunity to reflect on the existence that YHWH Elohim had personally given to him, on the relationship that he shared with his Creator, and on himself as God's likeness(Cross Reference **Revelation** chapters 2-3). Although it may have taken a lifetime to appreciate, YHWH Elohim could not have provided Adam with a better setting in which to gain an appreciation for God's personal revelation(**Genesis 1:1-2:4a** and The Revelation of the Messiah).

The Rebellion Within Man and the Creation

It may be futile to estimate the amount of time that passed within the creation between the completion of the Heavens and the Earth in **Genesis 2:4a**, the commencement of the age of the Earth and Heavens in **Genesis 2:4b**, and the time when Adam was formed in **Genesis 2:7**. It may also be futile to make assumptions, at least without further information, about what events took place during each transitional period. The Bible only provides a few details about the times that preceded Adam's creation and life in the garden of Eden(**Genesis 1:1-2:4a; Job 38:4-7** Cross Reference "Rahab" **Psalm 87:4, 89:10; Isaiah 51:9).** What can be known with certainty is that Adam's/man's perception of God and God's message to humanity became convoluted early on in our history(Cross Reference **Genesis 3:1-24** and **Revelation** chapters **2-3**). And void of the Light that gives life to the creation, each man has blindly pursued his own fraudulent representation of the Truth("Ye shall be as God, knowing good and evil" **Genesis 3:5**).

The ability to clearly perceive God's message is of vital importance, especially to the Messianic body of believers. A clear perception of **Genesis 1:1-2:4a** does more than make a relationship with the Creator of the universe possible, reveal the God given identity that Adam was divested of in the garden of Eden, and unravel the message and mystery of Genesis chapters 1 and 2. A clear perception of God's word can also eliminate the confusion surrounding troubling passages such as **Romans 1:18-32** and **Psalm 82:1-8**, as well as expose the entities who exist to keep man from ever coming to the Truth: the Synagogue of Satan, the Seven-Headed Ten-Horned Beast, and the dual-pronged False Prophet of **Revelation 2:9, 3:9** and, **13:1-18**(Cross Reference **Matthew 24:1-31; Mark 13:1-27; Luke 21:1-28**).

When understood in their proper contexts, **Romans 1:18-32** and **Psalm 82:1-8** help to make sense of humanities present condition. These two passages focus on the man who was created in the image of God and offer insight into how and why humanity was destined to replicate the conditions prevalent on the earth in the days of Noah(**Genesis 6:1-7** Cross Reference **Matthew 24:37-39; Luke 17:26-30; Revelation 6:1-14:20**).

Romans 1:18-32

18. For Gods wrath is revealed from heaven on all ungodliness and unrighteousness of men, holding the truth in unrighteousness,
19. Because the thing known of God is clearly known within them, for God revealed it to them.
20. For the unseen things of Him from the creation of the world are clearly seen, being understood by the things made, both His eternal power and Godhead, for them to be without excuse.
21. Because knowing God, they did not glorify Him as God, nor where they thankful; but became vain in their reasoning's, and their undiscerning heart was darkened.
22. Professing to be wise, they became foolish,
23. And changed the glory of the incorruptible God into a likeness of an image of corruptible man, and of birds, and of four-footed animals, and creeping things.
24. Because of this, God gave them up to uncleanness in the lust of their hearts, their bodies to be dishonored among themselves;
25. Who changed the truth of God into the lie and worshiped and served the created thing more than the Creator, who is blessed forever. Amen.
26. Because of this, God gave them up to dishonorable passions, for even their females changed the natural use to that contrary to nature.

27. And likewise, the males also forsaking the natural use of the female burned in their lust toward one another, males with males working out shamefulness, and receiving back in themselves the reward which was fitting for their error.
28. And even as they did not think fit to have God in their knowledge, God gave them up to a reprobate mind, to do the things not right,
29. Having been filled with all unrighteousness, fornication, iniquity, covetousness, malice; being full of envy, murder, quarrels, deceit, evil habits; becoming whisperers,
30. Slanderers, God-haters, insolent, proud, braggarts, devisers of evil things, disobedient to those who engendered them,
31. Without discernment, perfidious, without natural affection, unforgiving, unmerciful;
32. Who knowing the righteous order of God, that those practicing such things are worthy of death, not only do them, but also applaud those practicing them.
Romans 1:18-32

Contrary to accepted Church doctrine, the focus of **Romans 1:18-32** is not the perverse state of humanity that resulted from Adam's sin, and verses **26-28** are not disparaging comments about homosexuality. **Romans 1:18-32** gives background information on the sinful angels(**Genesis 6:1-7; Psalm 82:1-8; 2Peter 2:4; Jude 1:6**) who were able to take advantage of humanities compromised heavenly kingdom(our spiritual bodies), which came about as the result of Adam's sin. Verses **26-28** of **Romans 1** pinpoints the flaw within the men created in the **Image of God** who rebelled against their own individual God given masculine and feminine nature. The rebellion of which resulted in arrogance and the violent, narcissistic, overbearing, domineering, obsessive, and compulsive abuses that are detailed in verses **29-32**. Any sane person should know that homosexuality does not result in the transgressions that are described in verses **29-32**, any more than heterosexuality does. Physical attraction is not the issue in **Romans 1:29-32**. The "men" who are being addressed are the angelic beings, the sons of God created in the image of God(**Genesis 1:27**), who were made caretakers of the macrocosmic reality, and who correspond to the "messengers" within each man and woman's microcosmic Kingdom of Heaven. Their error, their refusal to "Be Fruitful and Multiply(**Colossians 1:9-11**)", resulted in the corruption of the various aspects of each their own feminine and masculine natures, resulting in the various spiritual, mental, psychological, and emotional maladies that are detailed in the passage.

Consequently, what happens in heaven is reflected on the earth, and what happens on the earth is reflected in the heavens; "As Above so Below, As Below so Above(**Matthew 18:18**)".

Adam, and subsequently humanity, is only indirectly referenced in **Romans 1:23** as the "glory of the incorruptible God". This phrase, "changed the glory of the incorruptible God", is an oxymoron that should tip readers off. God Himself and His personal glory are incorruptible but Adam, God's glorious creation(**1Corinthians 11:7**), was not immune to corruption. It was humanity, via Adam, who was made subject to the likeness of the image of corruptible men, and birds, and four-footed animals, and creeping things(Cross Reference **Genesis 1:27-28** and **Genesis 6:1-7**).

The men who were being addressed in **Romans 1:18-32** cannot be common men. They were gods. A man being considered a god may sound implausible to many people, but the confusion should be rectified once you understand that a god, in the biblical and the generic sense of the term, is simply an individual or thing which has been placed as an example for other men and women to follow. A god can also be a source of information or of strength that men and women rely on, define ourselves by, or look to for justification. Additionally, according to **John 10:34-35**(Cross Reference **Psalm 82:6**) anyone to whom the Word of God comes, is a god. I would therefore admonish you, reader, to "Know Thyself".

Romans 1:18-32 can only possibly be applied to one of two groups of men who were both, considered to be gods and who had enough influence within the created order to effect humanity's existence on the earth. The first group of men, were created in the image of God in **Genesis 1:27**, commanded in **Genesis 1:28** to be "Fruitful and Multiply", and given authority over the existing creation. In **Genesis 9:1-7** the second group of men were given the responsibility of repopulating the earth. They were also commanded by God to be "Fruitful and Multiply", given authority over the planet earth, and they were made responsible to officiate over judicial matters. One significant difference between the two groups of men to whom the word of God was given is that the first group of men were created in the image of God. The second group of men only came to be in the image of God(**Genesis 9:1-7**) as the result of the first group being physically removed from the earth for their sins(Cross Reference **Genesis 6:1-7**).

Psalm 82:1-8 corresponds with **Romans 1:18-32** to clarify which group of men, those created(**Genesis 1:27**) or those who came to be(**Genesis 9:1-7**) in the image of God, is being addressed in the epistle to the Romans for their sin of corrupting the human species.

Psalm 82:1-8
A Psalm of Asaph
1. God stands in the assembly of God. He judges in the midst of the gods.
2. How long will you judge unjustly, and lift up the faces of the wicked? Selah

3. Judge the poor and fatherless; do justice to the afflicted and needy.
4. Deliver the poor and needy; save out of the hand of the wicked.
5. They neither know nor will they understand; they walk in darkness; all the foundations of the earth are shaken.
6. I have said you are gods, and all of you sons of the Most High.
7. But you shall die as man, and fall like one of the rulers.
8. Rise, O God, judge the earth; for you shall inherit all the nations.

Psalm 82:1-8

In **Psalm 82** God stands in the midst of the assembly, reprimanding the gods for their failure to uphold His righteous standard. In **Psalm 82:6** these particular gods are called sons/children of the Most High(Cross Reference **Genesis 6:2,4**). This fact is crucial to differentiating between the gods who were created in the image of God and those who came to be in God's image. A son/child of God is a man(or a woman) who, like Adam(**Luke 3:38** Cross Reference **Genesis 2:7**) and the men who were created in the image of God(**Genesis 1:27**), obtained his/her existence directly from the God of gods. This fact reveals the gods in **Psalm 82** to be men other than a congregation of Noah, Shem, Ham, Japheth, and/or their descendants -i.e. conventional men- who had received the word of God. Noah nor any of his sons, who are all descendants of Adam, could be called sons of the Most High(Cross Reference **Exodus 4:22** "Israel is My son even My firstborn:". The nation of Israel is the direct creation of the Most High God and prefigures the prophesied Israel of God: **Isaiah 49:1-7; Luke 1:54; Galatians 6:16** Cross Reference **Romans 9:6-7**). The earth's human population is indirectly referred to in the Psalm(**Psalm 82:3-5**) but **Psalm 82** is addressed to the men who were direct creations of God and to whom the word of God was revealed(**Genesis 1:27-28**).

Psalm 82 and **Romans 1:18-32**(Cross Reference **Genesis 6** and **Psalms 2:2-3**) are passages that are intended to shed light on the men who were given an authoritative identity and commissioned with the responsibility of maintaining order within God's creation(**Genesis 1:27-28**), but who instead left their former habitation to intermingle their seed among the earth's living organisms(**Genesis 6:1-13** Cross Reference **2Peter 2:4; Jude 1:6**).

Conclusion

Humanity was destined to repeat the sins and to be impaired by the blindness of long ago because the root of corruption that overtook humanity in the days leading up to the flood of Noah's day(**Genesis chapter 6**) was embedded within our DNA.

Humanity was alienated from God and we all took on a new spiritual identity when Adam ate the fruit of the tree of knowledge of good and evil. In that very day Adam died(**Genesis 2:17**), and he gave up the Spirit of Life that YHWH Elohim had been breathed into him(**Genesis 3:1-24**). The genetic code of every man, woman, and child was corrupted when humanity succumbed to the pestilence that came to define the days of Noah(**Genesis 6:1-13**). Even Noah, a perfectly righteous man, needed the grace of God(**Genesis 6:8-9**) to escape the flood that wiped man from off the face of the earth because he and his bloodline -parents, siblings, cousins, aunts, uncles, and in-laws- had also been tainted("All Flesh Had Corrupted Its Way On The Earth", **Genesis 6:12**). Man, angelic and human, deserved to be swept away by the flood waters that overtook the earth in the Days of Noah because the spirit and soul within humanity had/has no life, light, nor resemblance to the identity of the Creator of existence.

The **Genesis 1:1-2:4a** revelation of God that was given to the man who was created as His likeness in **Genesis 2:7** was intended to function as more than just a habitable environment. The Heavens and the Earth, the flora and the fauna, and the man(plural) created in the image of God are the details of God's personal revelation and of Adam's heritage as God's likeness. Adam was unique. He was intelligent, creative, passionate, self-aware, and formed with an innate nature to walk in step with his Creator(Cross Reference **Genesis 6:9**). Adam's lifework was to live, to make use of his environment, to know his God, and to know himself. The moment that Adam ate the fruit of the tree of knowledge of good and evil, God's likeness in man became subject to corruption: fear and pride, sin and death. The Spirit of God was taken from Adam, and the message of God's word became clouded in mystery. In each successive age, man's hunger for meaning and thirst for significance has only served to further advance the subjugation of the human identity to a caricature of God's likeness("I shall be compared to the Most High" **Isaiah 14:14** Cross Reference **Genesis 3:1-24, 6:1-13** "The Abomination of Desolation": **Daniel 9:24-27; Matthew 24:15; Mark 13:14**).

Humanity has been lost, desperately flailing in the darkness of a corrupt existence, unconsciously grasping after a stolen birthright. What has taken hold of us in the darkness and goaded us to chase the significance that we are continually led to believe has been missing from our lives, has only served to take us further out of the way of Truth and Life(Cross Reference **Genesis 3:1-24**). The path back to the existence that humanity was deprived of is beset on every side with adversity, and the road ahead is full of uncertainty. But for those of us who can overcome the identities that have come to define each of our individual experiences, the Light is at the end of the tunnel.

Notes:

CHAPTER 4
Yeshua Is LORD?

1Timothy 3:14-16
14. I write these things to you, hoping to come to you shortly.
15. But if I delay, that you may know how to behave in the house of God, which is the faithful community of the living God, the pillar and foundation of the truth.
16. And confessedly, great is the mystery of godliness: God was manifested in the flesh, was justified in Spirit, was seen by angels, was proclaimed among the nations, was believed on in the world, was taken up in glory.
1Timothy 3:14-16

    Understanding the correct identity of the Messiah is of vital importance to the Messianic body of believers because as **1Timothy 3:15** says, God's faithful community is "the pillar and foundation of the truth(Cross Reference **Revelation 3:12**)". The Messianic body is to stand upon and to uphold the truth that God was manifested in the flesh, was justified in the Spirit, was seen by angels, was proclaimed among the nations, was believed on in the world, and that He was taken up in glory.

    If the pillar and foundation of the truth were to be corrupted then its attempts to transmit the truth would, at best, be rendered ineffectual. The worst thing that could happen is that the corrupt pillar would gain followers and continue to spread(Cross Reference **Genesis 3:1-7**). The latter case has been the history of the multifaceted Church organization. The one Church organization has been divided into many movements, organizations, denominations, congregations, factions, sects, and cult groups; each with a strong following of supporters professing their particular brand of "truth".

    Questions and disagreements over biblical understanding are to be expected, after all the Bible is a unique compilation of documents. I would even go so far as to say that questions and disagreements over the Bible are healthy. Having conversations aimed at working through confusion or coming together to understand another individual's experience and perspectives are essential parts of any healthy relationship. The ability to constructively push against resistance, the willingness to engage in conversation, and taking the time necessary to understand another individual are character building qualities that lead to maturity. But this has not been the case with the Church organization. One particular issue has been taken beyond the realm of Christian edification and has been the cause of more disagreements which have resulted in dividing the Christian Church. Although this particular issue is addressed many times and in many ways in both testaments of the Bible, men and women from Christian, secular, as well as unaffiliated religious backgrounds still have questions about the identity of Yeshua of Nazareth.

Who is Yeshua of Nazareth?

I have personally heard many conflicting theories concerning the identity of Yeshua of Nazareth. I have heard that He is God, that He is a god, and that He is neither. I have heard that He was one of many enlightened individuals. I have heard that He was a magician and a deceiver. I have heard that He is Michael the archangel. I have heard that He is the brother of Satan. I have heard that His story is a retelling of the death of the Egyptian god Osiris and the birth of the god Horus. I have heard that Yeshua of Nazareth descended from native Egyptians who left Egypt after the death of Pharaoh Akhenaten. I have heard that He was the great great grandson of a Ptolemaic ruler. I have heard that He was the bastard son of a Judean whore and a Roman soldier. I have heard that He is the forefather of European royalty. I have seen him portrayed in paintings, sculptures, and in cinema as an African, an Asian, an Arab, and a European. And I have heard that He never actually existed but is only an invention of the Roman Catholic church.

Questions surrounding the identity of Yeshua of Nazareth, such as whether or not He should be understood as God, an enlightened man, or just regarded as a fictional character, really depend on two things. The first, depends on what each individual is willing to accept or reject as evidence. The second, depends on whether an individual is willing or unwilling to believe no matter what the evidence may say(Cross Reference: the ongoing debates surrounding the identity of the ancient Egyptians, Israelites, and Judeans). The truth simply 'IS'. Whether we know it, are ignorant of it, accept or reject it, man cannot affect the truth, and it will always exist. The truth may appear to be influenced by each individual's perspective but, contrary to the beliefs of many, the truth is not relative. It is not the truth, but how each individual relates to the truth that is relative*.

Cross Reference the epistles of Paul, James, Peter, and John with each other; and compare the four Gospel accounts to observe the different relationship that each apostle had with the Word of God. Also recognize that in both Testaments of the Bible, each individual man of God -Noah, Abraham, Moses, David, Yeshua's disciples and apostles, etc.- is only an individual man(or woman), of God.

A skeptic can argue that Yeshua was a fictional character based on his missing skeleton and the inability to replicate or scientifically verify the miracles that He is said to have performed. A believer can argue that Yeshua was real based on His genealogical record, the fact that the people who personally knew Him willingly died in defense of their faith in Him, and the fact that Christianity began and continues in His name to this very day.

According to the accounts given in the New Testament gospels of Matthew(**1:1-16**), Luke(**3:23-38**), and John(**1:1-5,14-18; 3:16-18**) Yeshua of Nazareth is the only begotten Son of God. He was conceived by the Holy Spirit of God in the womb of a Judean virgin and born in the Judean town of Bethlehem. Mary(Maria or Mariam), the espoused wife of a Judean man named Joseph, was blessed to be the human vessel that God used to bring His Salvation(Strong's Concordance Reference #**H3444**), His Yeshua(or Yehoshua #**H3091**), into the world.

Mary's being impregnated by the Holy Spirit has been the focus of some scornful humor by Bible critics. The humor is offensive, but it is understandable. We're all human and each of us tends to doubt. Only some of us go too far and ridicule what we don't understand(consider race and religion). When people mockingly ask me if I believe that God had sex with Mary to impregnate her, I ask them if they believe that God would have had to stick His penis in the soil of the earth after He brought it into existence, to fertilize the earth with trees and plants. Implanting the seed of Life in a woman who already had reproductive capabilities sounds like a much easier feat than shaping existence, as well as man(**Genesis 1:27,2:7**), out of non-existence.

All jests aside, the identity of Yeshua of Nazareth and the reliability of the Bible are two questions surrounded by confusion that demand an answer. But what the Biblical text declares, the evidence that it provides, and what many people are willing to accept may, simply, not be compatible. God requires belief(**Hebrews 11:6**), but man requires tangible evidence(Cross Reference **1Corinthians 1:18-31**).

Essentially, the Bible is a document that speaks to the spirit and soul of humanity. And unbeknownst to most, the central figure of the Biblical text is actually YOU, the reader. Consider that God cannot be affected nor changed. The only one who can be affected, changed, or benefit from the words of the Bible is You(Cross Reference **John 17:21** "That they all may be one; as Thou, Father, art in Me, and I in Thee, that they also may be one in Us..."). It is clear that the reception of the Bible's message is not guaranteed, as its message is prone to be manipulated by iniquitous influences(Cross Reference **Genesis 3:1-5**). It is a fact that the text of the bible has been altered over the ages and that men and women have manipulated the meaning of the Bible's passages to suit their personal aspirations. The existence of the multifaceted Church organization testifies to the fact that man is his own greatest obstacle to receiving the word of God. Yet, in spite of mankind's inadequacies, the Bible is able to authenticate its origin and to deliver its message.

Putting Trust in A Physical Document That Can Be Tampered With
(Cross Reference **2Peter 1:19-21**)

I trust the Word of God and I have confidence that the Bible is a reliable document because I can readily see the connections linking each of the individual Old and New Testament books of the Bible to one another. The consistency exhibited between the Old Testament's 5 books of Law/Moses, 12 historical books, 5 books of poetry and wisdom, 17 prophetic books, and the New Testament's 4 Gospels, 1 historical book of Acts, 21 epistles, and 1 prophetic book of Revelation may not seem that impressive unless you can appreciate the fact that the Bible that exists today as one coherent document was written by dozens of authors who lived in different countries and who were separated by hundreds of years. Considering the advancements that have taken place in science, psychology, and human relations in just the last 100 years the Bible's consistency looks no less than supernatural.

I am confident that the authors of the Bible were inspired by the Spirit of God to record their own life experiences, the experiences of their heroes, and of their adversaries, all in relation to the God whom they served because I accept the Bible as the work of one supernatural Author. I do not believe that it is possible for a document whose clarity depends on the correspondence between the individual authors who happened to be separated by time and distance, to be able to exist as one coherent document with one consistent message, without supernatural guidance(**Isaiah 28:10-13**). I believe that ONLY a supernatural author Who is not limited by time, has insight into the nature of reality and perception into the universal qualities and capabilities of man, Who can influence the lives of self-conscious beings, has the compassion to address the needs of all mankind, and that could have the ability to communicate a message of salvation and eternal life to audiences of any language or time period and also, and more importantly, be able to provide the means of attaining it. I do not believe that such an exceptional Being could be any less than the Author of existence.

I am confident in the accuracy of the Bible's prophetic outlook for the future of mankind because of the reliability of its revelations from the past. I am confident in the Bible's all-encompassing prophetic picture because I recognize the consistency and accuracy of the individual prophetic patterns that saturate the biblical text from **Genesis 1:1** through **Revelation 22:21**(For one example of a prophetic pattern Cross Reference **Genesis 1:27-Genesis 6:7** with **Daniel 2:31-45**: Gold, Silver, Bronze, Iron: The various ages of man detailed in the opening chapters of the book of **Genesis** prefigure the Gold, Silver, Bronze, and Iron ages of man prophesied in **Daniel 2:31-45**). I personally believe the Old Testament prophecies which foretell when, where, why, and how God would reveal Himself as the Redemption and Salvation of humanity(**Jeremiah 31:31-34** Cross Reference **Genesis 3:15; Genesis 22:8; Isaiah 49:1-7,**

52:13-53:12; Daniel 9:25-26) because I believe humanity to be lost in confusion, at war within ourselves, and incapable of escaping our self-destructive nature without supernatural involvement. I believe the Old Testament's prophesies concerning the Salvation of God and Redemption of humanity to have been fulfilled in the birth, life, ministry, death, and resurrection of Yeshua of Nazareth. All of which was confirmed by eye witness accounts that were recorded, compiled, and exist today as the New Testament of the Bible(**Luke 24:44; John 1:29, 36; 1Timothy 3:16; Revelation 5:6**).

I accept those things because I believe that a supremely compassionate, benevolent, righteous, just, powerful, and intelligent God shaped existence for the welfare of sentient beings who could understand and appreciate their own existence. I also believe that such a God wanting to communicate with a such an audience, could communicate His word through any and all barriers and not be restricted nor suffer the limitations of time, language, intellectual acuity, nor the ulterior motives of man. I believe that God is that God is and that, God does that God does. Not for any duty, commitment, or obligation to anyone nor to anything.

I am thankful that the Bible defies human logic and understanding. Its message is supernatural and therefore more reliable because it cannot be recognized, deciphered, nor understood by human reasoning in the absence of the Holy Spirit. Many, many, hundreds of years of Church history, Church seminary, Bible college, and independent Bible studies testify to that fact.

Besides of all those things, I believe the Bible because of my own life experience. This book is my testimony of the reliability of God's Word and evidence of the Spirit of God, the mediator through Whom I have the ability to testify(Cross

Reference **John 16:13***).

*Side note: I do believe understanding to be inspired by the Holy Spirit, but I believe that writing ability, grammar, sentence syntax, and paragraph structure are products of how well we pay attention in school.

IS YESHUA(JESUS) GOD?

The consistency existing between the individual books and both Testaments of the Bible is so astounding that some Bible critics, who fail to consider the number of authors and years that it took to complete the compiled text, suggest that the Bible's truths are substantiated by circular reasoning. The consistency of the Bible is not simply maintained from its beginning to its end but, even more than that, each book as well as each individual Testament of the Bible depends on that consistency for clarity and validation.

God, Satan, and the prophesied redemption of humanity would only amount to vain Old Testament concepts apart from being validated in the New Testament by the revelation of the Messiah. The entire New Testament of the bible could at best be considered as the spurious account of a shyster's exploits written by charlatans, had the identity and ministry of the Messiah not been affirmed in the Bible's Old Testament. In short, the New Testament revelation of the Messiah is supported upon the word of God as it was revealed to the prophets who testified in the Bible's Old Testament. And the Old Testament's prophecies are vindicated by the Word of God as He is revealed in the New Testament of the Bible.

The writers of the Old Testament declare YHWH Elohim to be the author of the Heavens and the Earth(**Genesis 14:19; Deuteronomy 10:14; Nehemiah 9:6; Isaiah 48:11-13**), the creation's only God of gods(**Deuteronomy 10:17; Joshua 22:22; Psalm 82:1-8; Daniel 2:47**), Israel's only Savior and Redeemer(Savior: **Isaiah 43:3,11; Hosea 13:4**. Redeemer: **Psalm 19:14; Isaiah 43:14, 44:6; Jeremiah 50:34**), and the Salvation of all mankind(Cross Reference **Genesis 3:15; Isaiah 49:6**). The New Testament writers professed the utmost trust in the Old Testament scriptures and saw no contradiction in declaring Yeshua of Nazareth to be the creator of Heaven and earth(**John 1:1-5; Colossians 1:16**), the God of their fathers(**Matthew 1:23; 1Timothy 6:14-16; Revelation 17:14**), the Savior of Israel(**Luke 2:11; John 4:42**), and the Redeemer of mankind(**Galatians 3:13; Titus 2:14**) Who had come in the flesh(**John 1:1-5,14; 1Timoty 3:16**).

According to the New Testament's gospel accounts, the 1st century A.D. Judean populace expected the prophesied Messiah to be revealed in their day(**Daniel 9:24-27** Cross Reference **John 1:19-27**). In light of their expectation, much of the Judean populace went out to be baptized and others went out to question John, the son of Zacharias(Cross Reference **Luke 1:5-17**{**Isaiah 40:3**}), as to whether or not he was the Messiah, Elijah, or the "prophet" whom they were all expecting(**Matthew 3:1-6; Mark 1:1-8; John 1:19-31** Cross Reference **Matthew 11:7-15**). John confessed that he was not any of those men whom the populace expected but identified Yeshua of Nazareth in **John 1:27** as the one "coming after me who is preferred before me, whose shoe latches I am not worthy to unloose". Not long after this confession John identified Yeshua of Nazareth as "the Lamb of God which takes away the sins of the world(**John 1:29,36** Cross Reference **Genesis 22:8**)".

John the Baptist, the Judean populace, the Judean religious leadership, and eventually Yeshua's own disciples each acknowledged in their turn that a significant occurrence had taken place in their day. According to one of the chief priests named Nicodemus(**John 3:1-2**), some of the Pharisees even went so far as to accept that the word of God had been realized in their day. But seeing the truth is not the same as accepting it. The significant difference between the men and women who came to faith in the Word of God and the men who were responsible for the murder of Yeshua of Nazareth is not complicated. Yeshua's disciples willingly forsook their own lives and devoted themselves to following the Messiah Who had been prophesied in the scriptures(**Matthew 4:19-20, 9:9; Mark 2:14** Cross Reference **Matthew 16:24; Luke 14:26; John 10:27**) and revealed to them in truth. But Yeshua's opponents, whether out of ignorance, fear, the love of money and distinction, or simply for the sake of pride, willfully sacrifice(d) the Truth of God's word in order to follow their own aspirations(**John 11:47-53** Cross Reference **Isaiah 14:13-14**).

What Yeshua's Opponents Understood

Matthew 26:63-66

63. But Yeshua kept silent. And answering, the high priest said to Him, I adjure you by the living God that you tell us if you are the Messiah, the Son of God.
64. Yeshua said to him, You have said it. Moreover I say to you, from this time you shall see the Son of man sitting on the right of power and coming on the clouds of the heavens.
65. Then the high priest tore his garments, saying, He blasphemed! Why do we have any more need of witnesses? Behold now you have heard his blasphemy.
66. What does it seem to you?" And answering they said, He is liable to death.

Matthew 26:63-66(Cross Reference **Daniel 7:13**)

Mark 14:60-64 records the same event as **Matthew 26:63-66**, only in Mark's account Yeshua's response to the high priest is more definitive, leaving no doubt about how Yeshua intended to be understood by the assembly.

Mark 14:60-64

60. And standing up in the middle, the high priest questioned Yeshua, saying, Do you not answer? Nothing? What do these testify against you?

61. But He was silent and answered nothing. Again the high priest questioned Him, and said to Him, Are you the Messiah, the son of the Blessed?
62. And Yeshua said, I AM! And you will see the Son of man sitting at the right of power and coming with the clouds of the heaven.
63. And tearing his garments, the high priest said, Why do we still have need of witnesses?
64. You heard the blasphemy. What does it seem to you? And they all condemned Him to be liable of death.
Mark 14:60-64

    Matthew 26:63-66 and **Mark 14:60-64** record the time that Yeshua of Nazareth publicly(Cross Reference **John 7:6, 17:1**) testified to being the Son of God and prophesied Messiah(Cross Reference **Genesis 1:26** and **3:15**).Yeshua made His confession before the assembly of priests, scribes, and elders because the time of His public revelation, trial, and execution had come, and the salvation of the world was at hand(**Matthew 26:18,39-42; John 12:23, 13:1** Cross Reference **Isaiah 52:13-53:12(Exodus 12:1-14)**). Yeshua's words before the assembly that are recorded in **Matthew 26:63-66** and **Mark 14:60-64**, included quotes from **Psalm 110:1 and Daniel 7:13-14**(Cross Reference **Mark 14:62**) that, instead of validating Yeshua's ministry, further incited the high priest and the members of the assembly to violence. With Yeshua's confession, the Judean assembly obtained the evidence that it wanted to justify murdering Him in accordance with their tradition.

    Yeshua's guilt in the eyes of the Judean assembly had been determined before he was captured in the field of Gethsemane(**Matthew 26:36-57; Mark 14:32-53; Luke 22:39-54; John 18:1-13**). It is recorded in **Matthew 12:14** and **John 11:47-50** that the Judean assembly had previously taken council together and decided that the ministry of Yeshua of Nazareth was a threat to their way of life. It was then decided that His capture and murder were necessary for them to maintain their status as heads of the nation.

Even before either of the councils that decided Yeshua's fate had officially convened, the Judeans had sought on several occasions to kill Him. Each time that Yeshua's life was threatened by the Pharisees, the Sadducees, the scribes, or the elders, came about as the direct result of the works that He performed and the words that He spoke before the Judean multitudes. One such instance is recorded in the 5th chapter of the Gospel of John. John 5 records the time that Yeshua healed a cripple man and told him to take up his bed and walk. The man who had been healed was later stopped by the Judean religious leadership and questioned about why he was carrying his bed on that particular day, which happened to be the Sabbath. The man later identified Yeshua of Nazareth as the One who had healed him and told him to take up his bed and walk. The Judeans confronted Yeshua and an argument ensued. Eventually the argument turned violent.

John 5:15-18
15. The man went away and told the Judeans that it was Yeshua, which had made him well
16. And because of this, the Judeans persecuted Yeshua, and lusted to kill Him, because He had done these things on a Sabbath day.
17. But Yeshua answered them, My Father works until now, and I work.
18. Because of this, therefore, the Judeans lusted the more to kill Him, for not only did He break the Sabbath, but also called God His own father, making Himself equal to God.

John 5:15-18

John's commentary note, "Making Himself equal to God", in **John 5:18** should eliminate any confusion that a reader may have about the intention of Yeshua's words, what John understood, or how the Judeans understood the meaning of Yeshua's words.

In fact, the erroneous belief that Yeshua of Nazareth never claimed to be God is refuted time and time again throughout Yeshua's ministry. **John 5:15-18** is only one of many places in the New Testament that Yeshua called God His Own Father, "thereby making Himself equal to God". In each instance that Yeshua of Nazareth called God His Own Father it is clear from the response of His listeners that the meaning of His words was clearly understood.

John 10:24-39 records another instance in which Yeshua of Nazareth was persecuted for His works and His words. In **John 10:24-39** Yeshua had again offended the Judeans because He, as He had done in **John 5:17**, called God is His Own Father. Only, in **John 10:24-33** Yeshua takes the declaration that God is His Father a step further, and the Judeans respond to His words in accordance with their understanding.

John 10:24-33

24. Then the Judeans encircled Him, and said to Him, How long do you lift up our soul? If you are the Messiah tell us publicly.
25. Yeshua answered them, I told you, and you did not believe. The works which I do in the name of My Father, these bear witness about Me.
26. But you do not believe, for you are not of My sheep, as I said to you,
27. My sheep hear My voice, and I know them, and they follow Me.
28. And I give eternal life to them, and they shall never perish to the age; and not anyone shall pluck them out of My hand.

29. My father who has given to Me is greater than all, and no one is able to pluck out of My Father's hand.
30. I and *my* Father are one!
31. Then again, the Judeans took up stones, that they might stone Him.
32. Yeshua answered them, I showed you many good works from My Father. For which work of them do you stone Me?
33. The Judeans answered Him saying, We do not stone you concerning a good work, but concerning blasphemy; and because you, being a man, make yourself God.
John 10:24-33

Maybe it's just me, and I'm saying this with a smile on my face, but Yeshua of Nazareth can come across as a bit of an instigator. He's standing amongst men who are looking for any reason to kill Him, telling them how secure His disciples are in His hands, and then He just happens to mention "Oh yeah, the God whom you claim to serve, He and I are one and the same!". Then He's almost surprised when the Judeans take up stones to kill Him. I know that He expected them to recognize Him for who He is and that He is very serious while He is addressing these men, but still, I have to smile. I don't know of any person whose understanding of and comfort level with their own identity is so natural yet transcends confidence to the extent that it comes across to others as arrogance(Cross Reference **Philippians 2:6**). In **John 10:26** Yeshua directly addresses the reason for the crowd's, as well as modern pundits, disbelief in His identity as the only begotten Son of God. These men are not His sheep and therefore have no association with His Father.

John 10:24-33 is clear and to the point. Yeshua not only affirms that He is the Messiah and that the work that He does testifies to that fact, but in **John 10:30** Yeshua eliminates any and all confusion about His relation to God. "I and the Father are one" is as clear as He could get. There is no "gray area" nor any need for interpretation. Upon hearing this declaration, the Judeans were forced to make one of two choices. They were forced to either accept Yeshua of Nazareth as the prophesied Messiah, their Lord and Savior, or to take up stones and kill Him. His words could not pass without one response or the other.

Continuing on in **John 10:34-36** Yeshua apparently diffuses the situation by quoting **Psalm 82:6**. Then in **John 10:38**, the Judeans are once again incited to lay hands Him when he says, "The Father is in Me, and I in Him".

John 10:34-36
34. Yeshua answered them, Is it not written in your law, "I said, you are gods'?
35. If He called them gods unto whom the word of God came, and the scriptures cannot be broken
36. Do you say of Him whom the Father sanctified and sent into the world, You blaspheme, because I said, I am the Son of God?
John 10:34-36

and,

John 10:37-39
37. If I do not the works of My Father, do not believe Me.
38. But if I do, even if you do not believe Me, believe the works that you may perceive and may believe that the Father is in Me, and I in Him.
39. Then they again sought to seize Him. And He went forth out of their hand.
John 10:37-39

What Yeshua's Disciples Had to Say

John 1:40-42a

40. Andrew, the brother of Simon Peter, was one of the two who heard this from John, and followed Him.
41. This one first found his own brother Simon, and told him, We have found the Messiah, which being translated is the Christ.
42. And he led him to Yeshua…

John 1:40-42a

The enemies of Yeshua of Nazareth continually sought to murder Him because of His works and His words. His disciples loved and followed Him for those same reasons. The disciples of Yeshua of Nazareth understood that they were accepting Him as the only begotten Son of God, the unique flesh and blood incarnation of the God of their fathers.

Matthew 16:15-16

15. He said to them, But you, whom do you say Me to be?
16. And answering, Simon Peter said, You are the Messiah, the Son of the living God.

Matthew 16:15-16

and,

Mark 8:29

29. And He said to them, And you, whom do you say Me to be? And answering Peter said to Him, You are the Messiah.

Mark 8:29

In **Matthew 16:15-16** Peter is quoted declaring Yeshua of Nazareth to be "The Messiah, the Son of the living God". Matthew, author of the Gospel of Matthew, includes this passage in his gospel because he also believed Yeshua of

Nazareth to be the Messiah, the Son of the living God.

Mark records Peter's words in **Mark 8:29** regarding the identity of Yeshua because He too believed in the divinity of the Messiah. **Luke 9:20**(Cross Reference **Galatians 6:16** "The Israel of God") seems to be a melding of the **Matthew 16:15-16** and **Mark 8:29** quotes.

Luke 9:20
20. And He said to them. But whom do you say Me to be? And answering Peter said, The Messiah of God.
Luke 9:20

John 6:68-69 continues in a similar vein to the Matthew, Mark, and Luke quotes.

John 6:68-69
68. Then Simon Peter answered Him, Lord to whom shall we go? You have words of everlasting life.
69. And we have believed and have known that You are the Messiah, the Son of the living God.
John 6:68-69

In the above section(**What Yeshua's opponents understood**) the arguments reached their climatic points every time that Yeshua said that He shared a unique affinity with God. It should be understood that Yeshua's disciples believed and followed Him because of that same unique affinity which they understood and accepted Him to share with the God of their fathers.

In **Colossians 1:12-20** the apostle Paul clearly acknowledges Whom he accepted Yeshua of Nazareth to be(Cross Reference **Colossians 2:9**).

Colossians 1:12-20

12. Giving thanks to the Father, who has made us fit for a share of the inheritance of the saints in the light,
13. Who delivered us out of the power of darkness and translated into the kingdom of the Son of His love;
14. In whom we have redemption, through His blood the forgiveness of sins;
15. Who is the image of the invisible God, Firstborn of all creation-
16. For all things were created in Him, the things in the heavens, and the things on the earth; the visible and the invisible; whether thrones, or lordships, or rulers, or authorities, all things have been created through Him and for Him.
17. And He is before all things, and all things consist in Him.
18. And He is the head of the body, the faithful community; who is Beginning, Firstborn from the dead, that He be preeminent in all things;
19. Because all the fullness was pleased to dwell in Him,
20. And through Him making peace through the blood of His cross, to reconcile all things to Himself through Himself, whether things on the earth, or the things in the heavens.

Colossians 1:12-20

Paul could be misunderstood in Verse **15** to be equating Yeshua's position within the creation to that of the angelic sons of God who were given authority in **Genesis 1:27**, when they were created in the image of God. But it should be taken into account that God's Salvation(Yeshua: Strong's Reference #**H3444**) did not come to 1st century Judea as a conquering king but instead He came to Judea in the form of a modest man, descendant of Judah, the son of Mary and heir of Joseph(**Genesis 49:22-26**), who was killed in the role of a suffering servant(Cross Reference **Isaiah 52:13-53:12, Daniel 9:24-26**).

But, in **Colossians 1:12-20** the apostle Paul really does capture the spirit of Genesis chapters 1 and 2. The reference to the "image of the invisible God, Firstborn of all creation", from **Colossians 1:15**, calls to mind the two men who prefigured the One Man Who would be the exact Image and Likeness of God. Only, the magnitude of Paul's reference is raised exponentially when in **Colossians 1:16** he states that all things in both the former and the later epochs of existence, in the Heavens(**Genesis 1:1-2:4a** Cross Reference **Colossians 1:16,20**) and of the Earth(**Genesis 2:4b-25** Cross Reference **Colossians 1:16,20**), were created in and through Yeshua the Son of God's love, in Whom we have redemption(Cross Reference **Genesis 1:26** "In Our image, according to Our likeness.").

Philippians 2:5-8 and **Hebrews 1:1-3** both agree with **Colossians 1:12-20** and confirm that Yeshua of Nazareth was accepted by His apostles as the physical incarnation of the invisible God Whom they worshiped.

Philippians 2:5-8
5. For let this mind be in you which also was in the Messiah Yeshua
6. Who subsisting in the form of God thought it not robbery to be equal with God,
7. But emptied Himself, taking the form of a slave, having become in the likeness of men,
8. And being found in fashion as a man, He humbled Himself, having become obedient until death, even the death of a cross.

Philippians 2:5-8

and,

Hebrews 1:1-3

1. In many parts and in many ways of old, God spoke to the fathers by the prophets;
2. In these last days He spoke to us as/in the Son, whom He appointed heir of all; through whom He indeed made the ages;
3. Who being the shining splendor of glory, and the express image of His person, and upholding all things by the word of His power, having made purification of our sins through Himself, sat down on the right of the Majesty on high,

Hebrews 1:1-3

The apostle Paul is not the only apostle to acknowledge Yeshua's unique affinity with the God of gods nor is he alone in ascribing the creation of the universe to the Messiah. The apostle John makes the same declaration in **John 1:1-3**.

John 1:1-3

1. In the beginning was the Word, and the Word was with God, and the Word was God.
2. He was in beginning with God.
3. All things came into being through Him, and without Him not even one came into being that has come into being.

John 1:1-3(Cross Reference **Genesis 1:1-2:4a**)

John continues from **John 1:1-3** to reveal that the One Whom he refers to as the Word is none other than Yeshua of Nazareth.

The translators and publishers of one edition of the bible that is used exclusively by one particular Christian group add the word '*other*' in italics to their translation of **John 1:3**. Rendering the verse "All *other* things came into being through him...(their later editions don't use italics)" thereby insinuating that at some time in the eternal existence of YHWH Elohim He carried on for a time without His own Word, that is until He created Him. Then, after first being brought into existence Himself, the Word of God was permitted by the God of gods to bring all other things into existence. The word 'other' is added to **John 1:3** to give support to the erroneous and misleading belief that Yeshua of Nazareth was only the physical incarnation of a previously created being, and not the God of gods. This belief contradicts the Biblical assertion that YHWH Elohim is eternal. If there ever was a time when YHWH Elohim was without His Own Word, His Own Wisdom, or His Own Spirit then He is Himself maturing and could not have continually existed as an all knowing, all powerful, or eternal God.

    The idea is also personally offensive. I don't believe that the all-powerful God of gods would send a mere angel to complete the work of accomplishing His word(**Genesis 1:26** Cross Reference **Isaiah 42:8; John 5:23, 10:30**). I cannot accept the idea that the God of gods would give the responsibility of redeeming His creation and reestablishing His relationship with man to a created being who cannot, because he is not the All Mighty, fully understand nor appreciate God's word, wisdom, will, compassion, or intelligence(Cross Reference **1Peter 1:12**). Adam's sin in the garden of Eden and the sins of the sons of God that are recorded in **Genesis** chapter **6** are enough evidence to convince me that the redemption of the creation and salvation of mankind could not be left in the hands of a mere created being. In each of God's works -the creation of existence and the man in God's image, as well as the formation of Adam and the garden of Eden- God gave of Himself for the benefit of man. I don't believe that YHWH Elohim could do any less than give Himself for the restoration of His ministries(Cross Reference **Isaiah 42:1-16**).

    It should be emphasized that a coherent word for word translation from one language to another is impossible. There are times in translations that adding a descriptive or explanatory word(s) becomes necessary to convey the intended message of the original language but adding the word 'other' in **John 1:3** is not one of those times. The word 'other' does not appear nor is it implied in any ancient text of **John 1:3**. More than that, adding the word 'other' not only contradicts the rest of **John 1** verse **3**, it is simply inconsistent with what the Old and New Testaments teach about God's servant(**Isaiah 49:1-7; Luke 1:54-55**) and the revelation of YHWH's Salvation(**Isaiah 43:11; 2Timothy 3:14-16**).

In the 20th chapter of the gospel of John, Yeshua is directly addressed as God by one of His disciples.

After the public revelation and murder of their teacher, Yeshua's disciples hid themselves out of fear of being persecuted by the Judean leadership. **John 20:19-28** recalls two of the times that Yeshua appeared to His disciples after being crucified and resurrected from the dead. At the first of the two recorded gatherings Thomas, one of the twelve apostles, was not present. And when the disciples later told Thomas about the encounter, he did not believe them. Eight days later the disciples were again gathered together, only this time Thomas was present when Yeshua appeared. Yeshua appearing in the midst of His disciples began to speak, "Peace to you",

John 20:27-28

27. Then He said to Thomas, Bring your finger here and see My hands; and bring your hand and thrust into my side, and be not unbelieving, but believing.
28. And Thomas answered and said to Him, My Lord and my God!

John 20:27-28

Thomas' response, "My Lord and my God!", to Yeshua's words are emphatically clear. Thomas was not only recognizing

Yeshua as his leader. Thomas was acknowledging that his slain teacher had risen again from the dead and was standing before him as both his leader and his divine Creator: "My Lord and my God(Cross Reference **John 1:1-5**)".

What Yeshua Had To Say About Who He Is

In **John 8:16-19** Yeshua answered the question of "Who He is".

John 8:16-19

16. But even if I judge, My judgment is true because I am not alone, but I and the Father who sent Me.
17. And in your law it has been written that the witness of two men is true.
18. I am witnessing concerning Myself, and He who sent Me, the Father witnesses concerning Me.
19. Then they said to Him, Where is your father? Yeshua answered, You neither know Me, nor My Father, if you had known Me, then you would have known My father also.

John 8:16-19

Yeshua finishes His statement about His relationship to the Father in **John 8** verse **19** by saying "If you had known Me, then you would have known My Father also". Yeshua is going further than saying that He shares some of the Fathers characteristics(Cross Reference the Image and Likeness of God). Yeshua is saying that He is the physical incarnation of the Father of creation. To know Him is to know the Father.

John 8:16-19 may not be conclusive enough, but in **John 10:27-33**(Also quoted above) Yeshua leaves no doubt about who He is.

John 10:27-33

27. My sheep hear My voice, and I know them, and they follow Me.
28. And I give eternal life to them, and they shall never perish forever; and not anyone shall pluck them out of my hand.
29. My Father who has given to Me is greater than all, and no one is able to pluck out of My father's hand.
30. I and the Father are one!
31. Then again the Judeans took up stones, that they might stone Him.
32. Yeshua answered them, I showed you many good works from My Father. For which work of them do you stone Me?
33. The Judeans answered Him, saying, We do not stone you concerning a good work, but concerning blasphemy; and because you, being a man, make yourself God.

John 10:27-33

In verse 30 Yeshua says plainly that He and the Father are one. This is quite a statement for anyone to make. No mere man nor angel of God would say that he and God the Father are one. In **Isaiah 14:12-14** Satan is quoted as aspiring to be compared to the Most High God, but aspiring to be compared to the Almighty God is still not going as far as claiming to have a share in the identity of the Almighty. **John 10:29** has been the cause some confusion and has led to questions such as, "How can Yeshua and the Father be one if Yeshua Himself admits that the Father is greater?" The answer is simple. The Father is the eternal God in Heaven. Yeshua of Nazareth was the physical incarnation of YHWH Elohim who hungered and thirsted, who walked and became tired, and who would be captured, would suffer, and who would die for the sins of humanity and the world(**Galatians 1:4; 1John 2:2**).

The Judeans took up stones to kill Yeshua, as it is recorded in **John 10:31-33**, because they understood Him to say that He was equal to the God of their fathers.

In **John 10:34-36** Yeshua temporarily halted the Judean's attack by referencing **Psalm 82:6**.

John 10:34-36
34. Yeshua answered them, Is it not written in your Law, I said, you are gods?
35. If He called them gods unto whom the word of God came, and the scripture cannot be broken,
36. Do you say He whom the Father sanctified and sent into the world, You blaspheme, because I said, I am the Son of God?

John 10:34-36

Psalm 82 is the record of God's dialog as He stands passing judgment in the assembly of gods. In verse **6** of **Psalm 82** the men who are being addressed are declared by God to be gods and sons of the Most High.

Psalm 82:6
6. I have said, You are gods and all of you sons of the Most High.

Psalm 82:6

After quoting **Psalm 82:6** and apparently diffusing the situation, the Judeans are again incited to kill Yeshua because of His words in **John 10:38**.

John 10:37-39
37. If I do not do the works of My Father, do not believe Me.

38. But if I do, even if you do not believe Me, believe the works, that you may perceive and may believe that the Father is in Me and I in Him.
39. Then they again sought to seize Him. And He went forth out of their hand.
John 10:37-39

There are at least two major issues with **John 10:34-39**(Cross Reference **John 10:15**). First, Yeshua states that those to whom the Word of God has come are gods. This means that Satan, who has stood before the throne of the Most High God, is a god. The man created in the image of God who received the command to be fruitful and multiply from God in **Genesis 1:28**(Cross Reference **Daniel 10:1-20**), Adam, Noah, Abraham, Moses(Cross Reference **Exodus 7:1**), and the prophets of God, are all considered to be gods among many other gods.* As the God of gods has the ability to create, establish, and ordain, the lesser gods have been given the ability, authority, and liberty to mold God's created order according to their own will(Cross Reference **Psalm 115:15-16**), whether it be in righteousness or impiety(**Genesis 1:28, 9:1,7** "Be fruitful and multiply". Cross Reference **Acts 3:19-21**). The lesser gods, in the heavens and upon the earth, do not have the ability to create existence out of non-existing material and must therefore influence or physically manipulate the works that were originally created by the Almighty God(**Genesis 1:1-2:4a, 2:4b-25** Cross Reference **Genesis 3:1-6; Romans 1:18-32** Cross Reference "the Abomination of Desolation").

*The Hebrew words that are transliterated as El and Elohim are translated into English as God, god, or gods; these words simply mean: strength(s), power(s), or mighty. Whether they are ordained by the will of God or by the submission of man(Cross Reference **Genesis 1:27-28, Genesis 3:1-6, and 11:1-9**), people, entertainment figures, political leaders, religious leaders, places* *and things, financial and educational institutions, adornments, news outlets, social class, skin color, etc.- can become gods; i.e. sources of authority, power, security, and information/knowledge that men and women rely on to provide us with the truths that we rely on to define our individual existence.*

Secondly, in **John 10:38** Yeshua says that the Father is in Him and that He is in the Father. It is commonly accepted that when the Holy Spirit of God descended upon and inhabited the body of Yeshua of Nazareth at His baptism(**Matthew 3:16, Mark 1:10; Luke 3:22; John 1:32**), the Father was 'in' Him. The flesh and blood man Yeshua of Nazareth could not have had a ministry nor a notable identity apart from the inclusion of His Heavenly Father. What has not been appreciated from Yeshua's statement in **John 10:38** is that Yeshua is saying that the Heavenly Father has never existed nor has He had His own identity apart from the inclusion of Yeshua, the revealed Word of God(**John 1:1-3**). Yeshua, the Son and Salvation of God, did not and does not exist in the form of a lesser god. Yeshua of Nazareth is the only begotten Son of God because He is the aspect of the Godhead's persona Who was sent out by the Lord YHWH and His Spirit(**Isaiah 48:16** Cross Reference **John 10:36; Philippians 2:5-8**) to the earth in the bodily form of a flesh and blood man, for the purpose of perfecting the work and word of God(Cross Reference **Genesis 1:26; John 5:17**).

In **John 14:6-10** Yeshua clarifies one of His disciple's confusion regarding His affinity to God while simultaneously reaffirming His statements that are recorded in **John 8:19** and **John 10:30**, that to know Him is to know the Father and that He and the Father are one.

John 14:6-10
6. Yeshua said to him, I am the Way, the Truth, and the Life. No one comes to the Father except through Me.

7. If you had known Me you would have known My Father also; and from now on you do know Him and have seen Him.
8. Philip said to Him, Show us the Father, and it is enough for us.
9. Yeshua said to him, Have I been with you so long, and you still do not know Me Philip? Whoever has seen Me has seen the Father. How can you say, Show us the Father?
10. Do you not believe that I am in the Father and the Father is in Me? The words which I speak to you I do not speak from Myself, but the Father who abides in Me, He does the works.
John 14:6-10

Verses **7-9** of **John 14** are so clear and to the point as to leave no mystery about how Yeshua intended to be understood. To see Yeshua is to see the Father. A secondary issue that is raised in **John 14** concerns **John 14:6**. Yeshua's words in **John 14:6** should be understood as "I am the only Way, the only Truth, and the only Life" because there is no way, there is no truth, and there is no life apart from that which can only be found in Him(**Genesis 1:1-2:25; Colossians 1:15-17 Cross Reference Genesis 2:17 and 3:1-24**).

In **John 17:20-21** Yeshua, praying to His Father, again states that His Father is in Him, that He is in the Father, and that the two are one. Yeshua made a similar statement in **John 10:38** that the Judean crowds understood to be a claim of equality with the God of their fathers and, which spurred on their desire to murder Him.

John 17:20-21

20. And I do not pray concerning these only, but also concerning those who will believe in Me through their word;
21. That all may be one. As You in Me, Father, and I in You, that they also may be one in Us, that the world may believe that You sent Me.

John 17:20-21

It would be easy to assume, without having an appreciation for what was accomplished by God's Redemptive work, that Yeshua was merely praying for His disciples to be in agreement with Him and His Father. But according to passages such as **Zechariah 14:6-9** and **Revelation** chapters **21-22** the relationship between the Messiah and His body of faithful servants in the New Heavens and New Earth will be a more substantial union.

Yeshua and His Disciple's Reliance Upon The Old Testament

Yeshua's ministry of Salvation and the apostle's faith in His word would amount to little more than boisterous claims and vain hopes had they stood apart from the word of God as it was revealed to the prophets(**2Peter 1:19**) in the Old Testament of the Bible. Yeshua of Nazareth regularly quoted the Old Testament to defend Himself against attacks(**Matthew 4:1-11; Mark 12:10-12**) and to validate His ministry(**Luke 4:17-21; John 2:19-22**). Yeshua's disciples depended on the scriptures to support their trust in His being the One whom they believed was prophesied to be sent from God as the Redemption of man and the Salvation of God.

In **John 1:45** Phillip, after encountering Yeshua of Nazareth himself, found Nathanael and, referencing the Old

Testament writers, he told Nathanael that, He Whom Moses and the prophets wrote about had been found.

John 1:45

45. Phillip found Nathanael, and said to him, We have found He whom Moses in the law, and the prophets did write, Yeshua the son of Joseph, from Nazareth.
John 1:45

In **John 5:46** Yeshua, in one of many confrontations with the Judean religious leaders, holds the Judeans responsible to know the books of Moses and to recognize Him as their Messiah because of what had been revealed in the scriptures.

John 5:46

46. For if you were believing Moses, you would then believe Me; for that one wrote concerning Me.
John 5:46

In **Luke 24:44**(Cross Reference **Luke 24:1-23**) after Yeshua had been crucified and then three days later resurrected, He appeared to His disciples. The disciples were shaken and afraid because of His appearance, believing that they were seeing the spirit of their departed teacher. To reassure His disciples, Yeshua instructed them to recall His words, that all of the recent events concerning Him were spoken of in the Old Testament books of Moses, the prophets, and the Psalms.

Luke 24:44

44. And He said to them, These are the words which I spoke to you, yet being with you, that must be fulfilled, all the things having been written in the Law of Moses, and the Prophets, and the Psalms, concerning Me.
Luke 24:44

The Law of Moses, the prophets, and the Messianic Psalms all pointed to the revelation of the Messiah. These prophetic books of the Old Testament foretold when, where, why, and how God's Salvation would come into the world. They served as the foundation of Yeshua's earthly ministry and even prophesied of Judea's rejection and murder of her Messiah. Yeshua could therefore rely upon the prophetic words of the scripture to comfort His disciples(Cross Reference **2Peter 1:19**) by reminding them that all things concerning His life, ministry, death, and resurrection(**Isaiah 52:13-53:12** Cross Reference **Genesis 22:1-14, Hebrews 11:17-19**) had been foretold.

In **2Peter 1:16-21** Peter recalls the time that he and two other apostles, James and John, were with Yeshua atop a mountain. The three apostles were witnesses to the voice of God from heaven which declared Yeshua to be God's beloved Son(Cross Reference **Matthew 17:1-5; Mark 9:2-7; Luke 9:28-35**). As powerful of an experience as that must have been for Peter, he admonishes the faithful servants of God to place even more confidence in the prophetic word of the scriptures which can more assuredly authenticate the revelation of the Messiah.

2Peter 1:16-21

16. For we did not follow cunningly devised fables when we made known to you the power and coming of our Lord Yeshua the Messiah, but were eyewitnesses of His majesty.
17. For He received from God the Father honor and glory when such a voice came to Him from the Excellent Glory: This is My beloved Son, in whom I am well pleased.
18. And we heard this voice which came from heaven when we were with Him on the Holy Mountain.

19. We also have the more sure prophetic word, which you do well to heed as a light that shines in a dark place, until the day dawns and the morning star rises in your hearts;
20. Knowing this first, that no prophecy of scripture is of any private interpretation,
21. For prophecy never came by the will of man, but holy men of God spoke, moved by the Holy Spirit.
2Peter 1:16-21

According to Yeshua's own words that are recorded in many places throughout the New Testament's gospel accounts, every question regarding the identity and purpose of the Messiah is revealed in the law of Moses, the books of the prophets, and in the Messianic Psalms(Cross Reference **Luke 24:25-27,44; John 5:39,46**).

I personally believe that **Isaiah 48:12-16**(Cross Reference **Isaiah 61:1-3{Luke 4:18-19}**) is one of the best passages in the books of the prophets to start with for an inquiry into the identity and purpose of the Messiah.

Isaiah 48:12-16

12. Listen to Me, O Jacob, and Israel My called: I am He; I am the first, I surely am the last.
13. My hand surely founded earth, and My right hand has stretched out the heavens; I called, they stood up together.
14. All of you gather and hear. Who among them has declared these things? YHWH has loved him. He will do his pleasure on Babylon; His arm on the Chaldeans.
15. I, I have spoken; yea, I have called him, I brought him, and he causes his way to prosper.
16. Come near to Me; hear this: I have not spoken in secret from the beginning. From its being, I was there; and now the Lord YHWH and His Spirit have sent Me.

Isaiah 48:12-16

In **Isaiah 48:12-16** YHWH identifies Himself as the speaker and it is YHWH who declares in verse **16** that the Lord YHWH and His Spirit "have sent Me"(To see Old Testament references to YHWH in two locations simultaneously refer to **Exodus 33:19-23**{**Exodus 34:5-6**} and references to "The angel of YHWH/the LORD". Also consider **Deuteronomy 6:4** in light of **Zechariah 14:9**). Verse 15 should include a few more capital letters as it is YHWH, in reference to the Servant of YHWH(Cross Reference **Isaiah 49:1-7**), who alone could declare that "YHWH has loved Him, He will do His pleasure on Babylon, His arm on the Chaldeans(v.**14**)" and", "I have called Him, I brought Him, and He causes His way to prosper." Isaiah **48:12-16** has been presumed by some Church groups to only be a prophetic reference to "Cyrus the great" who conquered Babylon and allowed the Judeans to return to their homeland but, this limited perspective fails to consider the eternal relevance of this prophetic passage and the fact that YHWH Himself is the One Who is being sent out by the Lord YHWH and His Spirit.

According to **Isaiah 49:1-7**(Cross Reference **Luke 1:54**{**Isaiah 49:8**} and **Galatians 6:16**) the Servant of YHWH would be sent upon the earth to establish the eternal identity of Israel in whom YHWH would be glorified.

Isaiah 49:1-7

1. Coast hear Me; and you people from afar, prick up your ears, YHWH called Me from the womb; He mentioned My name from My mother's belly.
2. And He made My mouth like a sharp sword; He hid Me in the shadow of His hand, and made Me a polished arrow; He hid Me in His quiver;

3. And said to Me, You are My servant Israel, You in whom I shall be glorified.
4. Then I said, I have labored in vain; I have spent My strength for nothing, and in vain; yet surely My judgment is with YHWH, and My work with My God.
5. And now, says YHWH who formed Me from the womb to be His servant, to bring Jacob back to Him: Though Israel is not gathered, yet I am honored in the eye of YHWH, and My God is My strength.
6. And He said, It is a little thing that You should be My servant to raise up the tribes of Jacob, and to restore the preserved ones of Israel; I will also give You for a light of the nations, to be My Salvation to the end of the earth.
7. So says YHWH, the Redeemer of Israel, His Holy One, to the despised of soul, to the hated of the nation, the servant of rulers, kings shall see and rise up; and chiefs shall worship; because YHWH who is faithful, and the Holy One of Israel; and He chose You.
Isaiah 49:1-7

The servant of YHWH is the prophesied Messiah, the literal and eternal personification of the Israel of God(Cross Reference **Isaiah 49:3; Galatians 6:16**), who would raise up the tribes of Jacob, restore the preserved ones of Israel, be a light to the nations, and be YHWH's Salvation(Yeshua: Strong's Reference #**H3444**) to the end of the earth.

Isaiah 48:12-16 and **49:1-7** are not two independent bible passages containing isolated concepts and should therefore, not be mysterious. Besides the many references to the revelation of God's Salvation(Yeshua: Strong's Reference #**H3444**) that can be found throughout the Old Testament, the identity of YHWH's servant(**Isaiah 49:1-7** Cross Reference **Matthew 12:18-21**) and the destination that YHWH is being sent to by the Lord YHWH and His Spirit(**Isaiah 48:12-16**) are both disclosed by the New Testament's revelation of the Yeshua the Messiah and Son of God, in ancient Judea(Cross Reference **Luke 1:54-55{Isaiah 49:8}**).

In light of the bible's many details concerning the revelation of the Messiah, doubt among Christians concerning the divinity of God's Salvation should not exist. But the existing doubt and confusion does serve a valuable purpose. The doubt surrounding the Messianic identity as a result of opposing Christian fellowships convoluting God's Word shines a very revealing light upon the multifaceted Church organization.

The New Testament has many cautionary admonitions about the deception and the blindness that would come to define the prophesied "End Time". Yeshua of Nazareth specifically told His disciples to be aware of false prophets and false messiahs that would arise and who, showing great signs and wonders, would if it were possible, deceive even the very elect of God(Cross Reference **Matthew 24:11,24; Mark 13:22**). The apostle Peter warned of false prophets among the people and false teachers among the brethren who, in his day, had introduced damnable heresies and even denied the Lord Who bought them(**2Peter 2:1-3**). The apostle John warned the servants of Yeshua that the prophesied "Last Days" were upon them, and sighted the appearance of false prophets(**1John 4:1-3**) and antichrists(**1John 2:18,22; 1John 4:3; 2John 1:7**) who, in that day, denied the revelation of the Messiah, as evidence. If the apostles understood the prophesied last days to have begun during their lifetime, why are churches telling their congregations to watch for future calamities to begin? According to **Revelation 12:1-17**, after the Child is born and then caught up to God there is a war in heaven and Satan and his angels are cast down to the earth. With that in mind, it should be clear why the apostles understood the prophesied Last Days to have begun in their time.

The confusion regarding the incarnation of the divine persona goes far beyond being a simple matter of biblical illiteracy. The revelation of the Messiah of God is stated so clearly and so often in the bible's Old Testament that to deny His revelation in the New Testament(New Covenant: **Jeremiah 31:31-34**) is to doubt God's spoken word(Cross Reference **Genesis 1:26**) and to question YHWH Elohim's reliability(Cross Reference **Genesis 3:1-5**). The multifaceted Church organization with its many opposing Christ figures is itself a testimony to the endurance of God's word and the bible's accurate depiction of the prophesied "Last Days". The Church's confusion regarding God's Salvation affirms YHWH Elohim's ability to communicate His word to the one audience who alone has the ears to hear His message(**Revelation** chapters **2-3** "He that hath an ear, let him hear what the Spirit saith" Cross Reference **Genesis 2:7,15-17**) and the understanding to recognize the times(**Matthew 24:42, 25:13; Mark 13:33-37; Luke 21:36** Cross Reference **Matthew 16:2-4**).

There are details in the Old Testament concerning the Messiah's revelation that could be and have been attributed to different men, living in various places, and existing at different times, but many, in fact most, of the details that are given in the Old Testament concerning the man who would be God's eternal Salvation can only be attributed to one specific man, living at one particular time, and ministering in one distinct place. **Isaiah 48:12-16** and **Isaiah 49:1-7** specifically reveal the identity of the Messiah and the purpose of His ministry. The precise timing of the Messiah's revelation was also foretold in the Old Testament. The angel Gabriel delivered a 70-week prophecy that concerned the Judean people, the city of Jerusalem, and the revelation of the Messiah to a Judean man named Daniel. Daniel's record of the experience is preserved in **Daniel 9:24-27**.

Daniel 9:24-27

24. Seventy weeks are determined upon thy people and upon thy holy city, to finish the transgression, and to make an end of sins, and to make atonement for iniquity, and to bring in everlasting righteousness, and to seal up the vision and prophecy, and to anoint the Most Holy.
25. Know therefore and understand, from the going forth of the word to restore and to rebuild Jerusalem unto the Messianic Prince shall be seven weeks and sixty-two weeks. The street shall be built again, and the wall, even in times of affliction.
26. And after sixty-two weeks the Messiah shall be cut off, and not be. And the people of the coming prince shall destroy the city and the sanctuary, and its end shall be with a flood, and unto the end of the war desolations are determined.
27. And he shall confirm the covenant with many for one week: and in the midst of the week he shall cause the sacrifice and the offering to cease, and because of the overspreading of abominations he shall make desolate, even until the consummation, and that determined shall be poured out on the desolator.

Daniel 9:24-27

It is clear from reading **Luke 3:1-22** and **John 1:15-51**(Cross Reference **Matthew 3:1-17; Mark 1:1-8**) that the 1st century A.D. Judean populace understood that the 69th week of Daniel's 70-week prophecy(**Daniel 9:24-27** Cross Reference **Matthew 26:18; John 19:30**), which prophesied the timing of the Messiah's revelation, would be fulfilled in their day. It is also clear that the Judeans understood that the manifestation of God's Messiah would be a physical incarnation. They were so eagerly awaiting the Savior whom they apparently expected to overthrow the Roman authority and lead them in strength before the nations, that they overlooked **Isaiah 52:13-53:12**, a passage which the Judean religious leadership must surely have been acquainted with.

Isaiah 52:13-15

13. Behold, My Servant shall deal prudently; He shall be exalted and lifted up and be very high,
14. Just as many were astonished over You; His face was so disfigured from man, and His form more than the sons of men
15. So shall He sprinkle many nations. Kings shall shut their mouths at Him; for they will see that which was not told them; yea, what they had not heard, they will consider.
Isaiah 52:13-15

Isaiah 53:1-12

1. Who has believed our report? And to whom is the Arm of YHWH revealed?
2. For He comes up before Him as a tender plant, and as a root out of dry ground. He has no form nor comeliness, nor beauty that we should desire Him.
3. He is despised and rejected by men; a man of sorrows and acquainted with grief. And we hid, as it were, our faces from Him; He was despised, and we did not esteem Him.
4. Surely He has borne our griefs and carried our sorrows; Yet we esteemed Him stricken, smitten by God, and afflicted.
5. But He was wounded for our transgressions, bruised for our iniquities; The chastisement for our peace was upon Him, and by His stripes we are healed.
6. All we like sheep have gone astray; We have turned, everyone, to his own way; and YHWH has laid on Him the iniquity of us all.

7. He was oppressed and He was afflicted, yet He opened not His mouth; He was led as a sheep before its shearers is silent, so He opened not His mouth.
8. He was taken from prison and from judgment, and who will declare His generation? For He was cut off from the land of the living; for the transgressions of My people, He was stricken.
9. And He made His grave with the wicked but with the rich at His death, because He had done no violence, nor was deceit in His mouth.
10. Yet it pleased YHWH to bruise Him; to put Him to grief. When You make His soul an offering for sin, He shall see seed, He shall prolong days, and the pleasure of YHWH shall prosper in His hand.
11. He shall see the labor of His soul and be satisfied. By His knowledge My righteous Servant shall justify many, for He shall bear their iniquities.
12. Therefore, I will divide Him a portion with the great, and He shall divide the spoil with the strong, because He poured out His soul unto death, and He was numbered with the transgressors, and He bore the sin of many, and made intercession for the transgressors.
Isaiah 52:13-53:12

    Isaiah 52:13-53:12 concludes inquiries into **Isaiah 48:12-16** and **49:1-7** and, substantiates **Daniel 9:26** by addressing the question of how the Servant(**Isaiah 52:13-53:12** Cross Reference **Isaiah 49:1-7**) of YHWH would be received in Judea upon being revealed. Each of these Messianic prophecies of the Old Testament are vindicated in the New Testament gospels. The New Testament not only details the birth of the Messiah and Judea's expectation for His arrival, but it also clarifies the apparent contradiction of Judea murdering her long-awaited Savior, YHWH's righteous Servant. The gospel accounts also provide insight into the men who expected His arrival to serve their own means -the elders, scribes, lawyers, Pharisees, and Sadducees-, and answers the question of why they could only find God's Salvation offensive(Cross Reference **Matthew 21:42; Mark 12:10-11; Luke 20:17-18; Acts 4:11-12; Romans 9:31-33; 1Peter 2:6-8**).

The rejection of the Messiah could possibly be misconstrued as an unfortunate misunderstanding by the Judean's, who were simply overburdened by the weight of the Roman occupation and overzealous in their defense of the name of God. After all the Judeans were a proud people(Cross Reference **Exodus 32:9; Deuteronomy 9:6**). But Yeshua's murder was not the result of a misunderstanding, and it involved a bit more than the Judeans being disappointed that Yeshua of Nazareth did not meet the criteria which they had established for a Messiah whom they were willing to accept(**John 5:43-44** Cross Reference **Matthew 11:1-19**). Although the Messiah's death was prophesied in the Old Testament and, His resurrection to eternal life would establish the New Covenant(**Jeremiah 31:31-34** Cross Reference **Romans 7:1-6**) which was prophesied to supersede the Old, **Mark 12:1-12; John 3:1-2**; and **John 11:47-53** reveal the motive behind the Judeans desire to kill Yeshua of Nazareth to be anything but altruistic.

Mark 12:1-12

1. And He began to speak to them in parables: A man planted a vineyard, and set a fence around it, and dug a wine-vat, and built a tower. And he let it out to vine-dressers and went away.
2. And at the season he sent a slave to the vine-dressers, that he might receive from the vine-dressers the fruit of the vineyard.
3. But taking him, they beat him, and sent him away empty.
4. And again, he sent to them another slave. And stoning that one, they struck him in the head, and sent him away, insulting him.

5. And again, he sent another, and they killed that one; also many others, indeed beating these, and killing these.
6. Yet having one son, his own beloved, then he sent him to them also, last of all, saying, They will have respect for my son.
7. But these vine-dressers said to themselves, This is the heir; come, let us kill him and the inheritance will be ours.
8. And taking him, they killed him and threw him outside the vineyard.
9. What, then, will the lord of the vineyard do? He will come and will destroy the vine-dressers and will give the vineyard to others.
10. Have you not even read this Scripture, The Stone which the builders rejected, this one became head of the corner;
11. This came about from the Lord, and it is marvelous in our eyes?
12. And they sought to seize Him, yet feared the crowd. For they knew that He spoke the parable against them. And leaving Him, they went away.

Mark 12:1-12

and,

John 3:1-2

1. But there was a man from the Pharisees, Nicodemus his name, a ruler of the Judeans.
2. This one came to Yeshua by night, and said to Him, Rabbi, we know that You have come as a teacher from God. For no one is able to do these miracles which You do, except God be with Him.

John 3:1-2

and,

John 11:47-53

47. Then the chief priest and the Pharisees assembled a Sanhedrin, and said, What are we doing, for this man does many miracles?

48. If we let him alone this way, all will believe into him, and the Romans will come and will take away from us both the place and the nation.
49. But a certain one of them, Caiaphas, being high priest of that year, said to them, You know nothing
50. Nor consider that it is profitable for us that one man die for the people, and not all the nation to perish.
51. But he did not say this from himself, but being high priest that year he prophesied that Yeshua was about to die on behalf of the nation,
52. And not only on behalf of the nation, but that He also might gather into one the children of God who had been scattered.
53. Then from that day they took counsel that they might kill Him.

John 11:47-53

Clearly, Yeshua of Nazareth was recognized in ancient Judea as a unique individual. The simple fact of the matter is that the Judeans murdered Yeshua because He was the direct threat to their position of authority within Judea, and His ministry impeded their aspirations of anointing a king(**Genesis 49:8-12** Cross Reference **1Samuel 8:6-9**) who would overthrow the power of their Roman oppressors. The Judeans essentially wanted the promises that God had given to Abraham and his seed(**Genesis 12:1-3,7; 13:14-17; 15:5,18; 17:7-8; 22:15-18** Cross Reference **Genesis 49:10-12; Galatians 3:16**) for themselves. They distinguished themselves as opponents of the revealed Word of God by refusing to give way for their own prophesied Messiah(Cross Reference the "Synagogue of Satan" mentioned in **Revelation 2:9, 3:9** "Who say that they are Judeans, and are not, but do lie."). The irony of the situation cannot be overlooked. The Judean's desperately waited for a savior, but these self-righteous men could only be offended by God's Salvation. The rejection and murder of Yeshua of

Nazareth in the New Testament confirms **Isaiah 52:13-53:12** with its graphic description of Judea's response to the revelation of God's Messiah.

The New Testament's confirmation of the Old Testament's prophesies concerning the birth, ministry, revelation, rejection, murder, and resurrection of the Messiah validates the revealed word of God, but the text of the bible has more to offer. Understanding of the Judean's motive for rejecting and murdering their prophesied Messiah unlocks a level of insight that goes deeper than validation. By understanding the Judean's motive for denying the Truth of God's word, a pattern can be traced forwards as well as backwards in time to give Bible readers insight into the rationale behind, Satan's attack on Adam in the garden of Eden(**Genesis 3:1-8**), the sons of Gods immorality in the days of Noah(Cross Reference **Genesis 6:1-7; Psalm 82:1-8; Romans 1:18-32**), the impropriety of the synagogue of Satan(Cross Reference **Revelation 2:9, 3:9**), and the campaign waged against the Messianic body of believers by the seven-headed ten-horned Beast and False Prophet(Cross **Reference Revelation 13:1-18**).

Early in the history of humanity Satan attacked man and set in motion his plan to be recognized as the Most High God. By disrupting mankind's reception(**Genesis 3:1-5**) of God's word, the serpent was able to give substance to his perverse ambition(Cross Reference **Isaiah 14:13-14**), to inculcate the perception of power in his own word(**Genesis 3:4-5**), and to fashion man according to his own identity(Cross Reference **Genesis 1:26** "Image...Likeness"). The murder of Yeshua of Nazareth in Judea was no less of an attempt to conceal God's revealed truth, to subject humanity to a false authority, and to redefine the human identity according to the image and likeness of a civil and religious regime of surrogate messiahs(**John 8:44;** Cross Reference the Seven-Headed Ten-Horned Beast, the False Prophet, and the Synagogue of Satan in the book of Revelation as well as **2Peter 2:4; Jude 1:6**). Fortunately for the sake of humanity, Yeshua of Nazareth satisfied the requirements God's law. His life and ministry fulfilled God's word that was revealed to the Old Testament's prophets(**Matthew 5:17**), His sacrifice redeemed humanity from sin and death, and orchestrated the renewal of God's creation(**Revelation 21:1-27**). In short, God's revealed Word crushed Satan's ambitions, his authority, and his kingdom(**Genesis 3:15** Cross Reference **John 1:1-5**).

On a hilltop in Judea the power and lie of Satan was exposed and defeated by the death of the Lamb of God(**Genesis 22:8** Cross Reference **John 1:29, Revelation 5:1-14**). And the resurrection of Yeshua the Messiah, God's Salvation, provided humanity with a new, unadulterated, impervious identity to take shelter under and to abide in(Cross Reference "Man" **Genesis 1:26, 2:7**). "And so it is written, the first man Adam was made a living soul; the last Adam was made a quickening Spirit" **1Corinthians 15:45**.

Conclusion

The message of the entire Bible is bound up in the identity of the one and only man whom God had prophesied would come into the world as the accomplishment of His stated will(**Genesis 1:26, 3:15, 22:8{John 1:29, Revelation 5:6-14**). To know Him is to know the Word of God(**John 1:1-5**), and to know the Word of God is to know the Father(**John 14:9-11**).

It has not been understood, nor has it been possible for church communities around the globe to recognize one subtle pattern of the bible that validates the Word of God in the Old Testament and substantiates the ministry of Yeshua of Nazareth in the New. This pattern; God codifying existence from the Heaven of heavens and YHWH Elohim descending upon the surface of the earth to accomplish His word, is the foundational methodology of God's interaction with His creation(Cross Reference **Genesis 1:1-2:25**). It is a principle that is firmly established in the opening chapters of the Bible, and which resonates throughout the scripture. Genesis chapters 1 and 2, God's works in Heaven and upon the surface of the Earth(Cross Reference **Exodus 33:19-23, 34:5-7**) are the working models of God's ministries in both the Old and the New Testaments.

The confusion surrounding the work and identity of Yeshua of Nazareth that has continued from ancient times up to the modern age, has served to distort God's personal revelation of Himself(i.e. **The Bible** Cross Reference **Philippians 2:5-6**) and humanity's reception of the truth. Thus, preventing man from ever coming to the Truth.

Still, the mysteries surrounding the identity of Yeshua of Nazareth have served an invaluable purpose. In ancient Judea, the ministry of Yeshua of Nazareth, the confusion, outright rejection, and murder of God's Salvation made a clear distinction between two groups of men and women. **Genesis 3:15** makes that same distinction(Cross Reference the "seed of the serpent and the seed of the woman"). The individuals who were bound to keep the 'Law', who depended upon their own works to justify them before God, and who could only be offended by the revelation of God's Salvation stood in stark contrast to the Lord's body of faithful servants who hear their Lord's voice(**John 10:26-27**) and who are justified by their faith in God's Word(**Galatians 3:1-11** "The just shall live by faith." Cross Reference **Habakkuk 2:4; Romans 1:17; Hebrews 10:38**). The identity of Yeshua of Nazareth makes a similar distinction in modern times between the men and women who continually sacrifice the Truth to man-made traditions(**Hebrews 9:24-28** Cross Reference **Genesis 3:3**) and those who lay down their own lives to partake of God's Salvation(**John 6:53-65**).

Arguments over biblical understanding are healthy, up to a point. But I'm convinced that very little to nothing can be accomplished once you take conversation past the point of understanding another individual's experience or beyond the realm of understanding for personal development. At the end of the day, after the arguments have been made and the emotional upheavals have settled down, each individual has to personally account for who you are actually trying to convince of your religious beliefs. Are you trying to convince a nonbeliever, yourself, or God(or the god whom you serve)? A nonbeliever should be expected to question the divinity of God's Salvation/Yeshua (Cross Reference **1Corinthians 1:18**) because they are not His sheep(**John 10:1-27**). Yourself? Personally, I could not and cannot trust myself to lead myself to the Truth. God? I trust that God knows what He's doing. Who am I to try and convince Him otherwise.

    I only hope to point out the Light, the Spirit will either draw or repel you.

    The one argument that has been at the center of more divisions concerning biblical understanding should, in all actuality, be the common denominator binding the various members of the Messianic body together(**1Corinthians 12:1-31**). The Old and New Testaments of the Bible are expressly clear on the identity of God's prophesied Messiah, in whom we all have Salvation. There is no middle ground on this particular issue, and it is inexcusable for any man or woman who calls themselves a child of God to doubt the divinity of the Shepherd of God's flock(**John 10:1-19**). I would even go as far as saying that to doubt the divinity and the revelation of the Messiah in ancient Judea is to call the entire Bible a fraudulent document(Cross Reference **Genesis 3:4-5**).

Postscript

    The Bible answers most of the questions that have been proposed in regard to the life, ministry, and identity of Yeshua of Nazareth. In accordance with the revelation of prophetic scripture, the creation's God of gods was incarnated and walked the earth as a flesh and blood man who suffered and died for the sins of the world. Questions about the missing skeleton of Yeshua of Nazareth are answered in the Bible by the resurrection(**Matthew 28:1-20; Luke 24:1-53**) and ascension of Yeshua the Messiah into Heaven(**Luke 24:51, Acts 1:1-11**). The miracles that Yeshua performed and that were recorded by eyewitnesses have not been replicated, they cannot be confirmed by modern science, and therefore they may not be answerable anytime soon. There are other questions surrounding the identity of Yeshua of Nazareth that are not addressed by the Bible, are unrelated to biblical understanding, but are none the less, legitimate.

Questions regarding the supposed European progeny of Yeshua of Nazareth, whether or not Yeshua of Nazareth is only an invention of the Roman Catholic Church, or even questions about the debatable ancestry of the Israelite and Judean people do deserve a brief comment.

Is Yeshua of Nazareth the Progenitor of European Royalty?

I do not personally know any figures of European royalty nor do I know whether or not any figures of European royalty claim to trace their lineage back to Yeshua of Nazareth but, there are books, two of which I own, as well as men and women who claim that an ancestral link between Yeshua of Nazareth and European royalty does exist. The subversive idea that Yeshua of Nazareth never actually died on the cross for the sins of humanity but instead traveled with his wife -Mary Magdalene- and fathered children, has been a source of debate and entertainment since before I was born. The idea is interesting, but quite problematic. It essentially declares Yeshua of Nazareth to be a liar and an impostor who did not come into the world to fulfill biblical prophecy. More than that, the idea implies that the Bible, its prophetic message of God's Salvation, and the revealed Word of God, is a lie. The belief that Yeshua of Nazareth lived and fathered children suggests one of two possibilities. According to the belief, one would have to assume that either God does not exist and there are no such places as Heaven and Hell, or if God does exist then He is incapable of accomplishing His will, Satan cannot be overcome, sin and death still rule over mankind, and all of humanity is destined for an eternal existence in the lake of fire(**Revelation 21:8**).

According to the bible Adam was created by YHWH Elohim to exist as a sovereign being(Cross Reference **Genesis 5:2** "He created them male and female, and blessed them, and called their name Man in the day when they were created."). Adam resembled his Creator, he was accepted by God, and he was justified by the Spirit of Life that had been breathed into him. The right of each man to rule over him or herself was usurped by the adversary of life, Satan. The belief that European royalty was given their right to rule over humanity by their presumed descent from a messianic figure who did not accomplish God's word does, among other things, equate Yeshua, and subsequently his presumed progeny: European royalty; with the seed of Satan(Cross Reference **Genesis 3:15**).

Is Yeshua of Nazareth an Invention of the Roman Catholic Church?

Looking at the history of the Catholic Church, its tradition based response to the word of God(Cross Reference **Hebrews 9:24-28**), its figurative interpretation of the bible's prophetic passages, its god(the Pope: meaning "father"; and Vicar of Christ: meaning "in the place of Christ"), doctrines and practices that contradict the Bible's teachings(Cross Reference **Matthew 23:9, 1Timothy 2:5, 1Corinthians 1:12-13**), and its repackaging of pagan holy-days(holidays) in presumably

"Christian" wrappings (Christmas=Saturnalia and Easter=Astarte), it is clear, at least to me, that the light that the Church(both the Catholic and Protestant branches) is shining in the world does not nor can it, reflect God's Truth. In addition to that, the Catholic Church's long history of political intrigues, sexual abuses, and its continued practice of ignoring, denying, mishandling, and outright lying about the molestations and rapes committed by its ordained clergy, are only a very short list of the reasons why I don't personally believe that Yeshua of Nazareth was invented by the Roman Catholic church.

Were the Children of Israel, Who Came Out of Egypt Under the Leadership of Moses, Actually Egyptians?

According to the bible the ancient Israelites and Judeans resembled the native Egyptians in physical appearance. According to history and archaeology the similarities between the children of Israel and the ancient Egyptians did not end with physical appearance. According to history the ancient Egyptians, as well as other African peoples, practiced circumcision* long before the children of Israel did. Moses, who resembled and was raised as an Egyptian in the Pharaoh's household for forty years, would have known this.

*According to the bible, each individual son of God was initially created with both a masculine and feminine aspect to their nature. Adam is also a son of God, who existed with that same masculine and feminine nature until the feminine aspect of his persona was taken out of his body in **Genesis 2:21**. Adam and Eve then existed as two distinct individuals; a male and a female. Circumcision was in ancient times and continues to be practiced today within many African cultures as the way of separating the "feminine" covering from the "masculine" penis. I assume, based off of my understanding of the practice of circumcision within African cultures, that YHWH Elohim* *ordained circumcision to be the sign of the covenant between Himself and Abram in order to commemorate Eve(Female) being separated from Adam's(Male) body.*

Moses would also have been familiar with the Egyptian religious texts, such as "The Book of The Dead/Book of Coming Forth By Day" which included passages such as the "42 Negative Confessions" and he would have recognized their compatibility with the Ten Commandments. Moses possibly would also have been familiar with Pharaoh Aketnaten's monotheistic religious reforms and the compatibility of those reforms with his own ministry. Moses may also have been familiar with the "disappearance" of Pharaoh Akhenaten's followers after the so-called 'apostate' Pharaoh's death. According to the Bible, Moses was familiar with the miraculous appearance of the children of Israel and the mixed multitude that came out of Egypt with them, on the borders of Canaan.

According to archaeologists there are items that exist in Egypt whose similarity to items used by the children of Israel defy coincidence. For instance, the stated cubit measurements of the ark of the covenant that resided in the most holy place within Jerusalem's ancient temple are the same cubit measurements of the stone chest found within the King's Chamber of the Great Pyramid in Giza, Egypt. Also, the Bible's stated measurement of the most holy place within the Jerusalem Temple is precisely the same as the measurement of the King's Chamber within the Great Pyramid of Giza.

The evidence connecting the native Egyptians and ancient Israel seems to be undeniable but, its validity is subject to the opinion of individual men and women. Prejudice tends to influence the response that we each hear from the existing evidence.

I'm not a historian, an archaeologist, nor a professionally educated/trained scientist, but I like all of them, ask questions. I personally believe that every question about the Bible can be answered, when assisted by the Holy Spirit, within the text of the Bible. It just may be that the answers to the questions that won't "Be revealed until the Lord returns to the earth(Christians often use this phrase as a rebuff to difficult questions about the Bible.)" are simply buried in archives, museum warehouses, or beneath the surface of the earth. I do find it interesting that Bible critics who readily dispute the resurrection and ascension of Yeshua of Nazareth are just as quick to accept that entire nations of men and women could mysteriously vanish, such as is the case with the indigenous Olmec and other pyramid building civilizations of central America.

For some apparent reason, whenever the identity of prominent historical figures or nations is linked directly to dark brown, brown, or copper skinned Africans or indigenous Americans their histories and lineages seem doomed to remain "mysterious", to have been dropped from European colonial ideologies that have been recorded and taught as history, or they were deemed to be "too pagan" by the Church establishment and thus declared fit only to be crushed, burned, or by some other means, destroyed(See **Daniel 7:7**; **Revelation 13:1-18**).

Notes

CHAPTER 5
Tradition, The Law, and Faith.

Tradition

Mark 7:1-13

1. And the Pharisees were assembled to Him, also some of the scribes, coming from Jerusalem.
2. And seeing some of His disciples eating bread with unclean hands, that is unwashed, they found fault.
3. For the Pharisees and all the Judeans do not eat unless they wash scrubbing the hands, holding the tradition of the elders.
4. And from the market, they do not eat unless they wash themselves. And there are many other things which they received to hold: washing of cups, and of utensils, and of bronze vessels, and couches.
5. Then the Pharisees and scribes questioned Him. Why do your disciples not walk according to the tradition of the elders, but eat bread with unwashed hands?
6. And answering He said to them, Well did Isaiah prophesy concerning you hypocrites; as it has been written: This people honors Me with its lips, but their heart is far away from Me;
7. And in vain they worship Me, teaching as doctrines the commandments of men.
8. For forsaking the commandment of God, you hold the tradition of men: washing of utensil and cups, and many other such like things you do.
9. And He said to them, Too well do you set aside the commandment of God so that you may keep your tradition.
10. For Moses said, Honor your father and your mother; and, He who curses father and mother, let him be put to death.

11. But you say, If a man says to his father or mother, Whatever profit you might have received from me is Corban, (that is, a gift),
12. And you no longer allow him to do anything for his father or mother,
13. Making the word of God of no effect by your tradition which you delivered. And many such like things you do.
Mark 7:1-13

    Religious traditions generally serve two purposes. First, traditions serve as reminders. Either to mark a significant event or to remind a devotee of God's(or a god's) involvement in their daily lives. Second, traditions serve as protective hedges that keep the limits of an ordinance(s), divine or otherwise, from being exceeded. From a religious perspective "tradition" is the rational response of an intelligent man or woman who is mature enough to acknowledge his or her inability to maintain the divine standard. Inevitably devotion to the tradition, that was intended to protect the divine commandment, surpasses the reverence that had once been given to the actual commandment of God(or god). Thus, making the man-made tradition the ordinance that is followed by devotees, and thereby rendering the word of God ineffectual(**Genesis 3:3** Cross Reference **Revelation 2:1-7**).

    Traditions may be initiated by men or women who have only the best of intentions but, as the serpent's successful attack on Eve in the garden of Eden(**Genesis 3:1-7**) proved, man-made traditions(or justifications) are only liabilities in the realm of spiritual warfare*.

Spiritual warfare is waged without and within man's heavenly kingdom {Luke 17:21** Cross Reference **Genesis 1:1-2:4a**} ;the realm of causes and personal cognition.*

Religious tradition is older than humanity's original sin. In **Genesis 2:16** YHWH Elohim had commanded the man Adam saying, "You may freely eat of every tree in the garden". YHWH Elohim then continued to say in **Genesis 2:17** that Adam was not to eat the fruit of the tree of knowledge of good and evil, "For in the day that you eat of it, you shall surely die". In **Genesis 3:1** when the serpent confronted Eve and asked her if it was true that she and Adam were not permitted to eat the fruit of any of the trees in the garden of Eden, she responded in **Genesis 3:3** to the serpent's question by misquoting the Word of God(Cross Reference **Deuteronomy 4:2, 12:32; Revelation 22:18-19**). Eve added an additional clause to the command that Adam had received from YHWH Elohim when she told the serpent that she and her husband were not permitted to eat the fruit of the tree that is in the middle of the garden nor were they allowed to touch it, lest they die(**Genesis 3:3**).

Apart from the resulting catastrophe, Eve's response to the serpent's question was very logical. It is in fact impossible to eat something that you never touch. Unfortunately for Eve, her tradition of not touching the forbidden tree did not serve as a protective hedge around the word of God. It only served to convince the serpent that Eve either 1) didn't know the word of God, 2) didn't understand the word of God, or 3) that she didn't respect the word of God. Eve's tradition-based response to God's word encouraged the serpent's attack by implying that she did not believe that the word of God was strong enough to stand on its own. And, in light of the fact that two trees existed and bore fruit in the midst of the garden of Eden, Eve's additional edict to God's command disclosed her uncertainty about how she was to relate to either the tree of Life or to the tree of Knowledge of Good and Evil. Eve's traditional approach to the two trees that were in the midst of the garden of Eden appears to also have served Satan by giving Eve a false sense of authority over the tree of knowledge of good and evil, and thereby adding a measure of curiosity to her imaginative mind(This is another reason why a literal response to the Word of God must precede personal expression. Cross Reference Eve's being made subject to Adam's authority in **Genesis 3:16**).

    I sincerely believe that Eve only wanted to follow God's command. There is nothing in the Bible that would suggest otherwise(Cross Reference **Genesis 3:13; 2Corinthians 11:3; 1Timothy 2:14**). Ironically, for all of Eve's intent to safeguard the word of God she only rendered it ineffectual by her tradition and exposed herself as a liability in the face of a hostile adversary.

    The Word of God is the Truth. It is humanities only defense against our common spiritual adversary, Satan, and his host of servants(Cross Reference Yeshua's temptation in the wilderness: **Matthew 4:1-11; Mark 1:12-13; Luke 4:1-13** with **Genesis 2:17** and, **Genesis 3:1-6** with **2Corinthinas 11:12-15**). The traditions of man effectively nullify the influence of God's Word (**Matthew 15:3-9; Mark 7:13**) because they, by definition, encroach upon God's Holy standard by venerating the word of man(**Genesis 3:17** Cross Reference **Isaiah 14:13-14**). Man-made additions, subtractions, and alterations to the text and the intent of the Bible may seem justifiable to men and women who do not know, do not understand, or who do not respect the word of God, but such alterations only challenge the authority God's recorded word, raise doubts about its authenticity, and give Satan opportunity.

    God's word and how man relates to it are the root causes of our existence. God gave Man two commands in the opening chapters of the book of Genesis. In **Genesis 1:28** the man who had been created in the image of God was told to "Be fruitful and multiply", in **Genesis 2:16-17** Adam was also commanded, and told that he was allowed to eat the fruit of every tree of the garden of Eden but, he was not permitted to eat the fruit of the tree of knowledge of good and evil. The first command was given to man to ensure that the standard of God was maintained throughout the creation. God's second command was given to preserve the existing relationship between Himself and the man whom He had created as His likeness.

The man who had been created in the image of God knew the standard of God, he was placed under an ordinance("Be fruitful and multiply" **Genesis 1:28**), and held accountable for his exploits(**Romans 1:18-20** Cross Reference **Psalms 82**). Adam also knew the word of God. He may possibly have had some concept of physical death but, being the first and only human to receive the anointing of the Holy Spirit of God(**Genesis 2:7** Cross Reference **Matthew 3:16; Mark 1:10; Luke 3:22; John 1:32**) as well as the first and only ordained representative of the human species, I am confident that Adam had little to no appreciation for the type of death and spiritual separation that YHWH Elohim's command was intended to keep him from experiencing. But Satan, experientially, did.

Adam did not earn his way into the garden of Eden nor was his appointment the reward due for services performed. All that Adam could do contribute to his situating was to trust God. Adam could rest assured in the fact that his relationship with YHWH Elohim, his ordination and appointment, and his right to remain in the garden of Eden were justified by his faith in and reliance upon the word of God(**Habakkuk 2:4, Romans 1:17, Galatians 3:11, Hebrews 10:38**).

The commands given to the sons of God who were created in the image of God(**Genesis 1:28**) and to Adam(**Genesis 2:16-17**) mark the first time that the concepts of 'Law and Faith' become relevant in the bible. Though 'Law and Faith' become relevant early on in the history of man(Cross Reference the command given to Noah and his sons in **Genesis 9:1,7**; and the faith of Abraham in **Genesis 15:1-6**), their significance in the lives of humanity does not necessarily become readily apparent to many Bible readers until Exodus chapter 20, when the Ten Commandments and the Law of Moses were given to the nation of Israel.

The Law and Faith
(Jacob and Israel)

In the book of Exodus after the children of Israel were delivered out of the hand of the Egyptian Pharaoh the Ten Commandments and the Law were given to them in Arabia, at the foot of Mt. Sinai(Mt. Sinai, where the Ten Commandments were given to the nation of Israel, is not in Egypt, Cross Reference **Galatians 4:22-26**).

In **Exodus 20:1-17** God gave the nation of Israel the Ten Commandments.

Exodus 20:1-17
1. And God spoke all these words, saying:
2. I am YHWH your God, who has brought you out from the land of Egypt, from the house of bondage.
3. You shall not have any other gods before Me.
4. You shall not make a graven image for yourself, of any likeness which is in the heavens above, or which is in the earth beneath, or which is in the waters under the earth;
5. You shall not bow to them, and you shall not serve them for I am YHWH your God, a jealous God, visiting the iniquity of the fathers upon children, on the third and on the fourth generation, to those that hate Me;
6. And doing kindness to thousands, to those loving Me, and to those keeping My commandments.
7. You shall not take the name of YHWH your God in vain; for YHWH will not leave unpunished he who takes His name in vain.
8. Remember the Sabbath day, to keep it holy;

9. Six days you shall labor and do all your work;
10. And the seventh day is a Sabbath to YHWH your God; you shall not do any work, you, and your son, and your daughter, your male slave and your slave-girl, and your livestock, and your stranger who is in your gates.
11. For in six days YHWH made the heavens and the earth, the sea, and all which is in them, and He rested on the seventh day; on account of this YHWH blessed the Sabbath day and sanctified it.
12. Honor your father and your mother, so that your days may be long on the land which YHWH your God is giving to you.
13. You shall not murder.
14. You shall not commit adultery.
15. You shall not steal.
16. You shall not testify a witness of falsehood against your neighbor.
17. You shall not covet your neighbor's house; you shall not covet your neighbor's wife, or his male slave, or his slave girl, or his ox, or his ass, or anything which belongs to your neighbor.
Exodus 20:1-17

The Ten Commandments are summed up by Yeshua of Nazareth in **Matthew 22:37-40** of the New Testament.

Matthew 22:37-40
37. And Yeshua said to him, You shall love the Lord your God with all your heart, and with all your soul, and with all your mind.
38. This is the first and great commandment.
39. And the second is like it: You shall love your neighbor as yourself.
40. On these two commandments all the Law and the Prophets hang.

Matthew 22:37-40

In the book of Exodus after the Ten Commandments are given to the nation of Israel the people were terrified and stood at a distance from YHWH Who was atop the mountain. The children of Israel told Moses that they did not want to hear from God but that he(Moses) should go near, speak with God, and then come back and report to them what God had said(**Exodus 20:18-19**). Moses then went alone near to the thick darkness where God was and YHWH gave Moses 600+ additional ordinances for the nation to follow. The 600+ ordinances are the "Law of Moses" that the children of Israel were to live by. No obvious explanation is given in the Old or New Testaments to explain why God added 600+ ordinances to the Ten Commandments, but a little indirect insight from the New Testament's gospel of Matthew helps to reveal the answer why.

Matthew 5:1-16 parallels the account of God descending upon Mt. Sinai and delivering the Ten commandments to the children of Israel in **Exodus 20:1-17**. **Matthew 5:17-7:29** parallels the account of Moses receiving the 600+ additional laws, the "Law of Moses". In both the Exodus and Matthew accounts the keys to the kingdom of heaven were given to the individuals who drew near to God and heard His words for themselves. Also in both the Old and New Testament accounts, the standard of God: The Law; that man must follow to personally attain righteousness was given to those who chose to remain at a distance.

In the 4th chapter of the New Testament book of Matthew after Yeshua's "temptation in the wilderness(**Matthew 4:1-11**)" He, Yeshua of Nazareth, began to preach, proclaiming that the kingdom of Heaven is near. Yeshua began to go around Galilee, to gather His disciples, to heal the sick, and to cast out demons. The report of Him spread throughout the land and crowds from Galilee and Decapolis, and Jerusalem, and Judea, and beyond the Jordan river followed Him(**Matthew 4:12-25**). In **Matthew 5:1** Yeshua of Nazareth and His disciples withdrew from the crowds to a mountain top. Beginning in **Matthew 5:1** and continuing through **Matthew 7:29** Yeshua delivered to his disciples what has come to be referred to as "the Sermon on the Mount".

Opening the sermon, in **Matthew 5:1-17,** Yeshua spells out the personal characteristics of the men and women who will inherit the kingdom of heaven.

Matthew 5:1-17

1. But seeing the crowds, He went up into the mountain, and seating Himself, His disciples came near to Him.
2. And opening His mouth, He taught them, saying:
3. Blessed are the poor in spirit. For theirs is the kingdom of the Heavens.
4. Blessed are they who mourn. For they shall be comforted.
5. Blessed are the meek. For they shall inherit the earth.
6. Blessed are they who hunger and thirst after righteousness. For they shall be filled.
7. Blessed are the merciful. For they shall obtain mercy.
8. Blessed are the pure in heart. For they shall see God.
9. Blessed are the peacemakers. For they shall be called sons of God.
10. Blessed are they who have been persecuted for righteousness' sake. For theirs is the kingdom of Heaven.
11. Blessed are you when they shall reproach you, and persecute you, and shall say every evil word against you, lying, on account of Me.
12. Rejoice and leap for joy, for your reward is great in Heaven; for in this way they persecuted the prophets who were before you.

13. You are the salt of the earth; but if the salt becomes tasteless, with what shall it be salted? For it has strength for nothing anymore, but to be thrown out, and to be trampled under by men.
14. You are the light of the world, a city situated on a mountain cannot be hidden.
15. Nor do they light a lamp and put it under a grain measure, but on a lampstand; and it shines for all who are in the house.
16. So let your light shine before men, so that they may see your good works, and may glorify your Father in Heaven.
17. Do not think that I came to annul the Law or the Prophets; I did not come to annul, but to fulfill.
Matthew 5:1-17

Matthew 5:16 completes Yeshua's address to the blessed who have inherited life, and **Matthew 5:17** begins the transition from the first to the second part of His sermon. Both **Exodus 20:1-17** and **Matthew 5:1-16**, God's precursory discourses given to the people whom He has called near to Him, could be summarized by the words love, compassion, and respect(**Matthew 22:37-40**). These three qualities are hallmarks of godliness, as well as a healthy relationship.

After Yeshua defines by encouragement, the qualities of the men and women who will inherit the kingdom of heaven, the focus of His sermon changes. The second part of Yeshua's sermon on the mountain is introduced in **Matthew 5:17-20** with a reference to the righteousness of the men who stood as perpetual adversaries to Yeshua's life and ministry. Then beginning in **Matthew 5:21** and continuing up to **Matthew 7:29** Yeshua delivers the standard that must be maintained in order for a man to be righteous in the eyes of God.

Matthew 5:17-20

17. Do not think that I came to annul the Law or the Prophets; I did not come to annul, but to fulfill.
18. Truly I say to you, Until the heavens and the earth pass away, in no way shall one yot or one tittle pass away from the law until all comes to pass.
19. Whoever therefore shall break one of these commandments, the least, and shall teach men likewise, he shall be called least in the kingdom of Heaven. But whoever does and teaches, this one shall be called great in the kingdom of the Heavens.
20. For I say to you, if your righteousness shall not exceed that of the scribes and Pharisees, in no way shall you go into the kingdom of Heaven.

Matthew 5:17-20

If you are vaguely familiar with the relationship between Yeshua of Nazareth and the 1st century Judean religious leadership who persecuted, abducted, convicted, and eventually murdered Him it is much easier to pick up on the tone of His words in **Matthew 5:17-20**. Although many Churches teach otherwise, Yeshua is not complimenting the righteousness of the scribes and Pharisees who had been prophesied to reject and murder Him(**Isaiah 52:13-53:12**{**Isaiah 49:6-8**}; **Matthew 23:1-39**; **John 2:24;**), and whom He declared in **John 8:44** to be "sons of the Devil", nor is He encouraging His disciples to adhere to their traditions which, according to His own words, were an affront to the Word of God(**Mark 7:6-9,13**). In **Matthew 5:17-18** Yeshua transitions His sermon from "Faith" and the men and women who will inherit the kingdom of heaven(**Matthew 5:1-16**) to the "Law" -the righteous standard of God- and the men and women destined to seek their own righteousness, by first commenting on the assuredness and reliability of the Law and the Prophets. In **Matthew 5:20** Yeshua then completes the transition of His sermon by commenting on the inefficiency of the righteousness that was pursued by the men who refuse(d) to draw near to the Son of God(Cross Reference **Exodus 20:18-21; Romans 10:3**).

Romans 10:3

3. For they being ignorant of God's righteousness, and going about to establish their own righteousness, have not submitted themselves unto the righteousness of God.
Romans 10:3

A similar, albeit even less apparent, transition from Faith to the Law is made in the book of Exodus when the children of Israel stood at the foot of Mt. Sinai. Recognizing this fact is invaluable(Cross Reference the differences between Genesis chapters 1 and 2), but recognition only serves as the **Introduction to Understanding**. To understand why the laws of righteousness follow both the "Ten Commandments" in the book of Exodus and the so-called "Beatitudes" in the Gospel of Matthew, it is necessary to first have an appreciation for what God's original intention for His people was.

In **Exodus 19:5-6** YHWH declares the original desire that He had for the nation of Israel.

Exodus 19:5-6

5. And now if you will surely listen to My voice, and will keep My covenant, you shall become a special treasure to Me above all the nations, for all the earth is Mine.
6. And you shall become a kingdom of priests for Me, a holy nation. These are the words which you(Moses) shall speak to the sons of Israel.
Exodus 19:5-6

YHWH had told Moses in **Exodus 19:5-6** to say to the children of Israel that if they would listen to the voice of YHWH and keep His covenant they would become a special treasure to Him; a nation of priests(Cross Reference "Adam in the garden of Eden.") and a holy nation. In a practical sense, the nation of Israel would fill the office that was vacated by Adam after he sinned and was expelled from the garden of Eden. The nation of Israel as well as the mixed multitude that came out of Egypt with them(**Exodus 12:38**) were being offered a unique relationship with YHWH; the right to hear His voice, to know His word, and the privilege of being a guiding light in the world leading all nations back to the Truth(Cross Reference **Leviticus 11:44-45; 19:2, 20:7,26,** and **21:8; Matthew 5:14; John 9:5**). The entire nation would have been deemed righteous because of their faith in and reliance upon the word of God(Cross Reference **Genesis 2:15-25; Romans 4:1-8; Habakkuk 2:4; Galatians 3:11**, "The just shall live by faith.").

The Ten Commandments were given to the children of Israel in **Exodus 20:1-17** as the terms of a contract, a contract that would have inducted the entire nation into a holy priesthood. The terms of the contract required the nation of priests to listen to the voice of YHWH, to love their God, to respect themselves, and to respect and show compassion for one another(**Matthew 22:37-40, Mark 12:29-31** Cross Reference **Genesis 2:17**).

In **Exodus 20:18-21** after YHWH had delivered the Ten Commandments(**Exodus 20:1-17**) to the children of Israel, the nation responded to God's offer.

Exodus 20:18-21
18. And all the people saw the thunders, and the lightnings, and the sound of the horn, and the smoking mountain. And the people looked, and they trembled, and they stood from a distance.
19. And they said to Moses, You speak to us, and we will hear. And let us not speak with God, that we not die.

20. And Moses said to the people, Do not be afraid, for God has come in order to test you, and so that His fear may be on your faces, that you may not sin.
21. And the people stood from a distance, and Moses went near the thick darkness where God was.
Exodus 20:18-21

Can you imagine the thunder, the lightning, the sound of the horn so loud that the ground shook, and the smoking mountain? I'm betting that some of the people there had wished that they had worn their brown pants.

The children of Israel were terrified. They stood at a distance and declared that they did not want to speak with God. Thus, the nation of Israel rejected the terms of the relationship offered to them by YHWH.

In response to the nation rejecting the terms of God's covenant, Moses was then told to deliver 600+ additional laws for the nation to follow. The "Law of Moses" is the standard that God, who is holy, required of a people whose ancestor covenanted(**Genesis 15:1-21** Cross Reference **Romans 3:1-3, 9:6-8**) with the Most High and, who must also be holy(**Leviticus 11:44-45** Cross Reference **Genesis 1:28** "Be Fruitful and Multiply").

Israel's refusal could not nullify the word of YHWH Elohim that had been given to Abraham(**Romans** chapters **9-11** Cross Reference **Genesis 17:1-27**). YHWH Elohim chose Israel to be the unique people, among all nations, through whom God's Salvation would come into the world. The salvation of humanity(**Genesis 3:15**) required the grace and mercy of YHWH Elohim but the transgressions of(**Exodus 20:18-21** Cross Reference **Romans 9:6; Galatians 3:16-19**) and rejection by the people who had been chosen by God to be a holy nation, determined that the Law was necessary(**Leviticus 11:45** "Ye shall therefore be holy, for I am holy").

The Law of Moses follows the Ten Commandments in the book of Exodus and the Laws of Righteousness follows the so-called "Beatitudes" in the gospel of Matthew because two distinct groups of men and women are being addressed in both the Old and New Testament accounts of God conversing with His chosen people on the mountain top. The Ten Commandments and the Beatitudes apply to the group of God's servants whose righteousness is attributed to them by their faith in God's Word. The laws of righteousness in both the Exodus and Matthew accounts apply to the group of men and women who stood at a distance from God, but who are bound to seek righteousness on their own account.

The differences between the two groups are as different as night and day. Righteousness and God's acceptance are settled issues for God's faithful servants(Cross Reference the apostle Paul's letters, particularly the letter to the Romans). The end result of faith in God, His word, and His righteousness is a relationship with YHWH Elohim. But righteousness, justification, and God's acceptance are continual burdens for anyone who has made righteousness their own responsibility. The end result of humanity's striving to maintain God's righteous standard is religious expression, self-righteousness, self-justification, self-empowerment, and encroachment -the need to control- upon the standard of God and upon the rights and righteousness of others(**Genesis 3:1-13** Cross Reference, "Cain and Abel" and "Lamech" in Genesis chapter 4, the "Brilliant Morning Star -the god who helps those who help themselves" in **Isaiah 14:1-27**, the "Anointed Cherub" in **Ezekiel 28:1-19**, and the Scribes, Pharisees, and Sadducees in the New Testament gospels).

Faith in The Old Testament

Faith accrediting righteousness to man(**Habakkuk 2:4; Romans 1:17; Galatians 3:11; Hebrews 10:38** "The just shall live by faith."), as opposed to submitting to the tenets of the Law to be justified, is not a concept that originated in the New Testament. Righteousness was imputed to man for trusting in the Word of God before Moses received the Ten Commandments and the Law on Mt. Sinai(Cross Reference **Romans 4:9,13; Galatians 3:17-18**) and long before the physical incarnation of YHWH Elohim's righteous Servant. The 11th chapter of the book of Hebrews names Abel, Enoch, Noah, Abraham, Sarah, Isaac, Jacob, Joseph, the parents of Moses -Amram and Jochebed-, Moses, Rahab, Gideon, Barak, Samson, Jephthah, David, Samuel, and the Old Testament's prophets of God as the elders(Cross Reference **Revelation 4:4,10** and throughout the book of Revelation) whose faith gained them a good report and was counted to them as righteousness. Interestingly, the Hebrews chapter 11 list of God's faithful servants does not include one practitioner of the Law, but it does include liars, drunkards, adulterers, and murderers. In fact, had the bible's three most highly venerated men -Abraham, Moses, and David-, who are on the list of God's faithful servants, been judged according to the tenets of the Law of Moses they certainly would have to have been considered some of the Law's worst offenders(Samson was also a character; **Judges** chapters **14-16**).

Abraham, the forefather of the children of Israel, lived 430 years before the Law of Moses was given(**Galatians 3:16-17** Cross Reference **Exodus 12:40-41**) yet, had he been judged according to the Law, Abraham would have been found guilty of several violations. Abraham repeatedly lied about his relationship with Sarah, his wife, in order to protect own his life. Abraham also accepted compensation from men who were only guilty of believing the lie that he told about his own wife(**Genesis 12:11-20, 20:1-18**). Still Abraham's faith in God's word is commended(**Genesis 15:1-6, 22:1-19; Hebrews 11:17-19** Cross Reference **Romans 4:3; Galatians 3:6**) and it was accounted to him as righteousness.

Moses was raised as an Egyptian in the Pharaoh's household. At the age of 40 he committed murder and fled into Midian(**Exodus 2:11-15**) where he met and married his first wife, Zipporah, a native Midianite woman(Cross Reference Joseph's, son of Jacob, marriage to an Egyptian woman that is mentioned in **Genesis 41:45,50**. Israel was prohibited from intermingling with nations that would corrupt their relationship with YHWH Elohim. Joseph's marriage to an Egyptian woman, Moses' marriage to Zipporah, and his later marriage to an Ethiopian woman were not violations of God's standard). Yet Moses was chosen by YHWH Elohim to be His representative before the Pharaoh and to lead the children of Israel out of Egypt. Although there is no record of infidelity nor of a formal divorce from his first wife, Moses entered into a second marriage(**Numbers 12:1**) with an Ethiopian woman. Moses was also guilty of misrepresenting YHWH to the children of Israel in **Numbers 20:8-12**. For all of his faults Moses was allowed to draw near to YHWH Elohim and it was he who personally received the "Law" that the rest of the nation was to follow. Although Moses regularly spoke face to face with YHWH Elohim(**Exodus 33:11** Cross Reference **Leviticus 16:1-34**) and received the ordinances that the Levitical priests of God were to abide in, he never practiced the tenets of the Law himself.

1Samuel 21:1-6 records the time that David, on the run from king Saul and his soldiers, ate the sanctified bread that was reserved for the priests of YHWH Elohim. **1 Samuel 21:10-15** recalls the time that David feigned insanity to escape a hostile king's court. After becoming king, David coveted a married woman, committed adultery with her which resulted in a pregnancy, and had Uriah the Hittite -Bathsheba's husband- murdered after failing in his attempt to hide their sin(**2Samuel 11:1-27**). Yet for all of his faults, David's faith in YHWH Elohim is commended throughout the Bible and he is even acknowledged in both the Old and New Testaments as a man after God's own heart(**Acts 13:22** Cross Reference **1Samuel 13:14**).

Abraham, Moses, and David may appear to have been men who had been given a license to sin, but they were not above the Law of God(Cross Reference **Romans 6:1-23**). These three highly venerated men as well as the other Old Testament saints and the New Testaments apostles were normal men and women who experienced weaknesses(Cross Reference **Galatians 2:11-12**), who made mistakes, and who had successes. Abraham, Moses, and David did not live above the law, they were just not subject to keep its ordinances in order to be accepted by God. The distinguishing characteristic that was shared by each saint in the scriptures is the same characteristic that continues to separate all of God's saints from all past, present, and future practitioners of the Law. That characteristic is faith in the Word of God(Cross Reference **Hebrews 11:1-40**. Sainthood is determined by each individual's relationship with God, not by the will nor the vote of a tradition-bound religious council). As it is stated many times in the bible, "The just shall live by faith(**Habakkuk 2:4; Romans 1:17; Galatians 3:11; Hebrews 10:38** Cross Reference **Romans 3:19-28**)".

The Law
(Cross Reference Ezekiel 33:11-20)

The "Law" is good(**Romans 7:1-25**). With it there is no favoritism nor compromise. The Law does a thorough job of backing every man and woman into a corner and showing us that we are all hopeless sinners. The Law eventually leads man to a cross-roads and forces him or her to accept either that YHWH Elohim alone justifies man(**Matthew 9:12-13** -quoted below- Cross Reference **Deuteronomy 27:26; Galatians 3:10; James 2:10**) or that they must, in spite of the Truth(**Matthew 11:12**), continually seek after a form of righteousness in order to attain their justification(Cross Reference **Genesis 3:5** "You shall be as God, knowing good and evil.").

Matthew 9:12-13(Cross Reference **Isaiah 64:4-6**) has a comment on the righteousness of man and the righteousness of God.

Matthew 9:12-13

12. But Yeshua hearing, He said to them, The ones who are strong have no need of a physician, but the ones who are sick.
13. But go, learn what it means, I desire mercy, and not sacrifice. For I did not come to call the righteous, but sinners to repentance.
Matthew 9:12-13

In **Matthew 9:12-13** Yeshua states that He did not come for the righteous, who are identified as the "the ones who are strong", but to call sinners, who are identified as "the ones who are sick", to repentance. Yeshua's declaration reemphasizes the difference between the men and women who put their faith in and are justified by YHWH Elohim, and those individuals who pursue a righteousness of their own(Compare the Ten Commandments and the "Beatitudes" with the Law of Moses and the Law of Righteousness). A faithful man or woman puts their trust in the Word of God because he and she recognize that we are all lost and hopeless sinners apart from the Salvation of God. A self-righteous man or woman could only be offended by God's Salvation/Yeshua because a holy, righteous, and just God could only stand as an obstacle to a self-righteous individual's own self-image of righteousness(Cross Reference Satan, the serpent: **Isaiah 14:13-14** and **Genesis 3:5** "You shall be as God, knowing good and evil").

    Yeshua of Nazareth did not come to ancient Judea to annul the law, nor did He come to make a way for gentile peoples to practice the law alongside Jewish proselytes who adhere to ancient Judean religious traditions. Yeshua of Nazareth is the literal Word of God. He is the Truth revealed in the flesh. He is the embodiment of God's standard(Cross Reference, the "Likeness of God" and the "Last Adam": **Genesis 1:26; 2:7,15-25; 5:1-3; 1Corinthians 15:45**). Faith in Yeshua, God's Salvation, is trust in the Word of God(**Romans 10:4**). And it is that faith, in the ability of the literal incarnation of God's Word to justify man, that is accounted to each man and woman as righteousness(**Romans 4:3-9; Galatians 3:1-6** Cross Reference "The just shall live by faith." **Habakkuk 2:4; Romans 1:17; Galatians 3:11; Hebrews 10:38**).

Limitations of the Law
(Cross Reference Galatians 4:21-31)

    Trying to walk the so-called "Christian walk" or to hold yourself to the requirements of the law of Moses only serve as evidence that you have not died to the law(**Romans 7:1-6**) and that you either don't know, don't understand, or don't respect the grace, mercy, and Word of God. You cannot be reborn in the Spirit of God nor walk in the newness of life(**Romans 6:3-4, 8:1-17**) because God's Salvation is of no value to you(**Mark 2:17**).

    The Law requires duty, and with man, duty inevitably expects compensation, monetary or otherwise. If you follow the law, then it is your duty to keep the entire Law. To break one ordinance of the Law of is to be guilty of breaking the entire law(**Galatians 3:10; James 2:10**). Without a standing temple, an altar for sacrifices, or a holy place for the high priest to enter into once a year to make atonement for sins, the ordinances of the Law could not, during the Babylonian captivity, and cannot, in the modern age, be kept. Therefore, man-made traditions, which can only circumvent the holy standard of God, have been and must be substituted to compensate for man's inability to keep the Law. As well intended as men and women who strive by tradition to keep the Law of God may be, they, Christians and Jews, do not serve the Almighty God but are in all actuality promoters of sin(Cross Reference **Romans 7:1-25**{**Genesis 3:3** and the result of Eve's tradition.}).

The Law is necessary because of man's improprieties and Faith is available because of YHWH Elohim's grace and mercy but, it is not possible to substitute one commitment with the other. Deficiencies in Faith cannot be supplemented by keeping the Law, and any inability to keep the Law cannot be augmented by having Faith. The Law and Faith are two mutually exclusive institutions.

The Freedom of Faith

To have Faith is to have a trusting relationship with the Word of God. The duty of the faithful is to agree with God(Walk with God: **Amos 3:3** Cross Reference **Genesis 6:9** "Noah walked with God".) and accept that God has and will continue to accomplish His word(Cross Reference **Genesis 15:6; Hebrews 11:17-19**). A faithful man or woman understands that he or she is the temple of God and the habitation of the Holy Spirit(**Hosea 6:6; 1Corinthians 3:16, 6:19**). The continual challenge of the faithful is to work out their salvation with fear and trembling(**Philippians 2:12-15**) because God's command to "Be fruitful and multiply(**Colossians 1:9-12**)" is understood as the call to aspire to the identity that Adam, who was created to walk as God's likeness, was divested of in the Garden of Eden. In this pursuit there is no competition. In life, which should be the continual pursuit of perfection, there are only opportunities to personally mature one moment at a time.

Repentance

Salvation is not a license to test the limits of God's grace, mercy, or forgiveness. And repentance is not a daily routine of apologizing to God for making mistakes or for thinking bad thoughts. Repentance does not require you to physically punish yourself, drown yourself in guilt, or to wallow in self-pity. Repentance is a change of life that does not happen overnight, and it is not merely exchanging an old sickness for a new one.

Repentance begins with seeing yourself as you truly are, not merely as you believe yourself to be. The ability to recognize your mistakes, understand your faults, take responsibility for your actions, and stop making the choices that continually lead you astray is not acquired by simply wanting it. You must come to the end of yourself. (Please do not take this next statement in the literal sense and end your physical existence) You must die, be born again of the Spirit of God(**John 3:5-8**), and walk in the newness of life(**Romans 6:1-23**). Have faith in God as a child of God's. And accept God's command to "Be fruitful and multiply" as a personal obligation to continually become better at being alive(**Colossians 1:10** Cross Reference **Galatians 5:22-23**).

For some time, I have been settled on the idea that whether God has called me to paradise or has condemned me to Hell, I'm not going to change His mind. Therefore, I don't live my life as if it were a competitive sport. I live my life actively doing what I can to be better at living my individual experience in the midst of this grand occasion because, the more that I learn and the more I mature, the more appreciation and less frustration I have throughout my days. I trust that God knows what He's doing.

I thank God for every day that He gives me to make less a fool of myself. This is a tree of life(**Proverbs 3:13-18; 11:30; 13:12; 15:4**).

Notes

CHAPTER 6
GOD THE KING, GOD THE PRIEST

The Bible is unique among all books. The individual books of the Bible are man's written record of God's work and His Word in action, and they reveal the result that nefarious influence has had within God's creation. The Bible speaks directly to each individual man and woman, it addresses the universal qualities inherent in all of mankind, it offers readers insight into the Creator of the heavens and the earth, and it offers hope. The Bible describes humanities past history, it explains our present circumstances, and prophesies of our future destiny. It describes God's personal involvement within the human experience and it gives a detailed account of how mankind has reciprocated that attention. The Bible is also a prophetic text, and the Creator of existence is able to speak directly to man through the words on its pages.

Another defining quality of the Bible is its complex simplicity. For all of its details, prophetic insights, and revelations of God and man(as well as the root of human conflict), the entire Bible's story can be explained in the first three chapters of the book of Genesis. Similarly, the Bible has the ability to break down all of life's complexities and to offer humanity manageable solutions to life's problems. The Bible offers solutions, and to me, solutions are like buried treasure.

Yet, for all of the Bible's simplicity, delving deeper into its pages reveals; the complexity of the kingdom of heaven, the corroding influence of Satanic meddling, and the detailed outline of YHWH Elohim's plan to restore His original work.

The bible's simplicity is inviting, and its complexity is engaging(and very often, intimidating).

The complex simplicity of the first two chapters of the book of Genesis is particularly interesting. **Genesis** chapters **1-**

2:4a and **2:4b-25** are each independent histories that contain details and messages that depend on each other for clarity, validation, and confirmation. God's initial work that began in **Genesis 1:1** and was complete in **Genesis 2:4a** is validated and its message clarified by YHWH Elohim's work which began in **Genesis 2:4b**. YHWH Elohim's work which began in **Genesis 2:4b** and continued through **Genesis 2:25** is established upon and confirms the reliability of the Word that founded the Heavens and the Earth in **Genesis 1:1**(Cross Reference **John 1:1-3**). The mutual dependency existing between the opening two chapters of Genesis is so vitally important to the Biblical text that without it the accumulation of each chapter's details, and subsequently the details of the Bible, could be perceived as little more than interesting mythological tales and the message of each respective chapter could not be discovered, understood, nor trusted.

Genesis chapters 1 and 2 are also interesting because of how the two chapters correspond to and correlate with the Old and New Testaments of the bible. The Old and New Testaments of the bible actually share the same kind of dependency as do **Genesis** chapters **1** and **2**. In the same way that **Genesis 1** and **2** depend on each other for clarity, validation, and confirmation, so to do the Old and New Testaments of the Bible. Even more than that, the manner in which God relates to His creation and man in Genesis chapters 1 and 2 is also the same in both Testaments of the Bible.

Many Bible students recognize the correspondence between the Bible's Old and New Testaments(The Old Testament supports the New, and the New Testament validates the Old.). Few may even acknowledge that Genesis chapters 1 and 2 share a similar type of relationship, but, to my knowledge none have recognized the correlating ministries that link Genesis 1 and 2 to the Bible's Old and New Testaments. This recognition is vitally important to the Bible's core message because it is the signature of what is possibly the Bible's most imposing prophetic revelation.

The singular message of Genesis chapters 1 and 2 and that of both Testaments is fairly simple to recognize. It is God's revelation of Himself(Cross Reference **Exodus 3:14**, "I AM"), given to the man who was created as His likeness. Only, the specific details of the Genesis chapters 1 and 2 revelations of God are necessarily different from the details of the Old and New Testament revelations because the circumstances under which each revelation is made happens to be so different. In **Genesis 1:31** God had seen to it that everything that He had made was "Very good". And, after God's implementation of the seventh day, the Sabbath in **Genesis 2:3-4a**, God's personal revelation was ready to be delivered. In **Genesis 2:7** the recipient of God's message had been formed and then he was placed in the garden of Eden. But, in Genesis 3 the recipient of God's message, Adam, forfeited his anointing. A first result of God's likeness being defiled(**Romans 1:23; 1Corinthians 11:7**) was that sin and death were permitted to reign in the place of life within God's creation. The second resulting calamity was that humanity lost sight of its God given birthright. The third calamity was that the ministries of Genesis chapters 1 and 2 became veiled in mystery.

Fortunately for the sake of later generations of God's servants, the Bible has fail-safes in place to ensure that its ministries would persevere.

The Prophetic Details of God's Revelation

In the opening chapters of the book of Genesis two offices were consecrated for the newly created men to function in. The offices and the two men employed in them serve a number of functional purposes within the creation but even more important than their functional capacities, the men and their respective institutions work together for one particular purpose. The two offices and the men created to function in them are essential to Biblical understanding, clarification, and validation. The two men are essentially caregivers and besides providing the means for maintaining the creation's working order, the two offices work in conjunction with Genesis chapters 1 and 2 and both Testaments of the Bible by serving as additional details of one grand prophecy. The men and both offices support and verify the word of God that was revealed to the prophets in the Old Testament and they validate the life and ministry of Yeshua of Nazareth in the New. The men are the sons of God who were created in the Image and the Likeness of God. The two offices are that of King and of Priest.

When the sons of God, who were created in the Image and the Likeness of God failed to uphold their God given commissions, the ministry of the offices of "King and Priest" became convoluted(Cross Reference **Genesis 3:1-24, 6:1-7**). In time, the two offices were established within the nation of Israel and their ministries were revived. The tribe of Judah and the men who were ordained to rule as kings not only served to officiate over Israel and Judea, they also expounded upon the function served by the office of king. The tribe of Levi and the Levitical high priest not only interceded before God on behalf of the nation of Israel, the Levites also served as a representative explanation of the office that was initially instituted when YHWH Elohim created Adam in **Genesis 2:7**. It has not been obvious but the tribes of Judah and Levi and the men who were ordained to officiate in the offices of king and priest are actually microcosmic details of the Old and New Testament's macrocosmic revelation.

Throughout the bible, with three noteworthy exceptions - Melchizedek king of Salem and priest of the Most High God, the elders in the book of Revelation, and the Messiah of God(Cross Reference **Genesis 14:18-20; Hebrews 7:1-28; 1Peter 2:9; Revelation 5:10**)-, the offices of king and priest, and the men who were ordained to perform the duties associated with each office, were to remain distinct from one another. The men who were given the right to rule as kings could not officiate as priests and, the priests of God were not permitted to rule as kings(Cross Reference **Genesis 49:8-12; Numbers 3:10,18:7; Deuteronomy 18:1-5; 2Chronicles 26:16-21**).

    The reason for the separation between the offices and the men is not plainly stated in the Bible but, that separation is essential to understanding the Word of God. The fact is that, above all of the other purposes that they may serve, the offices of king and priest, the men created in the image and the likeness of God, the 1st and 2nd chapters of the book of Genesis, the royal tribe of Judah and the priestly tribe of Levi, as well as both the Old and New Testaments of the bible were all purposefully crafted as prophetic details to ensure the clarity of God's personal revelation.

The Ultimate Prophecy

Without question, it is maintained throughout the Old and New Testaments that there is only one true God of gods. Yet an inquisitive bible reader should quickly discover that at many times throughout the bible God "adapts" Himself to fit the needs of a given situation.

God resolved Himself to create existence, to sustain it, and to rule over it as the King of creation. Yet within the limitations of His own creation YHWH Elohim has served in the capacity of a Parent, a Gardener, a Messenger, a Teacher, and ultimately as Israel's Redemption and Salvation. Whether it be as the Spirit of God(**Genesis 1:2**), YHWH Elohim/God(**Genesis 2:4b**), YHWH(**Isaiah 48:1-17**), the Angel of YHWH (**Genesis 22:11-12**{**Exodus 3:1-22**}) or, as YHWH of hosts/armies(**1Samuel 1:3**) in the Old Testament, and as the Son of God in the New Testament, YHWH Elohim does not simply devote Himself to functioning in various capacities. YHWH Elohim "IS(**Exodus 3:14** "I AM")" the appropriate need Who responds to the given circumstance.

The idea that the persona of YHWH Elohim is a shared identity may be a difficult concept for some men and women to accept, but the concept is supported upon the pillars of the Old Testament. For instance, in **Exodus 3:2-15** Moses encounters the angel of YHWH in a burning bush that was not being consumed, Whom identified Himself as, "The God of your fathers" and the "I AM". **Isaiah 48:1-17** shows YHWH being sent out by the Lord YHWH and His Spirit. And **Zechariah 14:9** suggests that the one identity of YHWH is composed of individual personas, when it clearly states that the day is coming when there shall be one YHWH and His name shall be one.

Zechariah 14:9
9. And YHWH shall be king over all the earth. In that day, there shall be one YHWH, and His name one.
Zechariah 14:9

The Hebrew letters that are pronounced Yod-Hey-Wav-Hey make up the "YHWH", the personal identifier of God, and appear in English translations of the bible as LORD, Yahweh, the Name, and Jehovah.

Even though it is maintained throughout the Old and New Testaments that there is one true God of gods, many people, even some of whom attend church, have misunderstood the varying facets of YHWH's persona and have even gone so far as to encourage the belief that there are two different Gods of the Bible. According to the belief, the first God, who is referred to by some as the "God of the Old Testament", is understood to be a God of wrath and judgment. The second God of this theory, who is referred to as the "God of the New Testament", is understood to be a tolerant and loving God.

The simplest way to resolve the confusion that has resulted from the different manifestations of God's persona in the Old and New testaments is to first recognize that Genesis chapters 1 and 2 are two distinct revelations of the one God of gods. As far as I know, there has not been any question about the difference between the God who is responsible for the **Genesis 1:1-2:4a** creation and YHWH Elohim who formed Adam and Eve, the animals, and Who planted the garden of Eden in **Genesis 2:4b-25**. In fact most, if not all, churches and synagogues teach that the first two chapters of the bible are two recitals of the same event. The next step to resolving the confusion, is to understand that the Genesis 1 and 2 revelations of God serve as direct models of how God interacts with His creation in both the Old and New Testaments of the Bible. By pairing God's work in **Genesis 1-2:4a** with the Old Testament and YHWH Elohim's personal involvement in **Genesis 2:4b-25** with the New Testament, a clear picture of God's revelation in both testaments begins to materialize.

Reflect for a moment on Genesis chapters 1 and 2. **In Genesis 1:1-2:4a** God can be recognized as the authoritative Creator in the Heaven of heavens commanding His work into existence. God took six days to arrange His creation according to His own will and He bestowed authority upon the men whom He had created and appointed to be His representatives/messengers, and the guardians over His created order. In the **Genesis 1:1-2:4a** creation as well as throughout the Old Testament of the Bible God is clearly recognizable as the creation's King of kings.

In **Genesis 2:7**, by personally forming Adam, planting the garden of Eden, bringing the animal life into existence, placing Adam in the garden of Eden, giving Adam responsibilities, ordaining Adam to serve as humanity's representative, and providing a helpmate for the man, YHWH Elohim is recognizable in **Genesis 2:4b-25** as humanity's benefactor.

Before Adam's sin in Genesis 3 YHWH Elohim related to him more as a Father who held Himself accountable for His son's wellbeing, than as a disciplinarian or a priest who held Himself responsible for man's atonement(Cross Reference **John 5:17**). After Adam's sin YHWH Elohim sacrificed an animal to cover Adam's nakedness and after his expulsion from the garden of Eden in **Genesis 3:1-24** YHWH Elohim personally set in motion the events that would culminate in the ultimate sacrifice being made and which would bring about humanity's eternal reconciliation(Cross Reference the Lamb of God: **Genesis 22:8; John 1:29, 36; Hebrews 9:11-16; Revelation chapter 5**). As a result of the Yeshua's death and resurrection, His ministry is reflected upon throughout the New Testament and heralded as the consummation of God's word in **Genesis 1:26** and YHWH Elohim's work(**Genesis 1:26** "Image and Likeness of God" and **2:4b-25, 1Corinthians 15:45**. Cross Reference **John 5:17, 19:30** "It is finished!") that continued on from **Genesis 2:4b**.

The distinction between the epoch of the Heavens and the Earth(**Genesis 1:1-2:4a**) and that of the earth and heaven(**Genesis 2:4b-25**), the differences between the men created in the image and the likeness of God, the separation of the offices of king and priest, the dividing ordinations between the tribes of Judah and Levi, and the manner of revelation between both the Old and New Testaments is maintained throughout the Bible because without it the message of the Holy Spirit of God could not be received. Each of these individual details ministers and corresponds with the ministry of its counterpart to ensure the clarity of the Bible's grand prophetic revelation.

Just as the scripture reveals the Author of existence in **Genesis 1:1-2:4a** to be the same God Who was responsible for Adam's life of prosperity in the garden of Eden in **Genesis 2:4b-25**, the Spirit of God also reveals the King of kings in the Old Testament to be the same High Priest who sacrificed Himself to be mankind's ultimate propitiation in the New Testament(Cross Reference **Genesis** chapters **1** and **2; Isaiah 48:1-17**).

Each pair of details of the Bible's grandest prophetic revelation serves to communicate the message of the Holy Spirit of God that, "I AM(**Exodus 3:1-14** and **John 8:58**), and there is no other(**Isaiah 43:9-11**)!".

When the details of the bible's grandest prophetic revelation are understood, the scripture reveals the One God of gods to be the King of kings over the Heavens and the High Priest of humanity upon the earth(Cross Reference **Genesis 1:1-**

2:4a and **Genesis 2:4b-25** with the Old and New Testaments).

In the New Heavens and New Earth, the servants of YHWH will all know Him and will be with YHWH where He is(**Isaiah 65:17-25, Isaiah 66:20-23; Jeremiah 31:31-34; John 17:1-26; Revelation 1:5-6, 3:7-13(v.11), 5:10, Revelation 21**). In that day, the separation between the offices of king and priest will no longer exist because the unity between the King of creation, the High Priest of humanity, and the body of the Messiah will be complete. In the day that YHWH shall rule as king over all the earth, YHWH shall be one and His name one(**Zechariah 14:7-9**).

Notes

CHAPTER 7
IN THE BEGINNING, REVELATION:
An Interesting Connection Between The Book of Revelation and The Book of Genesis

Apocalypse: A prophecy or disclosure; any remarkable revelation. **Webster's Comprehensive Dictionary**

For a number of different reasons, the of book of Revelation's inclusion in the bible has been contested over the centuries. I have talked to different people about their views on the book of Revelation and the general consensus is that the book is a mystery. When do the events in the Revelation occur? Are believers of the Messiah on the earth when the events take place? Will there be mass killings of Christians leading up to the return of the Lord? What world leader is the anti-Christ? What does "666" mean? Legitimate yet difficult to answer questions such as these and the revelation's vivid and disturbing imagery, interpretational challenges, and debates surrounding the book's authorship, are all causes for disputes over the book of Revelation having a place in the bible. These type of questions and concerns are also the reason that the book of Revelation is generally ignored by many Christians.

Personally, I like the book of Revelation and have ever since I was a young child. The imagery that is used throughout the revelation is captivating and the book's references display the author's comprehension of prophecy, the law, the psalms, and the teachings of Yeshua the Messiah. I believe that any inquiry into biblical understanding could start with the book of Revelation because as I see it, the book of Revelation is essentially a condensed version of the entire bible.

The references that are used and the imagery that is described in the book of Revelation maintain consistency with the text and imagery that is used throughout both the Old and

New Testaments of the bible. But that consistency doesn't stand alone. There are subtle prophetic patterns that saturate the biblical text, and which are not only included in but also reach their climactic conclusions in the book of Revelation.

The Bible's Prophetic Patterns

The offices of king and priest and their connection to the Old and New Testament's revelation of YHWH Elohim, is just one example of a prophetic pattern.

Another example of a subtle prophetic pattern in the text of the bible concerns the Old Testament book of Daniel. The details of this prophetic pattern validate a king's dream, authenticate the dreams interpretation, certifies the dream and its interpretation's legitimacy as a chapter of the bible, and it confirms the understanding that two distinct men were created in the opening chapters of the book of Genesis.

In the 2nd chapter of the book of Daniel, a young Judean man named Daniel who was being held captive in Babylon was asked to recall and then interpret king Nebuchadnezzar's dream. In the dream king Nebuchadnezzar saw a great image composed of four metals that were divided into five sections. The head of the image was made of gold, its breasts and arms were of silver, its belly and thighs were of bronze, its legs were made of iron, and its feet were partly of iron and partly of clay. A stone, not cut with hands, struck the image on its feet and destroyed it. All of the metals were scattered by the wind and not a trace of them was to be found(**Daniel 2:31-45**).

Daniel's interpretation of the dream revealed that the metals represented four distinct ages of human kingdoms. The golden head represented king Nebuchadnezzar's Babylonian kingdom(**Daniel 2:36-38**). According to **Daniel 5:31**(Cross Reference **Daniel 8:20**) and recorded human history the conjoined kingdoms of Media and Persia(Cross Reference Adam and Eve, **Genesis** chapters **2** and **3**) succeeded king Nebuchadnezzar's Babylonian kingdom and are represented by the silver breasts and arms of the great image in the dream. The bronze belly and thighs of the image are revealed to represent the Grecian kingdom that succeed the Medo-Persian empire(**Daniel 10:20** Cross Reference **Daniel 8:1-27{20-21}**). The fourth human kingdom, which is represented by the iron legs that terminate in the impure feet of the great image is not specifically named in the book of Daniel. But the New Testament as well as recorded human history reveal that the iron legs and impure feet of the image, which succeed the bronze belly and thighs of the Greek kingdom, belong to the ancient and the renewed Roman empire(Cross Reference **Revelation 17:1-18**).

The great metal image that is described in **Daniel** chapter **2** and how it depicts, from Daniel's perspective, future human kingdoms itself is very interesting but the dream's connection to the book of Genesis is awe inspiring, and no less than supernaturally designed. The gold, silver, bronze, iron, and iron mixed with clay that compose the great image in king Nebuchadnezzar's dream do not only represent the succession of human kingdoms; from Babylon to Medo-Persia, to Greece, to Rome. The metals and the kingdoms of men that are associated with each metal directly correspond to the successive ages of man that are described in the first six chapters of the book of Genesis.

The golden head of the great image in **Daniel 2:37-38** and Daniel's interpretation of it correspond to man's first age, when the man who had been created in the image of God was given authority over the creation in **Genesis 1:27-28**; Man's "Golden Age". Daniel's interpretation of the inferior/lower(**Daniel 2:39;** inferior/lower **H772**: Earthly) silver kingdom that succeeded the golden Babylonian kingdom in **Daniel 2:39** corresponds to the age of man/Adam who was formed from the dust of the earth in **Genesis 2:7**(**Genesis 2:7-3:24**); Man's "Silver Age". The bronze kingdom that is described in **Daniel 2:39** corresponds to the generations of Adam's descendants that are detailed in **Genesis 4:1-26**; Man's "Bronze Age". The kingdom of iron that is described in **Daniel 2:40** and the corrosion of that mighty kingdom which is represented by the iron mixed with clay in **Daniel 2:41-43** corresponds to the ancient age of man in which humanity greatly multiplied throughout the earth in **Genesis 5:1-32**, Man's "Iron Age", and later succumbed to the angelic corruption that is described in **Genesis 6:1-7,13***, "Iron mixed with Clay". The stone that struck the image on the feet in **Daniel 2:34-35, 44-45** corresponds to the judgment of God that came as a flood and wiped mankind from off the face of the earth in the days of Noah(**Genesis 7:10-24**).

*There are three earth shaking desolating abominations(Cross Reference **Daniel 9:27, 11:31; Matthew 24:15; Mark 13:14**) recorded in the Bible. The reference to the "iron mixed with clay" in **Daniel 2:41-43** represents, from Daniels perspective, the future age of the third occurrence. Although each occurrence of the desolating abomination directly targets God's chosen people(or individual man, in Adam's case) the event resonates throughout all of humanity. The first desolating abomination was perpetrated in Genesis 3 by the serpent and resulted in Adam's corruption and expulsion from the garden of Eden. The second event is recorded in Genesis 6 and describes the corruption of man by the sinful angels in the days leading up to the great flood.*

A third example of the Bible's prophetic patterns, and the focus of this chapter, involves the conversation that was had between YHWH Elohim, Adam, Eve, and the serpent in **Genesis 3:9-19**. The **Genesis 3:9-19** conversation has a direct correlation to the seven letters addressed to the seven Messianic communities in the 2nd and 3rd chapters of the book of Revelation. In addition to linking the book of Genesis with the book of Revelation this particular pattern serves to substantiate the book of Revelation's placement as the bible's concluding testament. Like all of the other prophetic patterns in the bible this particular pattern has a personal and a universal relevance. That is to say that the details of the pattern: The **Genesis 3:9-19** conversation and the **Revelation** chapters **2-3** letters; although intended for a specific audience, are relevant to all of humanity, from the past, in the present, and who will exist in the future.

Similar to the interdependence that is shared between Genesis chapters 1 and 2 there is an interesting level of correspondence between the **Genesis 3:9-19** conversation and the **Revelation** chapters **2-3** addresses. Yet, also like **Genesis 1** and **2**, each individual address(in **Genesis 3:9-19** and in **Revelation 2-3**) has its own unique message that allows it to stand on its own.

The **Genesis 3:9-19** conversation between YHWH Elohim, Adam, Eve, and the serpent is uniquely significant to humanity because it shows the origin of our sorrows, the result of our choices, and what lay in store for the entire human species. The seven letters to the seven believing communities in **Revelation** chapters **2-3** are uniquely significant to prophesy because they provide the framework for the past, present, and future history of the Messianic body and, they also describe the potential and the ineptitude that is present within all of humanity.

The GENESIS 3:9-19
And REVELATION 2-3 Connection

Adam and Eve should be understood to have been two individual flesh and blood human beings. But the message of the

Genesis 3:1-24 "Fall of Man" is universal and speaks to the human soul. **Genesis 3:1-24** recalls the moment in history that Satan gained influence over humanity and how we were collectively divested of our birthright. The passage also explains why we have been denied the truth of our common manhood and why humanity has been denied access to YHWH Elohim. In spiritual reckoning, the terms male, female, and serpent are not gender nor even species-specific terms. They are terms that describe attributes of the human soul which give personality and individuality to each of us(Cross Reference **Genesis 1:1-2:4a**).

The seven believing communities that are addressed in the 2nd and 3rd chapters of the book of Revelation were actual communities that existed in Asia Minor when the apostle John was told to record and send a copy of the Revelation of the Messiah to each of them. The letters are addressed to specific communities of believers, but each message concerns the timeless Messianic body and speaks directly to each individual Messianic devotee. Each address describes the various obstacles, successes, and/or failures that members of the Messianic community have and will continue to experience until Yeshua the Messiah returns to the earth in glory.

The **Genesis 3:9-19** and **Revelation** chapters **2-3** conversations are two interconnected dialogues. The physical nature of Adam and Eve with the spiritual overtones of Genesis 3's message directly corresponds to the spiritual nature of the Messiah's Revelation and the book's physical undertones.

*Side Note: The Revelation of Yeshua the Messiah was revealed to the apostle John while he was in the spirit on the "Lord's Day", therefore you should not expect to see physical manifestations of the four horsemen(**Revelation 6:1-8**), demon locusts(**Revelation 9:3-11**), the great red dragon(**Revelation**

12:3-4,7-17), etc., walking the streets.

In **Genesis 2:7-8, 15-19** YHWH Elohim formed a man and placed him in the garden paradise that He had made and which had two timeless trees dwelling in its midst. The man was given command of the garden and a spouse with whom to share his experience. In **Genesis 3:1-7** the man and woman, Adam and Eve, partook in the event that would alter their reality, remove them from the garden paradise, and affect the lives of all present and future generations of humanity. In the event that has come to be known as 'The Fall of Man' Eve was deceived by the serpent and she ate the forbidden fruit of the tree of knowledge of good and evil. Adam disobeyed the command that YHWH Elohim had given to him, not to eat the fruit of the tree of knowledge of good and evil, and he followed Eve into rebellion. The eyes of both Adam and Eve were "opened" and they covered themselves with the leaves of a tree in an attempt to hide their nakedness. In **Genesis 3:8** YHWH Elohim returned to the garden of Eden to speak with Adam, whom He had appointed as the garden's guardian. But, instead of finding Adam at his post, YHWH Elohim discovered Adam and Eve hiding in the midst of the garden behind the tree of knowledge of good and evil. In **Genesis 3:9** a conversation ensued in which YHWH Elohim addressed seven statements, in the form of four questions and three judgments, to Adam, Eve, and the serpent who had caused Adam and Eve to stumble.

In **Revelation 1:10-20** the apostle John, "In the spirit on the Lord's day(**Revelation 1:10**)", is told to record what things he has seen, the things which are, and the things which will occur after what he was currently observing. John's record of the events, which is the apocalypse/revelation of the Messiah, was then to be sent to seven Messianic communities within Asia minor that existed in John's day: **Ephesus, Smyrna, Pergamos, Thyatira, Sardis, Philadelphia,** and **Laodicea.** Each community received its own copy of John's letter(the book of Revelation) which included, as a portion of the revelation, a personal address to each one of the seven communities. Thus, in addition to receiving the blueprint for humanity's future and the revelation of the Lamb of God, each one of the seven communities could read Yeshua's report on the progress or impropriety within their own particular community as well as that of each of the other six believing communities.

Each address has its own unique qualities, but some have qualities in common with other letters. For instance, the letters to the religious communities within the cities of Sardis and Laodicea, the fifth and seventh addresses, are interesting among the seven because their addresses are the two of the seven that receive only negative remarks. The addresses to Smyrna's and Philadelphia's faithful communities, the second and sixth addresses, are unique among the seven letters because theirs are the only ones that have references to the synagogue of Satan(**Revelation 2:9; 3:9**) and their communities are the only ones to receive strictly positive commendations from Yeshua the Messiah. The letters to Smyrna and Philadelphia are also significant to understanding prophecy, as certain elements within their letters offer clues that reveal why only three of the seven believing communities will be directly affected by the Great Tribulation. The address to the believing community within the city of Thyatira is uniquely significant because although her address contains elements which are present in the six other addresses, her believing community literally stands alone.

The seven statements that are delivered by YHWH Elohim in **Genesis 3:9-19** and the seven addresses of Yeshua the Son of God to the seven believing communities in **Revelation** chapters **2-3**, taken together, are particularly provocative. The seven statements of YHWH Elohim in **Genesis 3:9-19** directly correspond with Yeshua's seven addresses that are delivered in **Revelation** chapters **2-3**. YHWH Elohim's first statement in **Genesis 3:9** after arriving in the garden of Eden to speak with Adam, is paralleled by Yeshua's first address in **Revelation 2:1-7** to the Messianic community within Ephesus. The second statement of YHWH Elohim in **Genesis 3:11** coincides with the address to Smyrna, the second believing community that is addressed in **Revelation 2:8-11**, and so on through each corresponding Genesis **3:9-19** statement and **Revelation 2-3** community.

The Details

The conversation between YHWH Elohim, Adam, Eve, and the serpent takes place in **Genesis 3:8-19** after Adam and Eve have submitted themselves to the serpent and eaten from the tree of knowledge of good and evil. I have numbered (**1-7**) and highlighted the four questions and three judgments in **Genesis 3:9-19** so that they are easy to recognize.

Genesis 3:8-19

8. And they heard the sound of YHWH Elohim walking up and down in the garden at the breeze of the day. And the man and his wife hid themselves from the face of YHWH Elohim in the middle of the trees of the garden.
9. And YHWH Elohim called to the man and said to him, **(1) Where are you**?
10. And he said, I have heard Your sound in the garden, and I was afraid, for I am naked, and I hid myself.
11. And He said, **(2) Who told you that you were naked? (3) Have you eaten of the tree which I commanded you not to eat**?
12. And the man said, The woman whom You gave to be with me, she has given to me of the tree, and I ate.

13. And YHWH Elohim said to the woman, **(4) What is this you have done**?, and the woman said, The serpent deceived me, and I ate.
14. And YHWH Elohim said to the serpent, **(5) Because you have done this**, you are cursed above all beasts, and above every animal of the field. You shall go on your belly, and you shall eat dust all the days of your life.
15. And I will put enmity between you and the woman, and between your seed and her seed- He will bruise your head, and you shall bruise His heel.
16. He said to the woman, **(6) I will** greatly increase your sorrow and your conception; you shall bear sons in sorrow, and your desire shall be toward your husband; and he shall rule over you.
17. And He said to the man, **(7) Because you have listened to the voice of your** wife, and have eaten of the tree about which I commanded you, saying, You shall not eat from it, the ground shall be cursed because of you; you shall eat of it in sorrow all the days of your life.
18. And it shall bring forth thorns and thistles for you, and you shall eat the plant of the field.
19. By the sweat of your face you shall eat bread until you return to the ground. For you have been taken out of it; for you are dust, and to dust you shall return.
Genesis 3:8-19

Going in sequential order the statements are addressed to 1) **Adam**, 2) **Adam/Eve** 3) **Adam**, 4) **Eve**, 5) **the Serpent**, 6) **Eve**, and 7) **Adam**.

In Revelation chapters 2 and 3 the seven believing communities that John was told in **Revelation 1:11** to send a copy of the revelation of the Messiah to, are addressed. The seven communities are addressed in the following order: (1)**Ephesus**, (2)**Smyrna**, (3)**Pergamos**, (4)**Thyatira**, (5)**Sardis**,

(6)**Philadelphia**, and (7)**Laodicea**. Pairing YHWH Elohim's seven statements from **Genesis 3:9-19** to their corresponding communities in **Revelation** chapters **2-3** results in 1) **Adam || Ephesus**; 2) **Adam/Eve || Smyrna**; 3) **Adam || Pergamos**; 4) **Eve || Thyatira**; 5) **the Serpent || Sardis**; 6) **Eve || Philadelphia**; and 7) **Adam || Laodicea**.

1.
"Ephesus, Where Are You?"
(Revelation 2:1-7, Genesis 3:9)

In **Genesis 2:15-17** YHWH Elohim had given Adam a ministry within the garden of Eden. Adam appropriately performed his duties within the garden for a time but eventually failed to uphold his greatest responsibility. Adam forfeited the kingdom of heaven, ultimately, because he was more devoted to Eve, his wife, than he was to YHWH Elohim, his Creator(Cross Reference **Luke 14:26**). YHWH Elohim reprimands Adam in **Genesis 3:17**, for submitting to the words of Eve, whose tradition(**Genesis 3:3** Cross Reference **Matthew 15:1-9**) based relation to the word of God abetted the serpent's objective, and for disregarding God's word that would have protected him from the serpent's attack(**Genesis 2:17 and 3:17; Matthew 4:1-11; Ephesians 6:10-18**).

Adam's devotion to Eve is understandable. Eve was Adam's physical, emotional, and intellectual companion. She was the feminine counterpart to his masculinity and the integral component of his identity. Adam experienced the loneliness of existence(**Genesis 2:18-20**) before Eve was presented to him in **Genesis 2:22**, and the gratification of fulfillment after he was blessed with her companionship(Cross Reference **Genesis 2:23-25**). But that same sense of fulfillment that Adam discovered in Eve is what caused him to lose appreciation for the relationship that he had with YHWH Elohim. Adam wouldn't live without Eve(Cross Reference **Matthew 16:25, Mark 8:35, Luke 9:24,**

John 12:25), and it was Adam's devotion to his existence with her that drew him away from eternal life(Cross Reference **Luke 14:26**).

In **Revelation 2:1-7** the Ephesian believing community is the first of the seven believing communities to be addressed.

Yeshua's introduction to the Ephesian community in **Revelation 2:1**, "He walking in the midst of the seven golden lamp-stands", recalls **Genesis 3:8** where YHWH Elohim, upon returning to the garden of Eden, was heard walking up and down in the garden at the breeze of the day. YHWH Elohim's first question in **Genesis 3:9**, **(1)** "Where are you", directed to Adam equates with the condemning remark of Yeshua the Messiah to the Ephesian believing community in the book of Revelation "You have left your first love(**Revelation 2:4**)".

Revelation 2:1-7

1. To the angel of the Ephesian believing community, write: These things says He holding the seven stars in His right hand, He walking in the midst of the seven golden lamp-stands:
2. I know your works, and your labor, and your patience, and that you cannot bear evil ones; and you tried those pretending to be apostles, and are not, and found them to be liars.
3. And I know you bore up, and on account of My name you have labored, and have not wearied.
4. But I have against you that you left your first love.
5. Then remember from where you have fallen, and repent, and do the first works. And if not, I am coming to you quickly, and will remove your lampstand from its place, unless you repent.
6. But you have this, that you hate the works of the Nicolaitans, which I also hate.

7. The one having an ear, hear what the Spirit says to the faithful communities. To the one overcoming, I will give to him to eat of the Tree of Life which is in the midst of the Paradise of God.
Revelation 2:1-7

Although the Lord commends the Ephesian believing community for its works and labors, they are reprimanded for failing to uphold their most important commission(Cross Reference **Deuteronomy 6:5; Matthew 22:37; Luke 14:26**); which is to love the Lord their God. The Ephesian community was not devoid of love, her religious community had "left its first love". Another love had supplanted Ephesus' love of God. Ephesus apparently became so enamored with her service and works on behalf of the kingdom of God that her relationship with her Lord suffered. Ephesus' stumbling in regard to her devotion opened the door to a corrupt end. In contrast to Adam who did not over-come the Adversary in the garden of Eden and was denied access to the Tree of Life, the one(s) who was able to overcome the circumstances separating the Ephesian believing community from a relationship with "He holding the seven stars in His right hand", is given the right to eat from the tree of life(**Revelation 2:7**).

2.
"Smyrna, Who Told You That You Were Naked?"
(Revelation 2:8-11, Genesis 3:11)

Adam and Eve were provided with spiritual, emotional, intellectual, and physical companionship, which allowed their souls to be nourished in an environment that gave them shelter, food, and work to occupy their minds and bodies. Adam was given perfection in the garden of Eden, but the serpent was able to convince Eve that she had been cheated out of something that she deserved.

After God called out to Adam, **(1)** "Where are you" in **Genesis 3:9**, Adam confessed in **Genesis 3:10**, that he was hiding because he was naked. In response to Adam's admission YHWH Elohim asked him in **Genesis 3:11**, **(2)** "Who told you that you were naked?". This question is directed at Adam, but it indirectly points to Eve who was deceived by the serpent. The serpent was ultimately guilty of exposing Adam to a compromised existence because it was he who had convinced Eve to stray from the simplicity and security of the word of God.

YHWH Elohim's second question that is directed to Adam in **Genesis 3:11**, "Who told you that you were naked?", corresponds to Smyrna, the second believing community that is addressed in the book of Revelation(**Revelation 2:8-11**).

Revelation 2:8-11

8. And to the angel of the believing community of Smyrna, write: These things says the First and the Last, who became dead, and lives:
9. I know your works, and the affliction, and the poverty; but you are rich. And I know the evil speaking of those saying themselves to be Judeans, and they are not but a synagogue of Satan.
10. Do not at all fear what you are about to suffer. Behold, the Devil is about to throw you into prison, so that you may be tried; and you will have affliction ten days. Be faithful unto death, and I will give you the crown of life.
11. The one who has an ear, hear what the Spirit says to the faithful communities. The one overcoming will not at all be hurt by the second death.

Revelation 2:8-11

Although the religious community within Smyrna was not materially affluent and suffered continual attacks, she continued to do all that she had in her power to do. Smyrna held to her faith in the word of God and thereby retained her high esteem. The letter to Smyrna is short and sweet, and the only negative remark associated with this address is directed at the synagogue of Satan.

The evil speaking of the synagogue of Satan corresponds to the deceptive words of the serpent in **Genesis 3:1-5** that prompted YHWH Elohim to ask Adam in **Genesis 3:11**, "Who told you that you were naked?". Besides their false claim of being Judeans, the evil speaking of the synagogue of Satan is not detailed in the **Revelation 2:8-11** address to Smyrna. But I believe that it is safe to assume that the synagogue of Satan's evil words, like the serpent's words to Eve in **Genesis 3:1-5**, were intended to remove Smyrna from being an obstacle on the Satanic synagogue's path to usurp the Messianic identity.

The Messianic community within Smyrna is the first of only two **Revelation 2-3** communities to have nothing negative said about it. Much like Adam and Eve before their sin, in God's eye's, the faithful community within Smyrna was perfect. I find it interesting that Smyrna's encouragement was to remain faithful even unto death. There was no prison or affliction by Satan nor evil speaking of the synagogue of Satan that could separate Smyrna's faithful community from God as long as she relied upon His word. Contrasting with her then current state of poverty and affliction, Smyrna is told to be faithful unto death and she would be given the Crown of Life(**Revelation 2:10**).

The promise that was given to the overcomer within Smyrna's faithful community, "Not to be hurt by the second death(**Revelation 2:11**)", is also a contrasting detail, as it calls to mind Adam and the end of his relationship with YHWH Elohim. Adam failed to remain faithful to the word of YHWH Elohim and became submissive to the Adversary. In the very day that Adam ate from the tree of knowledge of good and evil he died, he lost his crown and his anointed position, and he was removed from the garden paradise.

3.
"Pergamos, Have You Eaten From The Tree of Which I Commanded You Not To Eat?"
(Revelation 2:12-17, Genesis 3:11)

It's reasonable to assume that Adam did not know who or what he was supposed to protect the garden of Eden from. But he did know the God who had formed him, taken him out of his native land, and given him the responsibility to care for the garden(**Genesis 2:7-8, 15-16**). Adam may also have lacked a full appreciation for the concept of death at the time that YHWH Elohim warned him not to eat the fruit of the tree of knowledge of good and evil, but Adam did know that the fruit of the tree of knowledge of good and evil was the one thing in existence that could alter the relationship that he shared with his Creator(**Genesis 2:17**).

The tree of knowledge of good and evil is the seat of power from which the Serpent was able to gain dominance over humanity. The word of YHWH Elohim was Adam's only defense against it. YHWH Elohim's third question to Adam in **Genesis 3:11,(3)** "Have you eaten from the tree of which I commanded you not to eat?", corresponds directly to the condemning letter that was written in **Revelation 2:12-17** to the believing community within Pergamos.

Revelation 2:12-17

12. And to the angel of the believing community in Pergamos, write: These things says He having the sharp two-edged sword:
13. I know your works, and where you dwell, where the throne of Satan is. And you hold My name, and did not deny My faith even in the days in which Antipas was My faithful witness; who was killed alongside you, where Satan dwells.

14. But I have a few things against you, that you have there those holding the teachings of Balaam, who taught Balaak to throw a stumbling-block before the sons of Israel, to eat idol-sacrifices, and to commit fornication.
15. So you also have those holding the teaching of the Nicolaitans, which thing I hate.
16. Repent! But if not, I will come to you quickly, and I will make war with them with the sword of My mouth.
17. The one who has an ear, hear what the Spirit says to the faithful communities. To the one overcoming, I will give to him a white stone, and on the stone a new name having been written, which no one knows except he receiving.

Revelation 2:12-17

The believing community within Pergamos existed where the throne of Satan was, and it suffered from continual attacks. Pergamos showed some resilience but still, her believing community let its guard down in the midst of a hostile environment. She compromised and allowed the teachings of Balaam and the Nicolaitans(**Revelation 2:14-15**) to infiltrate and influence her. She failed to rely entirely on the word of God and as a result she, like Adam, forfeited her God given identity. In **Revelation 2:16** Pergamos is spoken to as an adversary and told to repent of the corruption that had infiltrated her community or else the Lord would come upon her quickly and make war against her with the sword of His mouth(Cross Reference **Ephesians 6:17; Hebrews 4:12**). Hope, in the form of a new name and identity, is given in **Revelation 2:17** to the one(s) who could overcome the corruption within Pergamos and cling to the word of God. That promise, to the over-comer in Pergamos' believing community calls to mind Seth, Adam's third son who was born in **Genesis 4:25** after Cain had murdered Abel. Seth was in many ways a new beginning and a new identity for humanity.

4.
"Thyatira, What Is This You Have Done?"
(Revelation 2:18-29, Genesis 3:13)

God's fourth question from the Genesis 3(**Genesis 3:13**) confrontation in the garden of Eden, (**4**) "What is this you have you done?" is directed to Eve. Eve's sincere desire for understanding was taken advantage of and her assertive nature succumbed to the wiles of the Devil(Cross Reference **Ephesians 6:11**). It is clear from the conversation between YHWH Elohim and the three guilty parties in Genesis 3 that God knew exactly what Eve had done, but it was not clear if Eve comprehended the consequences of her actions. In addition to undermining Adam's leadership and upsetting the natural balance between the masculine and feminine qualities within the human soul, Eve served as the mediator between Satan and Adam. She thereby fostered the corruption that would overtake humanity and God's creation. YHWH Elohim's fourth question, that is addressed to Eve in **Genesis 3:13**, "What is this you have done?", is in itself interesting. For one thing, it is the first of YHWH Elohim's seven statements to be addressed directly to someone other than Adam. YHWH Elohim's question to Eve is also the dividing point between YHWH Elohim's four questions and His three judgments that follow. These points gain a greater degree of significance when their correspondence to Thyatira's believing community(**Revelation 2:18-29**) and the prophetic relevance of both addresses are taken into consideration.

Revelation 2:18-29

18. And to the angel of the believing community in Thyatira, write: These things says the Son of God, He having His eyes as a flame of fire, and His feet like burnished metal:
19. I know your works, and the love, and the ministry, and the faith, and your patience, and your works; and the last more than the first.
20. But I have a few things against you, that you allow the woman Jezebel to teach, she saying herself to be a prophetess, and to cause My slaves to go astray, and to commit fornication, and to eat idol-sacrifices.
21. And I gave time to her that she might repent of her fornication. And she did not repent.
22. Behold, I am throwing her into a bed, and those committing adultery with her into great tribulation, unless they repent of their works.
23. And I will kill her children with death; and all the communities will know that I am He searching the inner parts and hearts. And I will give to each of you according to your works.
24. But I say to you and to the rest in Thyatira, as many as do not have this teaching, and who do not know the deep things of Satan, as they say; I am not casting another burden on you;
25. But what you have, hold until I shall come.
26. And the one overcoming, and the one keeping My works until the end, I will give him authority over the nations,
27. And he will shepherd them with an iron staff, as the vessels of a potter they are broken to pieces, as I also have received from My Father.
28. And I will give to him the morning star.
29. The one who has an ear, hear what the Spirit says to the faithful communities.

Revelation 2:18-29

Thyatira had a few positive things said about her but, ultimately, she is guilty of mixing earthly aspirations with her heavenly commission. Thyatira allowed the teachings of Jezebel, a false prophetess(Cross Reference **Genesis 3:6-7, 1Kings** chapters **18-19**), to influence her community. She aspired to a powerful position in the world and, seeking that position apart from the truth of God's word that had been revealed to her, many within Thyatira's religious community delved into the mysteries of Satan.

    The reference to the "deep things/mysteries of Satan" in **Revelation 2:24** connects the worldly element within Thyatira to Eve who sought the hidden knowledge that was offered to her by the serpent. A brilliant, wise, and cunningly persuasive(**Genesis 3:1**) individual, who is an astute economist(**Ezekiel 28:16-18**) and a powerful spiritual entity with aspirations to not only exceed his peers in excellence but to replace YHWH Elohim as the sole authority figure over the creation(**Isaiah 14:13-14**) could only make for an attractive god to any mind that is ignorant of the Truth. Power attracts, and what power attracts it consumes. It only follows that the individuals within Thyatira(as well as those without) who were practiced in the mysteries/deep things of Satan would aspire to usurp the Messianic identity and seat themselves as the standard of righteousness(**Matthew 23:9** "Call no man your father upon the earth") and human authority(Cross Reference **Genesis 3:4-5, 3:17**, and the "Synagogue of Satan" **Revelation 2:9, 3:9**). In time and out of necessity these adepts in the Satanic arts would work to establish a "new" self-serving "truth/good" and to redefine the human identity in their own image and according to their own likeness(Cross Reference **Romans 1:18-32** and "The Abomination of Desolation" **Daniel 9:27, 12:11; Matthew 24:15**). By circumventing the ministry of the Spirit of God(Cross Reference **John 16:13-15**), adulterating God's word, subduing humanity to idol gods, and mediating between man and the Word of Truth these "Christian" ministers of

Satan(Cross Reference **Genesis 3:1-5, Revelation 13:11-18**) would imprison the hearts and minds of millions of men and women around the world.

Thyatira followed Eve's example from Genesis 3 by seeking clarity from a source other than the rightful head of her believing community. And like most, if not all men and women, the greatest obstacle for Thyatira to overcome is to see herself as she truly is. In **Revelation 2:26-28**, contrasting with the worldly authority that Thyatira sought after, true and everlasting power that can only come from the God of gods is promised to the one(s) who could overcome the circumstances within Thyatira that separated her religious community from the Truth.

5.
"Sardis, Because You Have Done This..."
(Revelation 3:1-6, Genesis 3:14-15)

Adam and Eve were apparently caught off guard by the serpent's temptation. And after their eyes were opened they hid, fearful of the condition that YHWH Elohim would find them in(**Genesis 3:7-8**). The serpent, on the other hand, acted confidently and was purposefully defiant of God when he deceived Eve and caused Adam to be alienated from his Creator. The serpent had no excuse for his actions and was not given the opportunity to offer a defense. In **Genesis 3:14-19** YHWH Elohim moved on from the questioning portion of the trial, and, beginning with the serpent, judgments were handed out to the three guilty parties. YHWH Elohim's judgment upon the serpent in **Genesis 3:14-15** began with, (**5**) "Because you have done this" and coincides with Yeshua's judgment upon Sardis' religious community in **Revelation 3:1-6**.

Revelation 3:1-6

1. And to the angel of the believing community in Sardis, write: These things says He having the seven Spirits of God, and the seven stars: I know your works, that you have the name that you live, but you are dead.
2. Be watching, and establish the things left, which are about to die. For I have not found your works being fulfilled before God.
3. Then remember how you received and heard, and keep, and repent. If, then, you do not watch, I will come upon you like a thief, and you will not at all know what hour I come upon you.
4. You also have a few names in Sardis which did not defile their robes, and they shall walk with Me in white because they are worthy.
5. The one overcoming, this one shall be clothed in white garments, and I will not at all blot out his name of the Book of Life; and I will acknowledge his name before My Father, and before His angels.
6. The one who has an ear, hear what the Spirit says to the faithful communities.

Revelation 3:1-6

Sardis was an apostate community. Her address in **Revelation 3:1-6** contradicts the perspective of every Christian man and woman who believes that the Church body will watch the devastating events that are unveiled in the later chapters of the book of Revelation, from a safe distance(Cross Reference "You" in **Matthew 24:4-25** with **Revelation 6:1-8:1**; the seven-sealed scroll). In **Revelation 3:1** Yeshua begins his address to Sardis by identifying Himself as the One "having the seven Spirits of God(**Isaiah 11:2**)", which is the complete Spirit of Life, Wisdom, Understanding, Counsel, Might, Knowledge, and the Fear of YHWH(**Isaiah 11:2**). Then in his next breath, Yeshua equates the religious community within Sardis to the serpent who misrepresented himself as a messenger of the truth to Eve in the garden of Eden. Sardis' religious community was dead and void of the light and life of God and, her apostate community did not have a share in the Messianic identity.

    Yeshua's allusion in **Revelation 3:3** to His unexpected return to judge the earth, furthers the connection between Sardis' believing community and the serpent who was judged in **Genesis 3:14-15** when YHWH Elohim returned unexpectedly to the garden of Eden. But contrary to the serpent, who is destined to spend eternity in the lake of fire(Cross Reference **Revelation 20:10**), the over-comer within Sardis' believing community is promised not to have his/her name blotted out of the book of life(**Revelation 3:5; 20:12-15**).

6.
"Philadelphia, I Will..."
(Revelation 3:7-13, Genesis 3:16)

    Eve was innocent and sincere in her desire to know the Word of God. And although she was deceived by the serpent because she did not have a full appreciation of the Word, she was not condemned by YHWH Elohim for her ignorance. Eve was guilty of naively overstepping Adam's anointed distinction and she was held accountable for establishing an identity apart from the head of her community(Cross Reference **Ephesians 5:23**). Therefore, YHWH Elohim's pronouncement, in **Genesis 3:16**, upon Eve does not begin with, "Because you have done this" like His judgments upon the serpent and Adam, who sinned while in full knowledge of God's command. God simply states how Eve, and womanhood, is destined to carry on from that day forth.

    Although she was sincere in her desire to know the truth of God's word, Eve's blind faith in the serpent made her a liability(**Genesis 3:1-6** Cross Reference **Matthew 15:14, 24:11; 1John 2:18**). Her susceptibility to the serpent's temptation, at the very least, suggests that faith in the word of YHWH Elohim must be accompanied by a fair measure of understanding.

Eve(**Genesis 3:1-7**) and the subsequent discipline that she received from YHWH Elohim in **Genesis 3:16** actually contrasts with a number of the elements of the **Revelation 3:7-13** address to the faithful community within Philadelphia. Eve had been formed to be a faithful supporter/pillar of the word of YHWH Elohim and companion to the head of her community, but she failed. Philadelphia's faithful community exemplifies the identity that Eve was created to follow in.

Revelation 3:7-13

7. And to the angel of the believing community in Philadelphia, write: These things says the Holy One, the True One having the key of David, He opening, and no one shuts, and shuts and no one opens;
8. I know your works. Behold, I have given a door being opened before you, and no one is able to shut it, for you have a little power and have kept My word and have not denied My name.
9. Behold, I will make them of the synagogue of Satan those saying themselves to be Judeans, and they are not, but they lie; behold, I will make them come and bow down before your feet, and they shall know that I have loved you.
10. Because you kept the word of My patience, I also will keep you out of the hour of trial which is going to come on all the habitable world in order to try those dwelling on the earth.
11. Behold, I am coming quickly. Hold what you have that no one take your crown.
12. The one overcoming, I will make him a pillar in the temple of My God, and he shall not go out anymore. And I will write the name of My God on him, and the name of the city of My God, the new Jerusalem which

comes down out of Heaven from My God, and My new name.
13. The one who has an ear, hear what the Spirit says to the faithful communities.
Revelation 3:7-13

The Messianic community within Philadelphia knew, understood, and trusted the word of God. Her faithful community is commended for its works and, because Philadelphia patiently waited for her Lord's return she is promised to be kept from the hour of trial which was prophesied to come upon the peoples of the earth. Philadelphia's believing community possesses a crown of authority(**Revelation 3:11**), and the over-comer within Philadelphia is promised to be made an unmovable pillar in the temple of God(**Revelation 3:12**). Contrary to Eve who established an identity apart from Adam and lost her place near God, the faithful community within Philadelphia is assured of her place in eternity because her identity is secured in the name of God and in the city of God which comes down out of Heaven.

7.
"Laodicea, Because You Have Listened to The Voice of Your..."
(Revelation 3:14-22, Genesis 3:17-19)

The final of YHWH Elohim's seven statements to the three guilty parties was directed in **Genesis 3:17-19** to Adam and corresponds to **Revelation 3:14-22** which is addressed to the religious community within Laodicea. In Genesis 2 Adam was given life, a relationship with his Creator, paradise, and an occupation(**Genesis 2:7-8, 15-20**). But, it was not until **Genesis 2:23**, after Adam was presented with Eve and he exclaimed, "At last, flesh of my flesh, and bone of my bone", that he was able to find contentment in the life that he had been blessed to receive. Eve came to be such a vital part of Adam's existence that he willingly forsook his God given designation to follow her into rebellion against the word of YHWH Elohim(**Genesis 3:6,17**). Ironically, in **Genesis 3:12** Adam, when faced with the consequences of his choice, laid the responsibility for his sin on YHWH Elohim who had given him life and his anointing, and upon Eve whom he loved.

The failure of Adam's ministry, his disparaging witness, indecisiveness(Cross Reference **Matthew 6:24; Luke 16:13**), disloyalty, negligence, self-preservation(**Matthew 16:25, Mark 8:35**), and the resulting judgment upon him directly coincide with Yeshua's Judgment in **Revelation 3:14-22** upon the apostate religious community within the city of Laodicea.

Revelation 3:14-22

14. And to the angel of the believing community of Laodicea, write: These things says the Amen, the faithful and true Witness, the Head of the creation of God:
15. I know your works, that you are neither cold nor hot. I would that you were cold or hot.
16. So because you are lukewarm, and neither cold nor hot, I am about to vomit you out of My mouth.
17. Because you say, I am rich, and I am made rich, and I have need of nothing, and do not know that you are wretched and miserable and poor and blind and naked.
18. I advise you to buy from Me gold having been fired by fire, that you may be rich; and white garments, that you may be clothed, and your shame and nakedness may not be revealed. And anoint your eyes with eye-salve, that you may see.
19. I, as many as I love, I rebuke and I chasten. Be zealous, then, and repent.
20. Behold, I stand at the door and knock: If anyone hears My voice and opens the door, I will go in to him, and I will dine with him, and he with Me.

21. The one overcoming, I will give to him to sit with Me in My throne, as I also overcame and sat with My Father in His throne.
22. The one who has an ear, hear what the Spirit says to the faithful communities.
Revelation 3:14-22

Similar to the address in **Revelation 3:1-6** given to Sardis' religious community, the letter to the Laodiceans contains only negative remarks(Cross Reference **Genesis 3:14-15** and **Genesis 3:17-19**, YHWH Elohim's judgments upon the serpent and Adam.). Nothing good could be said of Laodicea's believing community because she had found serenity in her own self-image and had become complacent in her ministry(**Revelation 3:15-16**). Like Adam and Eve, whose eyes were "opened" after they had eaten the forbidden fruit in Genesis chapter 3, Laodicea appeared before God wretched, miserable, poor, blind, and naked. Unlike Adam who hid in **Genesis 3:8** when he heard the sound of YHWH Elohim walking in the garden of Eden, Laodicea stood proudly, albeit ignorantly, defiant in the face of the Truth. Laodicea placed her trust in the opulence that she may have initially regarded as a blessing from God(Cross Reference **Genesis 2:23**, Adam's response to being presented with Eve.). But it is that same opulence that became the barrier which stood between Laodicea's religious community and a relationship with God. Yeshua the Messiah stood outside of Laodicea's religious community knocking, thus indicating that none within had a share in His Light or Life. A ray of hope is given to the overcomer within the community. The one(s) who could overcome the deprivation(**Revelation 3:17** Cross Reference **Luke 14:26** in light of **Matthew 6:31-33**) within the Laodicean community and come to the Truth, is promised communion with God and a place with Him in His throne(**Revelation 3:20-21**).

The correlation between the seven statements in **Genesis 3:9-19** and the seven letters to the seven believing communities in the 2nd and 3rd chapters of the book of Revelation serves to substantiate the Revelations placement as the Bible's final testament. That correspondence also collaborates with the correspondence existing between the Old and the New Testament accounts of God meeting with His chosen people on a mountain top(**Exodus 20** and **Matthew 5**) to deliver the keys to the kingdom, and thereby reaffirms the supernatural identity of Yeshua the Messiah(Cross Reference the chapter titled "God the King, God the Priest" in this book; **Zechariah 14:9**).

The Progression of The Believing Communities

Each address to the seven Revelation chapters 2-3 communities has the ability, like the Bible, to speak to man on many different levels. The seven Revelation chapters 2-3 Messianic communities were actual communities existing in real cities at the time that the Revelation was recorded. Each letter addressed real issues that were pertinent to the recipient community's particular circumstances. The letters were addressed to the community as a whole, but they spoke directly to each individual Messianic devotee. Each man and woman was notified of detrimental behaviors, that they may have been participating in and that effected their community's relationship with God. Each individual was also given encouragement and the opportunity to overcome those circumstances. Yeshua's assessments were honest and even though his words could and may be taken offensively, they need to be taken personally by each and every past, present, and future Messianic believer(Cross Reference **Philippians 2:12**. Recognize that the Bible is addressed the Messianic body but more importantly, recognize that it is addressed to YOU.).

The book of Revelation is, like the rest of the Bible, a prophetic text, and God is able to speak to man through it. The seven **Revelation** chapters **2-3** communities are a significant part of that prophetic revelation. Their message, similar to how the **Genesis 3:9-19** conversation gives a prophetic description of humanity's future on the earth, resonates throughout history as a time-line revealing the past history and future destiny of the Messianic community.

Recognizing the prophetic significance of the seven Revelation chapters 2-3 communities leads a Bible student to understanding why certain members of the Messianic body will be on the earth during the time period referred to in **Matthew 24:4-8** as the "Beginning of Sorrows(Cross Reference **Luke 21:7-22; Revelation 6:1-8**)". That recognition also explains why many members of the Messianic body will experience the "Time of Jacob's Trouble" and the "Times of the nations/gentiles"(**Jeremiah 30:7{Zechariah 14:1-2}; Matthew 23:31-39, 24:4-14; Mark 13:3-23; Luke 21:5-24**). Understanding reveals that some Messianic communities will exist on the earth throughout the time of the earth's "Great Tribulation(**Matthew 24:21-25; Revelation 13:1-18** Cross Reference **Revelation 2:22; Revelation 14:12-13**)" and during the time of man's final "Desolating Abomination(**Daniel 9:27, 12:11; Matthew 24:15; Mark 13:14**)".

Functioning in the capacity of details, the seven Revelation chapters 2-3 communities serve to describe the complete, past, present, and future experience of the Messianic body. Each address to the communities serves as one detail of the Messianic body's personal revelation and reveals its development from the so-called "Apostolic age" up to the "Apostate age" of the modern Christian Church. Each individual community also assists in the description of the Messianic body's progression by serving as one portion of a "Visual Aide".

The Complete Body

In **Revelation 1:11-20** the seven believing communities that the apostle John was told to send the revelation of Yeshua the son of God to, are represented as seven candles. The seven candles are distinct, but they are also all connected at their foundations. The seven individual lights are each a branch of one complete(7) menorah(Cross Reference **Exodus 25:31-37**; **Revelation 1:12, 20**). If you're not able to picture it in your mind, do an internet search for a "seven-branch menorah".

The menorah has four branches. Three of the four branches are parallel, and running east to west, make up the upper, middle, and lower branches of the menorah. The three parallel branches are supported upon the fourth and center branch which runs north to south and is itself supported upon a base. The six ends of the three parallel branches and the top of the center branch each hold one candle. Totaling seven candles. Each candle at the end of each branch of the menorah represents one of the seven believing communities that are addressed in the 2nd and 3rd chapters of the book of Revelation(**Revelation 1:20** Cross Reference **Exodus 25:31-37**).

The believing community within Ephesus is one end of the lowest and longest branch of the menorah that extends through the center branch and reaches to Laodicea at the other end of their shared branch. Smyrna is one end of the middle branch, which is shorter than the first but longer than the third branch, that extends through the center branch and reaches to Philadelphia at the opposite end of their shared branch. Pergamos is one end of the third, upper, and shortest branch of the menorah which extends through the center branch and reaches to Sardis at the opposite end of their shared branch. Thyatira stands alone as the center branch through which the three former branches -Ephesus, Smyrna, and Pergamos- pass through before culminating in their latter ends -Sardis, Philadelphia, and Laodicea(Cross Reference **Exodus 25:31-37**;

Revelation 1:12, 20).

In addition to the visual aide of the menorah, there are details within the dialogues of each pair of corresponding communities that link each to the other. For example: Smyrna and Philadelphia are opposite ends of one branch on the menorah. The crowns that are mentioned in both addresses are one correlating detail linking the two corresponding communities together. The crown that is promised to Smyrna in **Revelation 2:10** on the former end of their shared branch is in Philadelphia's possession of at the latter end of their branch in **Revelation 3:11**. The reference to the synagogue of Satan is another correlating detail connecting Smyrna to Philadelphia.

Each branch's former and later communities share characteristics, and their addresses share details that should be understood to involve more than simple correspondence. The fact is that the former communities of the menorah actually progress/mature into the latter communities on their respective branches. The faithful branch(Smyrna-Philadelphia) continued in faith but, the communities that relied on their works or allowed false doctrine to influence their communities at their former ends were worse off at their latter ends(Cross Reference **2Peter 2:20**). The details linking each corresponding pair of communities may not be as obvious as Smyrna and Philadelphia's "crown" but, Yeshua's description of each corresponding community's characteristics do reveal the progression/maturation. For example, Ephesus' devotion to its service("You left your first love." **Revelation 2:4**) matured into Laodicea's pride and self-reliance. The pairings and progressions of the Revelation 2-3 communities are as follows: the **1st** and **7th** communities, **Ephesus||Laodicea**; the **2nd** and **6th** communities, **Smyrna||Philadelphia**; and the **3rd** and **5th** communities, **Pergamos||Sardis**. The **4th** community, **Thyatira**, stands on its own as the center branch through which the former community of the branches are filtered and pass through before culminating in their latter ends.

Positioned in the midst of the seven Revelation 2-3 communities Thyatira acts as the "bridge" or "filter" through which the three former communities mature into the three latter. Thus, Thyatira intermediates between two distinct groups of communities. The two groups are further distinguished by a notable reference that is present in four of the seven letters, as well as by the orientation of two closing statements that are found in each one of the seven letters. In respect to the notable reference and the orientation of the two statements, Thyatira sits, like Eve did in the garden of Eden, in the position of intermediary. Thyatira's branch on the menorah has an association with the former community of branches and according to prophetic reckoning her believing community has existed from ancient times. But Thyatira is grouped with the latter communities by their shared references to the "Great Tribulation" and the orientation of each of their "Promise to the over-comer" statements. The letters to Thyatira, Sardis, Philadelphia, and Laodicea all include references to the "Great Tribulation" and, in each of their addresses the "Promise to the overcomer" statement precedes Yeshua's command to "Hear what the Spirit says to the communities". Just the opposite is true of the letters to Ephesus, Smyrna, and Pergamos. In the letters to Ephesus, Smyrna, and Pergamos, Yeshua's command to "Hear what the Spirit says to the communities" precedes the "Promise to the overcomer" statement and, none of these three addresses contain a reference to the "Great Tribulation".

The references to the "Great Tribulation" in the addresses to Thyatira, Sardis, Philadelphia, and Laodicea should cause all prophecy minded congregations(At least those holding pre-tribulation, mid-tribulation, and post-tribulation "Rapture" perspectives.) to pause and possibly reconsider their perspectives concerning the catching away, or the "Rapture", of the Messianic body.

Yeshua's sermon in **Matthew 24** concerning the prophetic "End Times" includes the warnings in verses **4** and **25** to "Take heed that no man deceives you...Behold, I have told you before(Cross Reference **Mark 13:5-23; Luke 21:8**)". Yeshua cautions His disciples to watch, to recognize, and to understand the times for many false Messiahs and false mediators professing to represent the word of God will go about and will deceive humanity(**Genesis 3:1-7** Cross Reference **Matthew 24:24; 2Corinthians 11:13-15**). These cautionary statements more than imply that members of the Messianic body will be on the earth during the prophetic "End Times". Yeshua's warnings should be understood to predict the existence of the multifaceted Church organization and to explain the confusion that is continually disseminated by the Church organization's many constituents and false prophets.

According to the book of Revelation, members of the Messianic body will exist on the earth up to the time that the "Vine of the earth is gathered and thrown into the wine-press of the great anger of God(**Revelation 14:17-20**)". Of the four addresses that have references to the "Great Tribulation" only the faithful community within Philadelphia is promised to be kept from that time. Thyatira, Sardis, and Laodicea, the three other members of Revelation 2-3's latter group of communities, do not receive any such exemption from those days. Philadelphia and Thyatira's communities can actually be understood to "bracket" the final age of the earth's submission to Satanic authority. Philadelphia is promised to be removed prior to "the hour of trial that is coming upon the whole earth(**Revelation 3:10**)", and Thyatira's believing community will exist on the earth throughout the time of the earth's great tribulation(**Revelation 14:12-13**) and man's final desolating abomination. Thyatira continues in the world up to the time that the Son of man comes to reap His meager harvest in **Revelation 14:14-16**. Thyatira's religious community is the final believing community to be removed from the earth(Cross reference **Revelation 11:13** and **13:7-10** "Sardis and Laodicea").

Genesis Revelation Conclusion

I find it interesting that the Bible begins with God revealing Himself to Adam in **Genesis 1:1-2:4a** and that it closes with God revealing "Adam" to himself in opening chapters of the book of Revelation. Boiled down to their fundamental messages, the Old and New Testaments of the Bible are basically the story of these two revelations(Cross Reference **Luke 17:21** "The Kingdom of God is within you"). Looking up and out from **Genesis 1:1-2:4a** we can see the majesty of the creation as evidence of a wise, almighty, beneficent, and righteous God. Looking down and in at **Revelation 2:1-3:22** we can understand the individual lives that we live as the evidence of our place in eternity(**Philippians 2:12**).

Although man's existence on earth began earlier, Humanity's portion of life's story essentially began in the garden of Eden. Mankind's history of confusion, conflict, and sorrow vindicate Adam's prophetic observation when in **Genesis 3:20**, before she had even given birth to her first child, he prophesied and declared Eve to be "The mother of all living". Humanity has in the past and continues up to this day to follow in the example set by our early ancestors. Yeshua's prophetic assessment in Revelation chapters 2-3 of the complete Messianic body is no less accurate.

Two fruit bearing trees exist(ed) in the midst of the garden of God(**Genesis 2:9**), having the power to affirm or to redefine man's God given nature. Adam was then, as mankind is today, given his choice of those two trees. Whether ignorantly or in full knowledge of our choice, we all eat from one tree or the other.

In consideration of the fact that Eve is the mother of all living and Adam is our father, the pertinent questions becomes, "Which Adam, the first one or the last(1Corinthians 15:45), will define your identity in the presence of the Most High God(**Revelation 20:11-15** Cross Reference **Genesis 3:1-24**)?"

Notes

CHAPTER 8
God, Satan, and Man:
Reflecting on The Beginning and Looking Toward The End.

Is God, consciousness, choice, desire, expectation, man, or the Devil to blame for all of humanities woes? Where does the responsibility for Adam's sin in the garden of Eden end for one party and begin for another? Does the story of Man involve more than one deadly choice? If eternity is truly written in our hearts(**Ecclesiastes 3:11**, "**World**", **H5769{Olawm}**: "**Eternity**" translated as "**World**" in many texts), then do we actually have the freedom of choice or are we are just given the opportunity to experience the trials and tribulations of life that serve as the evidence of our place in eternity?

For every conceivable distinction that sets humanity at variance with itself, one unshakable truth has always held fast. We are all ignorant. And in an ignorant mind the Truth itself becomes subject to the measure of that mind's ability to relate to it. Because we are all ignorant we are also, every one of us, slaves. Therefore, being ignorant and being slaves -whether to God, the Devil, our own passions, or to the will of others- what assurances, if we need them, do we have that we are submitted to the power and authority whose very existence is the standard of Truth that established and defines reality?

Proof of God's power and authority, and evidence of God's(or a god's) reliability lies in His ability to accomplish His stated will, aka His word(**Genesis 1:1-2:4a; Isaiah 55:8-11; 2Peter 1:16-21** Cross Reference **Isaiah 14:13-14**). Through time, language barriers, uninspired interpretations, and man-made alterations, the Old and New Testaments of the bible are able to communicate God's stated will. For validation, the quality of God's word can be checked against historical events and humanity's present-day circumstances.

Humanity's power to see, understand, and relate to either one experience or to the combined effect of all the experiences that define our lives, is founded within our spirit(**Job 32:8; Isaiah 29:10-14; Daniel 5:11-12; Romans 11:8; 1Corinthians 2:10-12** Cross Reference **John 16:13**). Whether it be the Spirit of YHWH Elohim or one of many Satanic apparitions, the spirit that is within each of us is the foundation and driving force of who we are and of how we each see, understand, and relate to the circumstances that constitute our personal experience. The evidence that we have to determine what kind of spirit is within each of us lies not only in our individual responses to life's circumstances but more importantly, in our personal response to the Word of God. Therefore, being slaves to the spirit that is within each us, and as it is exemplified by Eve's confrontation with the serpent in the garden of Eden(Cross Reference **Romans 6:16**), what assurances can we have that we are personally able to receive the message of God's word(Cross Reference **Genesis 3:1-24; Revelation** chapters **2-3**)?

Confusion dilutes the influence that the word of God is able to have within man and it gives Satan the opportunity to question God's reliability(Cross Reference **Genesis 3:1-5**). It is important to recognize that Satan did not gain his power over humanity by scaring us into submission. The deceiver appeared to Eve, in her time of weakness, as an angel of light(**2 Corinthians 11:12-15**) who had been ordained to mediate between her and the word of Truth(Cross Reference Adam, his role in the garden of Eden, and why his sin affected all of humanity). Satan gained Eve's trust and convinced her to follow his standard by enabling her to stand, in defiance of the Truth, enlightened upon a relative truth(Cross Reference **Genesis 3:1-7**; Cross Reference the prideful man and the anointed cherub: **Isaiah 14:13-14; Ezekiel 28:11-19**).

Adam was not ignorant of the word of God and he was not deceived by the serpent. Adam stood before YHWH Elohim as the representative of the human race, he fell from grace and lost his position of anointing because he chose to compromise the Truth that he had received.

Adam and Eve are the definitive examples of the universal qualities that are present within all of mankind. They represent who humanity is as a species and, their confrontation in the garden of Eden with the old serpent(**Revelation 12:9, 20:2**) is a precise depiction of the timeless battle waged within each of our souls for dominance over our individual spirits(Cross Reference **Matthew 4:1-11; Mark 1:12-13; Luke 4:1-13**). In a very dynamic way, the spirit which resides within each man and woman serves in the capacity of the cherubim who were placed before the garden of Eden in **Genesis 3:24**, to bar Adam's reentry. The spirit(or cherubim) within each of us mediates between us and the Word of Truth, which is the "Flaming Sword" that was placed in **Genesis 3:24** to guard the way to the Tree of Life. The spirit of man(Cross Reference **Genesis 2:17** and **Genesis 3:1-24**), as a result of Adam's sin, cannot apprehend the Spirit of God(**1Corinthians 2:11** Cross Reference **John 16:13; Romans 11:8; Revelation** chapters **2-3**) any more than a dead man can comprehend the Word of Life(Cross Reference **John 10:24-31**). It is because of this that the Word of God has remained unknown within the Church conglomerate as well as within the world at large. The truth of the matter is the Christian Church organization's modern derivatives of its same old erroneous interpretations, doctrines, traditions, and practices have done more to conceal than they could ever do to reveal the Truth of God's word.

When I was young and completely ignorant, I accepted the Christian Church and the Jewish Synagogue as God's proving ground. I believed that the men, women, and children who wanted to know God first needed to prove themselves in either community of God's servants to gain God's acceptance. Now that I am older and more mature, I understand that although each group has traditions and traditional doctrines dating back hundreds of years, neither group, the Church nor the Synagogue, has a relationship with God's revealed Word. I take the fact that neither group is willing to come to God on God's terms(**Matthew 11:12** Cross Reference **Matthew 5:20**{**Exodus 20:18-21**}) but instead, as if to spite the Spirit of Truth(Cross Reference **John 16:13**{**Jeremiah 7:23-28; Matthew 23:30-39**}), each group has clung to and lifted up their own private interpretations and their traditions concerning the Word of God(**Mark 7:6-9** Cross Reference **2Peter 1:18-21**{**Genesis 3:3**}).

The Days of Noah

The blind eye and the deaf ear that the world has turned to the word of God was long ago prophesied to overtake all of humanity in the days leading up to Yeshua's return to the earth

In **Matthew 24:37-39** and **Luke 17:26-30** Yeshua the Son of God makes a comparison between the men and women who will be living during the prophesied "End Times", the men and women who were living in days of Noah prior to the great flood, and the inhabitants of Sodom, Gomorrah and the cities of the plain, who were living in the days leading up to their destruction. **Genesis 6:1-13** and **Genesis 19:1-26** are the verses that describe the depraved state of humanity in the days of Noah and the perverse conditions existing within the cities of Sodom, Gomorrah, and the cities of the plain.

Genesis 6:1-13 recalls that in Noah's day mankind pursued perverse affinities and submitting to wickedness, contemplated only evil all the day long(**Genesis 6:5**). **Genesis 18:17-21** tells readers that the outcry against Sodom, Gomorrah, and the cities of the plain had reached up to heaven and that

YHWH had come down to see if the cry against the cities was justified. In **Genesis 19:1-25** two angels had come to Sodom where Lot entreated them to come into his home. Then the men, young and old, and other people of the village gathered at Lot's door demanding that Lot send his newly arrived visitors out to them, so that they could take turns raping them.

In both cases, in the days of Noah and in the cities of the plains, the wickedness of man was eventually punished. The great flood destroyed man in the days of Noah and fire from heaven came down and consumed Sodom, Gomorrah, and the cities of the plain. The limits of God's grace and mercy had been exceeded.

Both histories are graphic and very provocative. Only so much attention has been given to the depraved conditions of those times that most bible readers take the New Testament's references to those days completely out of context. Christians often imagine the prophetic "End Times" to be defined by kidnappers, human traffickers, liars, thieves, rapists, murderers, sexual perversion, depredation, strife, wars, and worldwide governmental abuses of power, genetic manipulation, and germ warfare(Right!?!) but, the references in **Matthew 24:37-39** and **Luke 17:26-30** to the "Days of Noah" and the "day that Lot went out of Sodom" are not nearly as focused on man's sinful nature as much as they are focused on humanities blindness to its coming judgment. **Matthew 24:37-39** and **Luke 17:26-30** simply make a comparison between man's blindness in ancient times to the blindness of man during the prophesied End Times.

Matthew 24:37-39
37. But as the Days of Noah, so also will be the coming of the Son of Man.
38. For as they were in the days before the flood: eating and drinking, marrying and giving in marriage, until the day Noah went into the ark,

39. And did not know until the flood came and took all away, so also will the coming of the Son of Man be. **Matthew 24:37-39**

and,

Luke 17:26-30

26. And as it was in the days of Noah, so also will it be in the days of the Son of Man.
27. They were eating, drinking, marrying, and giving in marriage, until the day Noah went into the ark, and the flood came and destroyed all.
28. And likewise, as it was in the days of Lot, they were eating, drinking, buying, selling, planting, building;
29. But on the day Lot went out from Sodom, it rained fire and brimstone from Heaven and destroyed all.
30. Even so it will be in the day the Son of Man is revealed.

Luke 17:26-30

Many bible readers assume that life must have been unbearable in the days of Noah and within the ancient cities of Sodom and Gomorrah. The reasons being that we believe ourselves to be more civilized, we have overactive imaginations, and we fail to appreciate the human nature of the men and women who were living during those times. We don't respect what we don't understand and too often we interject our own fears, pride, and rationale into the Bible's passages. We overlook the fact that no matter the time or place, the culture or beliefs, in fortune or famine, in peace time or war, even in chattel slavery; men, women, and children have the innate ability to emotionally and intellectually adapt to any condition that we find ourselves in. Although it is essential to our survival, that universally human ability to adapt is the cause of our past, present, and future blindness. We "Civilized" and "Cultured" men and women of the modern age can look down our noses at the events that transpired during Europe's religious inquisitions and purges, yet we fail to recognize that there is but little separation between

Roman crowds cheering to see prisoners be devoured by carnivorous animals in the Coliseum, American slave drivers and man hunters gathering -with their children present- to hang, to burn, or to watch dogs rip apart a captured freedom seeker, or watching terrorists kill or be killed on the internet. A man can always justify his own wickedness and despise the deeds of other men(Cross Reference **Genesis 3:5**).

    The men and women who were living on the earth in the days leading up to the great flood and within the cities of Sodom and Gomorrah before the cities of the plain were destroyed lived what they considered to be normal lives(Cross Reference **Matthew 24:37-39; Luke 17:26-30**). The men and women living during the prophesied "End Times" are said to carry on in their daily routines just as the men and women did in the former ages, marrying, eating, drinking, and working, tolerably ignorant of their own coming judgment. The relevant difference between the former and latter accounts of man's wicked state and God's ensuing judgments is that the Bible provides a window of perception into the foundational reality responsible for animating the latter age. The book of Revelation is that window.

    John, apostle of Yeshua the Messiah and chronicler of the Revelation, was given sight into and recorded his experience within the spiritual reality that animates our physical existence. John did not see a symbolic dragon, a mythical seven-headed and ten-horned beast, or other fictional monsters in his vision of the revelation. John saw Satan himself, in his actual form of a great red dragon, he saw the force/spirit empowering the Satanic empire that rules over the physical earth in its actual form of a seven-headed and ten-horned beast, and he saw the Church community as it exists in past, present, and future history. The revelation of Yeshua the Messiah is not a figurative event.

    The book of **Revelation** is the detailed account of the "End Time" events that are briefly touched on by Yeshua of

Nazareth in **Matthew** chapter **24**, **Mark** chapter **13**, and **Luke** chapter **21**. The Revelation's references are drawn from both the Old and New Testaments, and the imagery of the Revelation is consistent with imagery that is used throughout the bible. That consistency allows readers to use the bible as a glossary in order to accurately interpret the book of Revelation. The Lamb of God, the seven-sealed scroll, the 4 horsemen, the dragon, the seven-headed and ten-horned beast, the false prophet, the abomination of desolation, and the bride of the Messiah are all references that are drawn directly from other books of the bible. Searching out these references and relying on the Spirit of God to understand their practical relevance takes the reader on a tour through the scripture that unravels the mystery of God's Revelation.

The Lamb of God and The Scroll That is Sealed With Seven Seals

In **Revelation 5:1-2**, John records seeing a scroll "on the right of the One sitting on the throne" and a strong angel asking, "Who is worthy to open the scroll, and to loosen its seals". When it appeared, in **Revelation 5:4**, that no one worthy enough to open and to read the scroll could be found, John "wept very much". But in **Revelation 5:5**, one of the elders alerted John's attention to the Lion of the tribe of Judah, who was worthy to open the scroll and to loose its seals. In **Revelation 5:7** the Lion of the tribe of Judah, in the person of the Lamb of God, took the scroll and then in **Revelation 6:1** began to loosen its seven seals.

The Lamb of God is Yeshua the Messiah(**John 1:29,35-36** Cross Reference **Genesis 22:7-13**). He is the Lion of the tribe of Judah(**Genesis 49:8-12; Revelation 5:5**), the One prophesied Messiah(**Matthew 16:16; Mark 14:61-62** Cross Reference **Isaiah 48:12-16, 61:1-3{Luke 4:18-19}**), the great High Priest of humanity(**Hebrews 4:14** Cross Reference **Genesis 2:4b-25**), and eternal King of kings over the creation(**Revelation 17:14** Cross Reference **Genesis 1:1-2:4a**{**John 1:1-5**}).

The nature of the seven sealed scroll that is taken by the Lamb of God in **Revelation 5:7**(**Revelation 5:1-8:1**) and opened in **Revelation 6:1-8:1** is first described in the Old Testament book of Zechariah(**Zechariah 5:1-4**). On one hand, the scroll is a curse that is unleashed upon every man, woman, and child of the earth. On the other hand, the scroll serves as the deed to the planet and opening its seals begins to unleash the spiritual calamities(**Revelation 6:1-8:1**) that are described in **Matthew 24:4-8** as the "Beginning of Sorrows", which give rise to the final Satanic world empire.

The Four Horsemen of The Apocalypse

The four horses and their riders that were unleashed upon the world in **Revelation 6:1-8** are first introduced to bible readers in the Old Testament's prophetic book of Zechariah(**Zechariah 1:8-10, 6:1-8** Cross Reference **Matthew 24:3-14; Mark 13:3-13; Luke 21:5-11**). They are the initiating principles, i.e. spiritual forces, responsible for instigating and mobilizing the social, political, agricultural, and environmental strife that paves the way for the world-wide authority of the Revelation 13 seven-headed ten-horned beast and its false prophet.

The Dragon

The dragon that appears in **Revelation 12:3-4, 7-17** is clearly identified. **Revelation 12:9** states that the great red dragon is the old serpent(**Genesis** chapter 3) who is called the Devil(Cross Reference **Matthew 4:1-11; Luke 4:1-13**) and Satan(Cross Reference **Job 1:6-12, 2:1-7**).

After the death of the Lamb of God, the Lamb was resurrected and ascended to heaven, and a war took place in heaven. Michael and his angels fought against the dragon and his forces. The dragon and his angels were sent crashing to the earth(**Revelation 12:7-9**) where Satan was given authority to reign for a **Time, Times,** and **Half a Time**(Cross Reference **Daniel 7:25; 12:1-13**).

Looking at the biblical time-line from the perspective of the 21st century: Yeshua's ascension, the war in heaven, the dragon being cast to the earth, the opening of the scrolls seals, and the commencement of the earth's final Satanic kingdom were not prophesied to take place years from now at some undetermined point in the future. According to the biblical text, these prophetic events were set in motion the moment that Yeshua the Risen Messiah ascended to heaven(Cross Reference **Matthew 24:11,24; Mark 13:22; 2Corinthians 11:12-15; 2Peter 2:1; 1John 2:18** "Little children, **it is the Last Time**: and as ye have heard that antichrists shall come, even now there are many antichrists, whereby we know that **it is the Last Time**").

The Beast, The False Prophet, and The Synagogue of Satan

The Beast

In **Revelation 13:1** John, in the spirit on the Lord's day, standing on the sand of the sea saw a beast having seven heads and ten horns rise out of the sea. The beast was like a leopard with the feet of a bear and a mouth as of a lion. It was given its power to overcome the saints of God and its authority over every tribe, tongue, and nation of the world, by the Dragon(the old serpent called the Devil and Satan: **Revelation 12:9**) who had been cast down to the earth from heaven(See **Revelation**

12:1-17). The book of Revelation is not the first time that this beast is mentioned in the bible, and its earlier reference offers a great deal of insight. The seven-headed and ten-horned beast that rises out of the sea in Revelation 13 is the same terrible beast that Daniel, in the Old Testament book that bears his name, saw in his vision of the future.

In the seventh chapter of the book of Daniel a Judean native who was being held captive in Babylon had a vision in which he saw four very different beasts(**Daniel 7:1-28**). The first beast was like a lion that had eagle's wings. The second beast was like a bear. The third beast was like a leopard which had four bird's wings and four heads. The fourth beast that Daniel saw in the vision appeared fearful, terrifying, and very strong. It is described as having great iron teeth and bronze claws with which it devoured, and crushed, and trampled what had come before it(**Daniel 7:7,19**). The fourth beast of Daniel 7 was given power to make war with the saints of God and to overcome them(**Daniel 7:21**), until the Ancient of days came and the judgment was given to the saints of the Most High, and they, the saints, possessed the kingdom.

Daniel was told by "one who stood by(**Daniel 7:15-27**)" that the four beasts that he saw in the vision are the spirits of four different empires of men. The four human empires that are personified by the beasts in the vision are not mentioned by name in Daniel chapter 7. But, for the sake of interpretation it is very fortunate that the succession of the kingdoms is detailed throughout the book of Daniel. In the second chapter of the book of Daniel, Daniel was called upon to interpret king Nebuchadnezzar's dream. King Nebuchadnezzar dreamed of a great image that was composed of four metals. According to Daniel's interpretation the four metals represent four distinct eras of human kingdoms that were prophesied to exist from that day up until "The God of Heaven shall set up a kingdom which shall never be destroyed(**Daniel 2:44** Cross Reference **Daniel**

7:14, 26-27)". The succession of the metals in Daniel chapter 2 culminating in the end of their authority, and the God of Heaven setting up His eternal kingdom corresponds to the succession of the beasts in Daniel chapter 7, their end, and the kingdom being given over to the saints of the Most High God. Thus understanding that the four beasts of Daniel chapter 7 and the four metals of Daniel chapter 2 directly correspond to one another, the conclusion can be drawn that the golden head of the image in Daniel chapter 2, that represents the authority of King Nebuchadnezzar's Babylonian kingdom corresponds to the first beast, the "Lion" of **Daniel 7:4**. History as well as **Daniel 8:1-27(v.20-21)** reveal the second(silver) and third(bronze) metals of the image from King Nebuchadnezzar's dream in the second chapter of the book of Daniel to correspond to the Medo-Persian(Silver, v.**20**)and the Grecian(bronze, v.**21**) kingdoms. The beasts that Daniel sees coming after the Lion(Babylon) in the vision recorded in **Daniel 7:1-28** and that correspond to the succession of kingdoms are; the Bear of **Daniel 7:5** which is the spirit of the Medo-Persian kingdom and the Leopard of **Daniel 7:6** is the spirit of the Grecian kingdom. The fourth beast of Daniel chapter 7 is the amalgam of the three former kingdoms. Although the fourth beast is made up of the former kingdoms and their six distinct heads, it retains its own distinct identity. Thus, the number of heads; One head of the lion{**Daniel 7:4**} plus, one head of the bear{**Daniel 7:5**}plus, four heads of the leopard{**Daniel 7:6**} = 6 heads. Added to those six heads is the one distinct head of the fourth beast making for seven(7) heads.

If you were to place the description of the Beast of Daniel chapter 7 side by side with the seven headed ten horned beast of Revelation chapter 13 you will see that the beastly characteristics are in the opposite order. The explanation is that the seven-headed and ten-horned beast of Revelation 13 is the mirror image of Daniel chapter 7's(Cross Reference **Daniel 10:1-21**) fourth beast. In Revelation 13 John, looking from the back "End" of time observes first the complete Beast, then the leopard(Greek empire), then the bear(Medo-Persian empire), and lastly the lion(Babylonian empire) aspects of the beast, whereas Daniel looking forward in time sees the lion(Babylonian empire) first, next the bear(Medo-Persian empire), and then the leopard(Greek empire) before seeing the "complete" fourth beast. In both visions Daniel and John the apostle saw same seven-headed ten-horned beast that conquered and absorbed the nations, histories, traditions, and legacies of the former beasts, they both saw its reign of terror and, they both saw the beast's end and the kingdom being given over to the saints of the Most High Elohim

Daniel 2, **Daniel** chapters **7** and **8**, **Daniel 9:24-27**(is straight fire), **Revelation 13**, as well as **Revelation 19:1-21** are all various details of the same prophetic event. Each individual detail only serves to add clarity to the entire prophetic picture(Cross Reference **Isaiah 28:10,13**, "Here a little, there a little.").

The confusion that has surrounded the identity of the 7 headed 10 horned Beast of **Revelation 13:1-10** can be eliminated by using the various books of the Bible, written by multiple authors at different times and places, as reference material to understand the Revelation's imagery and prophecies. With this understanding in hand, keep at the forefront of your consciousness the understanding that John the apostle was seeing in the Spirit on the Lord's day. John was seeing the spiritual entities, the animating forces and powers behind the kingdoms of men. The 7 headed 10 horned beast of Revelation chapter 13 is not A Man. The beast is the Satanic(**Revelation 13:4**) force, the Satanic power, the Satanic spiritual foundation of the kingdom that came after and absorbed the kingdoms of Babylon, Media-Persia, and Greece. The 4th beast of **Daniel** chapter **7**, the coming Prince mentioned in **Daniel 9:26**, the 7 headed 10 horned beast of **Revelation** chapter **13:1-10** is the

Roman kingdom that eventually stretched far outside of Italy and conquered all of Europe, parts of North Alkebulan(called Afrika) and, the so-called Middle East.

It is important to recognize the fact that the Satanic Beast(**Revelation 13:1-10**) and its False Prophet(**Revelation 13:11-18**) hide at this very moment in plain sight, disguised behind traditional Christian doctrine and the belief that their appearance on the earth is yet future. In **1John 2:18** the apostle John wrote to assure the faithful community that the prophetic "End Times" had arrived in that day, as the appearance of antichrists at that time was the sign that "It was the last times".

The False Prophet

The second beast of Revelation chapter 13 rises out of the land. An aspect of its appearance resembles the Lamb(Cross Reference "The Lamb of God" **John 1:29,36; Revelation 5:6**) and it speaks as the Dragon(**Revelation 13:11** Cross Reference **Matthew 7:15** "Beware of false prophets, which come to you in sheep's clothing, but inwardly they are ravening wolves." and **2Corinthians 11:12-15** "for Satan himself is transformed into an angel of light." **Genesis 3:1-5**). This beast is, just as the seven-headed ten-horned beast is, a spiritual entity, and not an individual man. This beast pushes throughout the earth with its two horns of power. It is perceived by its various constituents and opposing congregations of devoted followers as the mediator between man and God. Although convincingly sincere and appearing as an angel of light(**2Corinthians 11:13-15** Cross Reference **Genesis 3:1-5**), in truth, the second Revelation chapter 13 beast fulfills a role initially executed by the serpent in the garden of Eden. This beast leads humanity out of the Way, misrepresents the Truth, and separates humanity from the Life and Light that can only be found in the Messiah of God.

The Second beast of Revelation chapter 13 is the False Prophet, and it is also an antichrist.

The term "Antichrist" trips many people up. The term can refer to individuals who oppose the Messiah, but the term also applies to initiating principles, spiritual entities and ministers of Satan, who place themselves as angels of light(Cross Reference **2Corinthians 11:13-15**).

The False Prophet* has often been misconstrued by church goers as an individual man who will arise during the future indeterminate prophetic "End Times" to aid the Satanic Beast in waging an open campaign of aggressive opposition against the Messianic body of believers.

For examples of how the Global Church aides and abets the European Conglomerate, search on the internet for "The Doctrine of Discovery(circa 1493)" as well as "The Curse of Ham".

The Bible and recorded history reveal that the ministers of Satan have not relied on overt force alone to gain the trust of their constituents. Just as the serpent, who led Eve astray in the garden of Eden(Cross Reference **Genesis 3:13**, "The serpent deceived me, and I ate".), Satan's agents have relied on manipulation and deception to subject the world(**Genesis 3:20** "Eve...became the mother of all living". Cross Reference **Matthew 24:24-25, 2Corinthians 11:13-15**). The description of the False Prophet in **Revelation 13:11**, as having an appearance(horns representing power or force) as of the Lamb and speaking as the dragon is particularly revealing. The False Prophet appears as the Lamb of God to its followers. This description goes so far as to explain why there is so much confusion and so many contradictory and erroneous interpretations of the Bible coming from every seemingly opposed division of the Catholic and Reformation/Protestant

Church organization(Organization is singular. The False Prophet is one beast having two significant horns of power.).

The Synagogue of Satan

The Synagogue of Satan is a third significant corporate entity that is mentioned in the book of Revelation(**Revelation 2:9, 3:9**) to stake a claim upon the Messianic identity. The synagogue of Satan is an assembly of Gentiles and their descendants(Cross Reference **Matthew 23:15**) who usurped the identity of the ancient Judean people and who adopted the Judean religious traditions that displaced the law of Moses(Cross Reference **Matthew 15:3-6, Mark 7:8-13**). The synagogue of Satan has no foundation in the truth of God's word but is rooted only upon the traditional teachings of the men who perpetually stood in opposition to God's Salvation(Cross Reference **Matthew 5:17-20**).

The men and women at the heads of these three Satanic corporate bodies are not masters of deception because they possess a degree of intellect that is higher than the average man or woman. They, like their father(s) before them(Cross Reference **John 8:44**), are masters of deception because the spirit that is within them inspires, compels, and justifies their need to invent ways and means of displaying, asserting, and maintaining their presumed right over man, the earth, and all of the earths living organisms(Cross Reference **Genesis 3:4-5; Genesis 4:5-8, 23-24; Isaiah 14:13-14**). Mankind's perception that each organization's anointing is apparent exists only because these corporate entities are organized and more or less unified, as opposed to the divided and conquered masses, in pursuit of a common goal and have for centuries exercised influence and control over humanity's access and our response to information(Cross Reference Eve's, who was prophetically named "the mother of all living", interaction with the serpent in

Genesis 3:1-6, 13,20). Each Satanic agency is driven by the spirit who can only recognize God, His Messiah, and God's chosen nation of men, women, and their descendants, as barriers to their own aspirations of authority, anointing, and favor(**Isaiah 14:14; Genesis 3:5,** "I will be like the Most High" and "You shall be as God").

The seven-headed ten-horned beast, the false prophet, and the synagogue of Satan are each an antichrist in their own right. They have each seated themselves before man as God's anointed and infringed upon the Messianic identity of Lord, Mediator, and Inheritor of God's promises. These three organizations are composed of men and women who are the literal flesh and blood seed of the serpent(**Genesis 3:15; Isaiah 14:29; John 8:44; Revelation 12:1-17**{**17**}Cross Reference **John 5:43**).

The Abomination of Desolation

The Abomination of Desolation(**Daniel 9:27, 11:31, 12:11; Matthew 24:15; Mark 13:14**) is not an act of defilement committed against a rebuilt temple in the modern day "Middle Eastern" city of Jerusalem. A modern Judaic temple in the city of Jerusalem built with human hands could only contradict the teachings of both the Old(**Isaiah 66:1-3; Jeremiah 31:33; Ezekiel 36:25-27**{**Hosea 6:6**}) and New Testaments(**Acts 7:48-50, 17:24; 1Corinthinas 3:16-17; 2Corinthians 6:15-16**), and would itself be an abomination. Stop and think for a second, why would the creator of all existence put any value in a man-made building and what purpose would it serve? Sacrifices? That box was checked with the death of Yeshua/God's Salvation. A place for the Holy Spirit to stay when not residing in the body of believers? No and No. Yet many Churches teach, and many Christians expect a new temple to be built in Jerusalem.

The Bible record's the different occurrences of the events that can be referred to as "The Abomination of Desolation". Each event has the same focus.

The abomination of desolation is an event of such magnitude that from the time of its inception until the return of the Messiah its effects have influenced all manner of human interaction. From the serpent's attack on Adam in the garden of Eden, to the angelic corruption of humanity in the days of Noah, up to its final occurrence in the prophesied "Last Days", the effect of each of these abominable acts has served to further desolate God's likeness in man(Cross Reference **1Corithians 3:16-17**, "Know ye not that ye are the temple of God, and the Spirit of God dwelleth in you?"). In each desolating abomination God's chosen people are targeted for corruption but, humanity at large suffers as a consequence(Cross Reference **Genesis 3-6; Romans 1:18-32**).

The most recent desolating abomination is the European and Islamic slave culture which impacts the world like no other event has, can, nor will. I've heard people say that those events happened so long ago that it is now time to move on from them. But how long would it take for you to move on from your mother being raped or from having your father murdered in front of you. How long would it take for you to move on if you saw your brother snatched out of your home, dragged and beaten all the way to a square where literally thousands of men, women, and their children had gathered in celebration to watch your brother be lynched, set afire, riddled with bullets and, then dismembered. Then for the charred remains of your relative to be taken home as souvenirs from the celebration of death. What if those memories and those experiences are embedded in your DNA. They are. What if your family's blood cries out to you? It does. Or does your DNA celebrate and justify the despotism that it has exercised over humanity. It is true that, as many European colonists have stated in defense of the form of slavery that has existed in the western hemisphere from the time of their arrival, "Slavery has existed on the earth from ancient times". Yes, this is true, servitude is not new within the human experience. But there is not a more Abominable act in the history of man than what is recorded in The United States annals of its history and throughout the African continent as legalized murder, legalized dismemberment, legalized rape, legalized kidnapping, legalized human trafficking and, legalized torture and human experimentation nor has any other institution of servitude robbed a people of their human, their family, or their national identity. My mind cannot conceive of a more Desolating condition to exist in than to have no rights over your own mind and body, to be a conscious being and to know and to be constantly reminded by every aspect of the dominating culture that your existence is subject to the will of another man. Christians have been taught that they will be persecuted for their beliefs, but some people can hide, lie about or, simply change their beliefs. Imagine being hunted and captured, tied up and put on display and auctioned and sold as an animal because of a quality or genealogical characteristic that cannot be hidden, lied about, nor changed such as the amount of melanin displayed in your skin. Man equating another man to an animal is, The Final Abomination of Desolation.

What are the depths of depravity of a mind that would attempt to justify, condone, or ignore these behaviors? For one to justify or condone such horrendous acts, or to continue to benefit from such horrendous acts, or to perpetuate such horrendous acts makes such a one an accomplice of those vile acts. Consider that no other people in history who were welcomed as guests into a foreign land, given shelter, fed, clothed and taught how to survive in the new county, no other people have turned on their host and enslaved them and taken over their land. No other humans have done nor apparently have even conceived of committing such a diabolical act but, there is one other being in the history of man's experience who has taken advantage of man's humane nature to the same degree that imperial colonists have: **Satan**, that old snake in the garden of Eden, the father of the lie. Consider that **Genesis 3:15** acknowledges that there are just two seeds inhabiting the earth, the Seed of the woman and the Seed of the serpent. Who's seed are you(Cross Reference **Matthew 7:21-23**)? This question points back to a sobering statement made earlier in this book, "One and only one branch of the multifaceted Church organization could possibly be right but, each and every one of them can be absolutely wrong".

Matthew 7:21-23

21. Not every one that saith unto me, Lord, Lord, shall enter into the kingdom of heaven; but he that doeth the will of my Father which is in heaven.
22. Many will say to me in that day, Lord, Lord, have we not prophesied in thy name? And in thy name have cast out devils? And in thy name done many wonderful works?
23. And then will I profess unto them, I never, knew you: depart from me, ye that work iniquity.

Matthew 7:21-23

    These lines aren't a guilt trip nor a pity party but if the descendants of abused communities in the Americas, Alkebulan(Afrika) and Australia(See "Post Traumatic Slave Syndrome" by Joy Degruy; Also see "Epigenetics") must bear the weight of societies founded on broken treaties, lies, inequality, betrayal and crimes against humanity, should they have to bear that weight alone or in silence?

    With that being said, I'll state freely that I do not believe that all Europeans are the seed of the Serpent. Nor do I believe that all indigenous peoples are righteous and Godly. I can't judge a man's nor a woman's spirit, intellect nor demeanor until I've had at least one insightful conversation with them.

Ezekiel 33:12

12. Therefore, thou son of man, say unto the children of thy people, The righteousness of the righteous shall not deliver him in the day of his transgression: as for the wickedness of the wicked, he shall not fall thereby in the day that he turneth from his wickedness; neither shall the righteous be able to live for his righteousness in the day that he sinneth.

Ezekiel 33:12

Time, Times, and Half a Time

The phrase "Time-Times-and Half a Time" that is used in **Daniel 7:25, 12:7**, and in **Revelation 12:14** has given rise to many speculative conjectures. The "Time-Times-and Half a Time" is often taught in Churches as only encompassing a microscopic 3½ year period at the end of Satan's rule over the earth. Limiting the scope of the "Time-Times- and Half a Time" to only a narrow 3½ year period of time not only bypasses the last 2000 years of recorded human history, but it also undermines the influence of prophetic revelation by allowing the Satanic Beast, the False Prophet, and the Synagogue of Satan to continue their influence over all manner of human interaction, undetected in the modern age. The "Time-Times-and divided/half a Time" began when the Messiah ascended to and took His place in heaven, Satan was cast down to the earth, and the Lamb of God took the scroll that was sealed with seven seals and began to loose its seven seals(Cross Reference **Acts 1:9-11; Revelation 6:1-8:1; Revelation 12:9**). Although the final 3½ years of Satan's earthly rule may very well be the most trying, the **Time** of Jacob's trouble(**Jeremiah 30:7**), the **Times** of gentile rule over the earth(**Luke 21:24** Cross Reference **Genesis 11:1-4{Revelation 13:1-18), and the Abbreviated/Shortened Time(Matthew 24:15-22; Mark 13:14**) period that is inaugurated by the Abomination of Desolation appropriately fills in the approximately 2000 year gap in biblical understanding.

The Rapture

1Thessalonians 5:9 states that "God has not appointed us to wrath, but to obtain salvation by our Lord Yeshua the Messiah". Therefore, it should be understood that Yeshua the Last Adam, Who became a Life giving Spirit, will return to the earth in order to keep His faithful servants from experiencing God's wrath that will eventually be poured out(Cross Reference **Genesis 6-7:24; 19:1-26**) upon the earth. Misunderstandings have arisen in church congregations that confuse the earth's "Great Tribulation", an event which Believing communities will experience(Cross Reference **Revelation 2:18-3:22, Thyatira, Sardis, Laodicea**), with God's Wrath(**Revelation chapters 15-16**). A "Rapture" event does take place in **Revelation 14:14-16** after the seventh angel blows his trumpet in **Revelation 11:15** and before the wrath of God is poured out in Revelation chapter 16 but, the actual event is yet future and its appearance to the naked eye is a mystery.

The instant physical removal of an indeterminate number of men, women, and children from off the face of the earth is a possibility(Cross Reference **Matthew 24:31; 1Corinthians 15:51-52; 1Thessalonians 4:16-17; Revelation 14:14-16**) but, considering that the Messiah sacrificed his body and became a life-giving Spirit(**1Corinthians 15:45**), and the physical members of the Messianic community are literally His flesh and His bones(**Ephesians 5:30**) on the earth and that, the kingdom of God is stated not to come with observation but to be revealed within humanity(**Luke 17:21**), consider that the revival, the "(En)rapture" of the Truth within each member of the Messianic body, is also a possibility.

The New Man and His Bride

The New Man

Genesis 1:27

27. And God created the man in His image; in the image of God He created him. He created them **male** and **female**.
Genesis 1:27

and,

Genesis 2:23-24

23. And the man said, This now, at last. Bone of my bone and flesh of my flesh. For this shall be called Woman, because this has been taken out of man.
24. Therefore, a man shall leave his father and mother, and shall cleave to his wife; and they shall become **one flesh**.
Genesis 2:23-24

and,

Matthew 19:4-5

4. But answering He said to them, Have you not read that He who created them from the beginning created them **male** and **female**?
5. And He said, For this reason a man shall leave father and mother, and shall be joined to his wife, and the two shall become **one flesh**.
Matthew 19:4-5

and,

Matthew 22:30

30. For in the resurrection they neither marry nor are given in marriage, but they are as the angels of God in Heaven.
Matthew 22:30

Androgynous angelic beings may sound strange until you can appreciate the fact that Adam, himself a son of God, once shared the same nature as the angels. Each of the sons of God who came into existence in Genesis chapters 1 and 2 were created both masculine and feminine. Only Adam, the man created as God's likeness, had the feminine aspect of his nature taken out of his body and then presented to him in **Genesis 2:21-22**. Adam and Eve were (re)united and, thus, becoming one flesh(**Genesis 2:23-24**), existed as He Who created man from the beginning had created them; male and female(**Matthew 19:4-5**).

    Many prophecy minded denominations teach that the Church is the eager and expectant bride of the Messiah. According to this line of thinking, when the Messiah returns to the earth He will gather His faithful community, judge and punish the wicked, and then marry His eager and expectant bride, i.e. the Church. This interpretation fails to consider the fact that the body of the Messiah is already the body of the Messiah, and not one nor many separate denominational entities. The union between the Messiah of God and His own body was sealed long ago in the Messiah's own blood(**Acts 20:28** Cross Reference **John 19:30**) and remains a completed issue for every man and woman who has died to the law and been reborn in the Spirit(**Romans 6:1-7:25**).

    In **Ephesians 5:23-33(23, 30-32)** Paul applied his understanding of the union between a husband and his wife to the relationship between the Messiah and His community of faithful servants.

Ephesians 5:23

23. Because a husband is head of the wife, as also the Messiah is Head of His faithful community, and He is Savior of the body.

Ephesians 5:23

and,

Ephesians 5:30-32

30. For we are members of His body, of His flesh, and of His bones.

31. For this a man shall leave his father and mother, and shall be joined to his wife; and the two shall be one flesh.
32. The mystery is great, but I speak as to the Messiah and as to the faithful community.
Ephesians 5:30-32

The Messiah is the head and Savior of His own faithful body(Cross Reference **Revelation 2:8-11, 3:7-13** "Smyrna and Philadelphia".). The faithful Messianic community is considered to be the flesh, bone, and physical body of the Messiah*. In the eyes of God, Yeshua and His faithful community of followers are one man(Cross Reference **Ephesians 5:30-32**). The gathering of the Messianic body is not yet complete but, understanding of the unity between the Messiah and His body should comfort the weary, as it alleviates doubts regarding the eternal status of the Messianic body and helps to unravel passages such as **Matthew 19:4-6, 22:25-30; Mark 10:6-9, 12:20-25**; and **Luke 20:29-36**.

**The union is spiritual, just as is the union between Satan and his flesh and blood offspring. Cross Reference the Seven-Headed Ten-Horned Beast, the False Prophet, and the Synagogue of Satan in the book of Revelation.*

The future bride of the Lamb of God is not, as many Christian congregations erroneously teach, the Church organization(Cross Reference "The False Prophet" **Revelation 13:11-18**). The Bride of the Lamb is clearly identified many times in both the Old and New Testaments of the bible.

The Bride

The Prophet Isaiah identifies the Bride of the Messiah in **Isaiah 62:1-5**(Cross Reference **Isaiah 49:14-21**).

Isaiah 62:1-5

1. For Zion's sake I will not be silent; and for Jerusalem's sake, I will not rest; until her righteousness goes forth as brightness, and her salvation as a burning lamp.
2. And nations shall see your righteousness, and all kings your glory. And you shall be called by a new name which the mouth of YHWH shall name.
3. You also shall be a crown of beauty in the hand of YHWH, and a royal diadem in the palm of your God.
4. You no longer shall be called Desolate. But you shall be called, My Delight is in Her; and your land, Married. For YHWH delights in you, and your land shall be married.
5. For as a young man marries a virgin, so shall your sons marry you. And as a bridegroom rejoices over the bride, so your God shall rejoice over you.

Isaiah 62:1-5

The entire 54th chapter of the book of Isaiah is dedicated to the city of Jerusalem and in the **5th** verse of **Isaiah 54** the prophet plainly states how dear she is to YHWH.

Isaiah 54:5

5. For your Maker is your husband; YHWH of hosts is His name; and your Redeemer is called the God of all the earth.

Isaiah 54:5

The apostle Paul witnesses to Isaiah's prophecy in **Galatians 4:26-27**.

Galatians 4:26-27
26. But the Jerusalem above is free, who is the mother of us all;
27. for it has been written, Be glad, barren one not bearing; break forth and shout, the one not travailing, for more are the children of the desolate rather than she having the husband.

Galatians 4:26-27 (verse **27** is a quote from **Isaiah 54:1**)

The identity of the bride is also stated in the book of Revelation(Cross Reference **Revelation 21:1-27**).

Revelation 21:2
2. And I, John, saw the holy city, New Jerusalem coming down out of Heaven from God, having been prepared as a bride, having been adorned for her husband.

Revelation 21:2

and,

Revelation 21:9-10
9. And one of the seven angels came to me, he having the seven bowls being filled with the seven last plagues, and spoke with me, saying, Come, I will show you the bride, the wife of the Lamb.
10. And he carried me in spirit onto a great and high mountain, and showed me the great city, holy Jerusalem coming down out of Heaven from God,

Revelation 21:9-10

The Bride of the Messiah must not be confused with the modern city of Jerusalem that is situated in the "Middle Eastern" country that has been called Israel. The Lamb of God's expectant bride is the woman who was prophesied in **Genesis 3:15** to bring forth the seed who would have enmity with the seed of the serpent and who would crush the serpent's head. She is the woman in Revelation chapter 12 who is clothed with the sun, having the moon under her feet, wearing a crown of twelve stars, and who gave birth to the male child in **Revelation 12:5**. As it is stated in the Old Testament and reaffirmed in the New, the bride of the Lamb of God is the New Jerusalem(**Revelation 3:12, 21:2**) which will come down from Heaven. She is mother, bride, and future residence of all of the faithful. But for the time being, respect the earth that all of our bodies come from and which all of our bodies will return to(**Genesis 3:19**).

A man marrying the land may sound illogical but as it pertains to prophecy, the pattern is consistent and enlightening from the beginning to the end of the bible. (See the Dictionary definition for "Husbandry")

God + His Messengers(Angels), the Sons of God = One Man;
The Creation = The Life-Giving Bride;

Adam + Eve = One Man;
The Garden of Eden = The Life-Giving Bride;

God + the Nation of Israel = One Man*;
The land promised to Abraham's seed = The Life-Giving Bride;

The Messiah + His Body of faithful believers = One Man;
The New Jerusalem = The Life-Giving Bride.

The general population of the nation of Israel rejected this relationship at the foot of Mt. Sinai. In response to their rejection the "Law" was given to them(Cross Reference **Exodus 19:6, 20:18-21; Romans 9:3-8). To the Christians who are eagerly waiting to be the "bride" of Christ; you were lied to. You're supposed to be the existing "Body" of the Messiah not a future bride.*

A Brief Summary of 2000 years of Revelation

Christians who are awaiting the prophesied "End Times" will be surprised to know that those days began not long after the resurrection of the Messiah, when the Lamb of God ascended to and took His place in Heaven. War broke out in Heaven and Satan, the great dragon, was cast down to the earth. Israel, the seed of the woman, was assailed and Jacob was scattered(**Revelation 12:1-17**).

Down on the physical surface of the earth the Roman empire, Daniel 7's fourth beast, adding to its control over portions of the former Babylonian, Medo-Persian, and Greek empires(Cross Reference **Daniel 2:36-42, Daniel 7:1-28, Daniel 8:1-27**{v.**20-21**}, and **Daniel 10:1-21** with **Revelation 13:1-10** and modern history's details of the Roman empire that succeeded the Grecian kingdom.), campaigned throughout North Africa and the Middle East, and spread its influence into every corner of the European continent. The Roman Catholic Church gained influence and also spread with the expansion of the Roman Empire. Islam* was born in the 7th century A.D. and aided by the Roman empire's own internal conflicts, temporarily halted the worldwide charge of the mighty Roman kingdom.

The Moors -Civically, militarily, and religiously trained African and Arab inheritors of Egypt's and Judea's masonic rites, who conquered large portions of Europe, ruled their conquered lands for roughly 700 years, and were directly responsible for Europe's "Age of Enlightenment", until their final stronghold, Granada, was overthrown in 1492- introduced the European's to literacy, science, law, government, civil order, culture, masonry(ideology, rites, attire, as well as stonework), mathematics(geometry, algebra, calculus), astrology and astronomy(time and the calendar),anatomy, art, agriculture, hygiene, chemistry and medicine, in addition to establishing *numerous universities, libraries**, and educational centers. The same cannot be said of European imperial colonialists who appropriated ancient knowledge, and in the name of spreading civilization and Christianity to indigenous peoples -particularly those of Alkebulan(the Afrikan continent)), Australia, and the Americas-, have left a legacy of discrimination, segregation, genocide, disease and war, drug and alcohol abuse, violence, illiteracy, famine, and extreme poverty, in their wake. All the while extracting commercial wealth from the lands.*

**The Phoenician Canaanites were responsible for introducing the written alphabet to the Greeks, which was later adopted by the Romans. In modern times we know this alphabet and the language associated with it as "Latin".

During this period, the so-called "Dark Ages -roughly 500 A.D. to 1492 A.D.-", Ashkenazim Jews appeared in Eastern Europe and Sephardim Jews appeared in Western Europe. Roman dominance reemerged out of the so-called "Dark Ages(**Revelation 17:8**)" and the European nations that comprised the former Roman Empire spread their identity, influence, and ideologies throughout Alkebulan(Afrika), Asia, the Near East, the Middle East, Far East, the Pacific and Atlantic islands, Oceania, and the Americas(**Daniel 7:7-8, 23-25; Revelation 13:1-10, 16-18**). European monarchies aided by the dual prongs of the Catholic and the eventual Reformation/Protestant Church(**Revelation 13:11-17**) systematically submitted the nations of the world to varying degrees of European colonialism. Dark brown, brown, and copper skinned indigenous peoples of Africa, Asia, Oceania, the Pacific Islands, and the America's were pushed to the fringes of society, and assigned designations that separated them from their inheritance/land, their family names, and their nationalities. Their histories were burned, defaced, trampled on, crushed, stolen, conveniently lost, and/or re-engineered. Their very lives and their birthrights were deemed the possessions of others(**Daniel 7:7,19** Cross Reference **Deuteronomy 28:15-68**).

Through the control of information, the use of multimedia, propaganda, infiltration and destabilization, intelligence agencies, and outright force, as well as through civil infrastructure, and public, private, religious, and military educational institutions, governing bodies around the world have been able to dictate the human identity to mankind and to quell resistance to their authority by indoctrinating the masses with Eurocentric ideals of culture and civilization and by enacting laws, encouraging conflict, offering sustenance, and supplying entertainment. All of these actions ultimately serve to augment the Beast's identity as mankind's supreme authority(Cross Reference **Genesis 2:15-22; 3:5**). Thereby consummating the theft(**Genesis 3:1-24**), perversion(**Genesis 6:1-13** Cross Reference **Romans 1:18-32**), and annihilation(**Daniel 9:26-27**) of man's God given identity("The Abomination of Desolation" **Revelation 13:16-18** "**666**"Cross Reference **Genesis 2:7, 5:1-2** "He made him in the likeness of God.").

From that fateful day in the garden of Eden when Adam ate the fruit of the tree of knowledge and good and evil up to today, Satan and Satanism has defined the spiritual identity of humanity(Cross Reference **Genesis 2:17**, "In the day that you eat of it, you shall surely die."). From the time that the sons of God cohabited with the daughters of humanity, corruption has festered at the roots of the human soul. And from 1492 up to the modern age, flesh and blood men and women at the head of governing bodies, religious and civil educational institutions, and corporate organizations of nations, cultures, languages, and dialects have compromised humanity in the ongoing pursuit to supplant the Truth and to redefine the human identity in their own image and according to their own likeness(**Genesis 3:5**{**Isaiah 14:14**} "You shall be as God", Cross Reference

Genesis 11:4; Revelation 13:1-18{Cross Reference **Revelation 17:1-18**}).

Conclusion

YHWH Elohim was, is, and will always be(Cross Reference **Exodus 3:14**). All things that exist have their existence for, through, and to the pleasure of Him. YHWH Elohim is the originator of existence, the standard of "Good", and the epitome of perfection. His Word is and can only exist as Truth. The Old and New Testaments of the bible are the written record of God's word within the experience of mankind. YHWH Elohim's love and compassion, knowledge and wisdom, power and ability to accomplish His word, and His desire to share of Himself are each displayed by and within His created order and recorded within the pages of the bible.

YHWH Elohim is not the authority over the creation because He worked more or harder, nor because He receives more prayers or devotion than other gods. YHWH Elohim is the God of gods and the definitive example of truth, Who gives wisdom, strength, and affluence to others because the existence of all things visible and invisible, in heaven, on earth, and under the sea, whether they be thrones, or dominions, or principalities, or powers, were created by and for Him to whom belongs the glory forever(Cross Reference **Romans 11:36, Colossians 1:16**). Amen.

God and Truth exist unchanged whether or not we acknowledge or accept them, and God has the right to give or to deny what is His to whom He pleases(**Romans 9:16 Cross Reference Matthew 20:1-16**).

On its surface and down to its core, the essential message of YHWH Elohim's word is, "I AM. There is no other(Cross

Reference **Isaiah 45:5-6, 21-22; Isaiah 46:9-10**)". Through time and space, language barriers, and man-made alterations to the text and its meaning, the Old and New Testaments of the bible can deliver and verify the supernatural origin of God's message. Man's general inability to understand or to corrupt the message of the scriptures is evidence that God's Word has endured intact and that it is reliable. This book, "The Unknown God. And The End Of Church And State", attests to the endurance and reliability of God's message.

God's message has proved itself reliable, but man's reception of God's word is not guaranteed(Cross Reference **Genesis 3:1-5**). The message can be hidden, our perception of it can be manipulated, its written record can be altered, and even after we have come into contact with it, not one of us has to accept that the Word of YHWH Elohim is true(Cross Reference **Exodus 20:18-21**).

Fortunately, through all time, places, and understandings, the Truth remains: singular, absolute, immutable, and eternal.

Just as Yeshua of Nazareth was persecuted, crucified, buried, and resurrected to eternal life after spending three days and nights in the heart of the earth(**Matthew 12:40**), at the end of the Time-Times-and-Half a Time the Truth too will be revived and restored to its proper place in the hearts and minds of YHWH Elohim's faithful servants, to be expressed in our bodies and through our works(Cross Reference **James 2:15-18**). In that day the power of Satan's lie(**Genesis 3:5** Cross Reference **Isaiah 14:13-14)** will be dissolved and the adversarial principalities and powers who dwell in the heavens(**Ephesians 6:12**), the authorities of man(**Revelation 2:9, 3:9; 13:1-18; 17:1-18**), and even Satan himself(**12:3-4,7-17**), will be done away with.

Post Script:

The Rights of Man

Only the God of gods has the authority to administer rights to mankind. I would therefore take great consideration of any past or present situation or nation in which a man or woman has had or would have to petition another man, woman, or government to receive rights. I would be even more suspicious of any man or woman who would have the audacity to presume the authority to constitute rights or righteousness(verses constituting the protection of man's God given rights) to another man or woman(Cross Reference **Matthew 23:8-10** and **Genesis 3:1-5** with "The likeness of God" **Genesis 1:26, 5:1**). The man or woman who would ask to receive rights from another man would either have to be completely ignorant of the Truth, be in submission to a Satanic authority, and/or seeking an inroad to usurp the position of the man or government who has him in submission.

The individual at the other end of the spectrum, the one who has placed himself in the position of authority over the rights and righteousness of man, from this day forward, can be considered as no less than an impostor(Cross Reference **Revelation 2:9, 3:9**), an instigator, an antichrist/false messiah(**Matthew 24:15-25, 1John 2:18-26** Cross Reference **Revelation 13:1-18**), and a devil, the seed of the serpent/Satan(**Genesis 3:15** Cross Reference **Isaiah 14:13-14**). Any nation of the world that would have the audacity to declare itself "Good(Cross Reference **Matthew 19:17; Mark 10:18; Luke 18:19**)" or that would misuse God's Word to justify the morals and the laws that it has constituted for itself(Cross Reference **Genesis 3:1-5**), or to validate the authority that it has taken unto itself, or to excuse itself for violating the rights and taking the land or property/inheritance of indigenous men and women, can be understood as no less than a Satanic State(Cross Reference "Rahab": **Job 26:11-13, Psalm 87:4, 89:10, Isaiah 51:9{Genesis 3:1-6, 6:1-13}**).

World Peace?

The very idea of world peace defies humanity's corrupt nature. The idea itself is just a carrot dangled before the hearts and minds of men and women who are ignorant of the truth. Reality is the stick that continually smacks our dumb asses(pun intended). Our spirits and souls are at war within each of our own bodies(Cross Reference "the kingdom of heaven" **Genesis 1:1-2:4a**.) and we wage war with our neighbors. The multifaceted Christian Church, the leaders of the world's diverse populations, and the many various means, religious or otherwise, that man has looked to in order to define or to justify our manner of living cannot lead man to eternal Life. The world can have no rest and humanity will have no peace until we first realize that we are all the subjects of liars, thieves(**Zechariah 5:1-4**), and ignorant children who destroy life for the love of accolades and shiny things(**Luke 11:43; John 12:43; 1Timothy 6:10** Cross Reference **Isaiah 14:13-14; Ezekiel 28:12-19**; and **John 8:44**, "You are of your father the Devil.". For all of the "isms" -race, sex, class, national, cultural, etc.- and distinctions that have been created by man, **Genesis 3:15** only differentiates between two groups of men and women living upon the surface of the earth: the {1}seed of the serpent who will continually hinder the {2}faithful seed of the woman{**Revelation 12:1-17**} and our walk/relationship with God{**Amos 3:3** Cross Reference **Genesis 6:9**}).

Man cannot constitute freedom, which was given to all men and women by God. The spirit that currently drives humanity only knows how to restrict the rights of others in order to exalt itself and to inculcate the perception of its entitlement.

Just as Satan, who would only see the power and might, the wisdom, and the majesty of the Most High God Whom he desired to emulate(**Isaiah 14:13-14**), man, the corrupted image and likeness of the Most High, can only aspire to a flawed perception of the Truth(**Genesis 3:5**).

It is my opinion, and I'm fine with being wrong, but I believe that the most underrated figure of the Bible, who the Bible narrative is about is YOU, the reader(Cross Reference **Luke 17:21**). God Cannot be added to, subtracted from, manipulated nor influenced. YOU can be and have been throughout your entire life. My hope for you is that daily you do change and increasingly you become the Likeness and the Image of Abundance, Wisdom, Care, Generosity, Power and Love: YHWH Elohim.

Psalm 115:17-18

17. The dead do not praise YHWH, nor do any of those who go down into silence.
18. But we will bless YHWH, from now on and forevermore. Praise YHWH.

Psalm 115:17-18 (Cross Reference **Joshua 24:15**)

Notes:

www.ingramcontent.com/pod-product-compliance
Lightning Source LLC
Chambersburg PA
CBHW070636160426
43194CB00009B/1475